Kingdom of Children

PRINCETON STUDIES IN CULTURAL SOCIOLOGY

Editors

Paul DiMaggio
Michèle Lamont
Robert Wuthnow
Viviana Zelizer

Kingdom of Children

CULTURE AND CONTROVERSY IN THE HOMESCHOOLING MOVEMENT

Mitchell L. Stevens

PRINCETON UNIVERSITY PRESS

PRINCETON AND OXFORD

Copyright © 2001 by Princeton University Press
Published by Princeton University Press, 41 William Street,
Princeton, New Jersey 08540
In the United Kingdom: Princeton University Press,
3 Market Place, Woodstock, Oxfordshire OX20 1SY

Third printing, and first paperback printing, 2003
Paperback ISBN 0-691-11468-4

The Library of Congress has cataloged the cloth edition of this book as follows

Stevens, Mitchell L.
Kingdom of children : culture and controversy in the
homeschooling movement / Mitchell L. Stevens.
p.   cm. — (Princeton studies in cultural sociology)
Includes bibliographical references and index.
ISBN 0-691-05818-0 (alk. paper)
1. Homeschooling—United States. 2. Educational sociology—United States.
I. Title. II. Series.
LC40.S74   2001
371.04′2′0973—dc21   00-068441

British Library Cataloging-in-Publication Data is available

This book has been composed in Janson

Printed on acid-free paper. ∞

www.pupress.princeton.edu

Printed in the United States of America

3   4   5   6   7   8   9   10

FOR THE PARENTS

Then children were brought to him that he might lay his hands on them and pray. The disciples rebuked the people; but Jesus said, "Let the children come to me, and do not hinder them; for to such belongs the kingdom of heaven."

Matthew 19:13–14

Contents

Acknowledgments

To ANY WHO HAVE grown cynical about the kindness of strangers, I say, meet some home schoolers. They will renew your faith. My first thanks are to the people of the homeschool movement, without whose help and trust this book could not have been written. I was delighted, and sometimes awed, by so many who were gracious to a researcher who always had more questions to ask. Though it would be impossible to thank each of them individually, I would like to note a handful of people and organizations that were exceptionally helpful. In Illinois, the HOUSE chapter I attended regularly for over two years paid me the compliment of treating me like a native. Its members' reception enabled me to learn innumerable little lessons that took me far toward a big picture. The National Homeschool Association and the Home School Legal Defense Association both gave me access to personnel, archival materials, and their distinctive national views of home schooling. The people I here call Deirdre Brown, Robert and Martha Edwards, and Susan and Steve Jerome not only talked with me at length and on multiple occasions; they also took the time to read portions of my manuscript for accuracy. The meetings in which we worked through the manuscript together are high points of my ten years of homeschool research. I doubt that Deirdre, Robert, Martha, and the Jeromes will agree with everything in the following pages, but I hope that this book offers them a little bit of what they gave to me: a privileged and thoughtful perspective on their cause.

Several organizations generously provided financial support for this project. A dissertation fellowship from the Spencer Foundation gave me early outside confirmation that I was doing something worthwhile, as well as the means for a full year for research and writing in 1992. The Indiana University Center on Philanthropy's Governance of Nonprofit Organizations Program provided travel and transcription funds that enabled me to study home schooling as a national movement. Northwestern University supported travel and the purchase of many homeschooling texts. A research grant from St. Lawrence University facilitated travel in 1996. Many others helped in kind. Michael Burkin, Patrick Cox, Jessica Dietrich, Leslie Golden, Kevin Henson, and Mark Porter opened their homes to me during my research trips, offering good food, spare beds, and probing questions at the end of research days. My parents, Wendell and Lola

Stevens, encouraged me for years in this effort and gave timely financial and spiritual support along the way.

Over the last five years, many at Hamilton College have made my work considerably easier. The office of the Dean of Faculty consistently funded research travel and offered a course release to help me complete the manuscript. The capable staff at Burke Library assisted cheerfully with research tasks large and small. In the Department of Sociology, student assistants Bethany Baker, Rebecca Hamm, Rebecca Hornbach, Scott Richard, and Peter Shelton got me up to speed on such disparate topics as home schooling on the Internet and Montessori education. Carole Freeman and Marcia Wilkinson graciously helped me ascend an impressive mountain of transcription and correspondence work. Fellow faculty in the department both took this effort seriously and gave me the temporal space to get it done. Add it all up, and one would be hard pressed to find a better home for scholar-teachers than Hamilton.

A long list of people shaped my head in a manner that made it possible for me to put the pieces of this puzzle together. I cannot thank them all, but I will name some. Laura Adams, Elizabeth Armstrong, Howard Becker, Amy Binder, Steve Brint, Kevin Henson, Jeff Livesay, Michael Lounsbury, Doug McAdam, John Meyer, Francesca Polletta, Chris Smith, Lisa Staffen, and Steve Warner all offered encouragement and criticism for the project at timely moments. Eileen Eisenberg showed me that how we talk about children has consequences for how we nurture them, an intellectual gift that has informed much of my subsequent thinking. Paul Lichterman, Art Stinchcombe, Brad Wilcox, and Viviana Zelizer read parts of the manuscript and kindly helped me navigate relevant literatures. Steve Ellingson, Chris Honde, Kirk Pillow, Peter Shelton, and April Wyckoff read the entire manuscript and provided excellent criticism, sometimes on a page-by-page basis. Elisabeth Clemens provided collegial assistance at many stages in this effort and offered a very helpful critique of the penultimate draft. Deft in his role as series editor, Robert Wuthnow generously read two entire versions of the manuscript, each time directing me toward greater clarity and precision. David Sikkink was a thoughtful fellow scholar for several years and was particularly helpful in the final days of manuscript preparation.

Several people nurtured the dissertation this once was and encouraged the book it has become. Arlene Daniels agreed to shepherd me early on, before I knew very much about home education or had very much to say about it. Nicki Beisel believed that the movement could tell a broader story about contemporary American politics and consistently pushed me toward larger questions. She also shared her remarkable talent for giving incisive criticism while looking its recipient squarely in the eye. Wendy Espeland frequently reminded me of the pleasure of intellectual work and nurtured my appreciation for theoretical equipment I once thought beyond my ken. Carol Heimer allowed me to honor the complexity of the movement as I saw it and taught me the analytic discipline I needed to untangle it all. Although I may have yet to meet them, her high standards for excellent and humane scholarship have become my own.

As the dissertation became a book, several colleagues and friends lent their expertise to the legal and ethical questions inherent in writing about real people in real time. Thanks to Howard Becker, Carol Heimer, Joe Miller, and Susan Shapiro in this regard. In what has become a years-long, ongoing conversation, Dan Chambliss has helped me negotiate these and many other puzzles of fieldwork.

At Princeton University Press, Mary Murrell did me the favor of expressing interest in this project years before it was done and has availed me of her professional acumen and cosmopolitan smarts ever since. Also at the Press, Fred Appel, Susan Ecklund, and Tim Sullivan pointed out spots that needed polish while capably seeing the book and its author through production. This is a better, clearer book because of them.

I reserve final thanks for Kirk Pillow, who entered my life when I thought this study was nearing completion—six years ago—and who, in innumerable ways, has been instrumental in seeing it to the end. Kirk has encouraged, advised, scheduled around, and in general put up with me, lending intellect, heart, and humor all along the way. I am especially grateful for his helping me attend to the complicated emotional dimensions of fieldwork over these many years. In doing so he has taught me a lesson about scholarship and subjectivity that I will remember for a long time.

Any errors or shortcomings of this book are entirely my own, of course, but any credit for its merits will be enjoyed in good company.

Kingdom of Children

Introduction

ON FEBRUARY 13, 1983, the *Seattle Times* reported that some local citizens were taking the law into their own hands. Among them were Michael Farris, an Olympia attorney, former executive director of the state's Moral Majority chapter, and his wife, Vicki, parents of three. In 1983, Washington law required that all children attend public or state-approved private schools. Mike, Vicki, and the parents of some five thousand Washington youngsters were risking twenty-five-dollar-a-day fines to teach their kids at home. "Firm Beliefs Foster Defiance of School Laws," the headline read.

Just what were people like the Farrises up to, and was it good for their children? The article explained that most home schoolers in the state were "Christian fundamentalists." Their incentive, apparently, was a mix of religious conviction and a suspicion that the public schools were not adequately doing their job. "My first and highest goal for our kids is to love our Lord," Vicki Farris explained. The Farrises also had become convinced that conventional classrooms were bad places for their children academically. They cited the work of some educational researchers who claimed that early schooling is detrimental to young children's motor and cognitive development.

The article carried quotes of both Farrises, but it represented Vicki as the homeschool teacher. The lead photo featured a close-up of her, poring over a book with seven-year-old Christy at the kitchen table. Vicki described homeschool motherhood as rewarding but taxing, too. "In a way it's fulfilling some of my needs. Sometimes I felt all I was doing was cleaning up spills and washing clothes, so it's been stimulating, but sometimes I'm ready to pull out my hair," Mrs. Farris confessed, "but I still think it's worthwhile."

Meeting the journalist's imperative to paint a balanced picture, the *Times* duly reported some dissenting voices. Reporters used an interview with Joanna Nichols, principal of King's Elementary, a local Christian day school, for the contrary position. After some research Nichols had, according to the newspaper, "concluded that home-schooling is a phenomenon destined to burn out," for a number of reasons. "While the one-to-one teaching ratio at home is great, she says, sometimes teaching needs to be 'carefully geared to meet individual learning needs, and a trained teacher is the best resource for that.'"

This book is about the men and women who ignored such wisdom, the parents of the estimated one million American children who are now being educated at home. It is about how homeschool advocates have convinced these parents that their children's bodies are too fragile to be squeezed into desks all day, their needs too distinctive to be handed over to strangers, their minds too pliant to be subjected to secular teachers. It is about why ordinary mothers and fathers have felt the conviction to make an extraordinary life choice, and about the organizational scaffolding they have built to support their decision. It is about what made it possible for Michael Farris, a small-town attorney in 1983, to grow a national organization with a multimillion dollar budget and more than sixty thousand members before he and Vicki had finished homeschooling their own children.

Finally, this book is about the many ways in which home schooling is different upon close inspection than it seems at first glance. Initially one may expect home schoolers to be isolated in their homes, inadequately socialized. One of the first lessons home schoolers teach the careful observer is that in fact home schooling is a collective project. Home schoolers have always worked together to surmount the multiple challenges that come with doing things unconventionally. In conversation with one another, they become convinced about the troubles of schools. In support groups, they swap words of wisdom and stories of uncomprehending in-laws. In regional and national associations, they lobby legislatures and education departments to ensure their freedom to homeschool. In magazines and publishing houses, on the Internet, and through small businesses and ministries of every description, home schoolers have built a lively and talkative world of their own, one that supplies parents and children alike with wide possibilities for friendships, political experience, and, sometimes, lucrative careers. Home schooling is, in short, a social movement, with a rich history and an elaborate organizational apparatus.

At first glance some critics see all the Vicki Farrises—full-time mothers in what appear to be traditional household roles—and assume that home schooling is a reactionary, antifeminist cause. In fact home schooling bears clear imprints of the liberal feminism that was blossoming when many of today's homeschooling mothers came of age. Like most women, homeschooling mothers take for granted that the idealized domesticity of the 1950s housewife is a thing of the past. Like their more conventional neighbors, homeschooling women face hard choices between paid work and parenting. Where they differ is in how they decide to navigate those choices.

At first glance, home schooling appears to be the logical purview of evangelical and fundamentalist Christians. In fact, one would be hard-pressed to find a social movement peopled by a wider spectrum of faiths and philosophies. The plurality of home schoolers makes them harder for the rest of us to comprehend. On what could fundamentalists and atheists, Muslims and Mormons, Buddhists and Baptists all agree? I found that despite their varied backgrounds, home schoolers agree that children have enormous potential for distinctive accomplishments and that standardized ways of educating children temper or even squelch this potential. Home schoolers also are wary of state intrusion into family life and generally are skeptical of the ability of bureaucracies and "experts" to meet the task of child rearing. Because these beliefs are rooted in some cherished American cultural traditions, they are compelling to a wide range of people.

The points of shared sentiment have not, however, made it easy for home schoolers to cooperate. Home schooling's earliest adherents differed not only by faith but also in the histories they inherited. Some of them cut their teeth as activists in the liberal "free school" movement of the 1960s and 1970s. These activists were familiar with the highly democratic organizational forms favored by attendant causes of that era, namely, the New Left student movement and, a bit later, the nascent feminist movement. From the beginning they have imagined a diverse and democratic home-school cause, a big-tent movement with plenty of room for political and philosophical disagreement. Those who became homeschool leaders in the evangelical and fundamentalist world, however, did so with contrary understandings of what a social movement ought to look like. In that world, hierarchical divisions of labor and authority are generally regarded as appropriate, as is the exclusion of those who do not share one's religious faith. Given such striking differences in what I came to call the organizational sensibility of home schoolers, it is not surprising that they have often disagreed.

This book is about home schooling, but it also about the mechanics of social movements more broadly. I argue that people who build social movements, people like Michael and Vicki Farris, are appropriately thought of as entrepreneurs.[1] They see troubles in their surrounding culture and cannily find ways to define them in novel and compelling ways. They create practical technologies for fixing the trouble. They figure out how to share their vision with amenable audiences. And like all entrepreneurs, they take risks in the interest of the cause. They may forgo stable careers to do the thing they believe in. They may abandon the comfortable ken of a more respectable cause and strike out precariously on their own. Many, with empty pockets and nary a footnote in the history books, lose the gamble. But to the successful go many spoils: the glamour and excitement that come from taking risks in the short term; the long-term promise of making history; the intellectual buzz of rethinking what others take for granted; the sublimity of transcending the rules.

Entrepreneurs do not work in vacuums. Just as in business, where particular regulatory environments, fluctuating market conditions, and spotty information require opportunity-takers to be knowledgeable and nimble, in the business of social movements entrepreneurs must do their work in a manner that is sensitive to context. The factors that shape the fate of movement-builders are numerous. Some are structural: the legal organization of a society, for example, which determines the outside costs of doing things unconventionally and provides the rules for voicing official dissent. Some are cultural: the intellectual traditions that shape the heads of potential recruits; the larger culture's stock of legitimate ways of making sense of things; and the organizational sensibilities that characterize people's sense of how they can appropriately be glued together into groups.

The people who laid the foundations for home education in the early 1980s, people like Michael Farris, did so in a legal context that was very favorable to their cause. The United States is distinctive among Western industrialized nations in the extraordinary decentralization of legal rules regarding schooling. Public schooling is governed largely by states and localities in this country, and this kind of legal structure creates lots of wiggle room for educational innovators. One can fight local battles to change the rules or move someplace where the regulatory climate better suits one's pedagogical imagination. And since the question of just who ultimately is responsible for the education of children (parents? the state?) has never been squarely resolved in America, the country has accommodated many alternatives to public schools.

Farris and his peers also have done their work in a particular historical context. Theirs is a post-1960s America, a nation now sensitized profoundly to the fact that state officials and school bureaucrats can abuse their powers, a nation that has grown rather more accustomed than it used to be to groups that do things unconventionally, to people who live their ideals. Many of today's homeschool sages became adults in the 1960s and 1970s. Many participated in the cultural innovation and experimentation of those decades. Even years later, they think of themselves as their own people, a bit outside the mainstream. Notably, I found this sentiment to be as pervasive among conservative Protestants as among other home schoolers. These are people who have self-consciously done their own thing, or the right thing, regardless of what the neighbors or the in-laws might think.[2]

But homeschool advocates are not homogeneous. They come from different sectors of American society and have pursued their cause in contextually specific ways. Michael Farris has made his career in the organizationally robust world of conservative Protestant America, a world composed of thousands of local congregations and a vast constellation of businesses, ministries, and national advocacy groups. This is a place rich with opportunity for entrepreneurs of all sorts, a place in which someone with a big idea and a willingness to work hard can, with God's grace and with help from his brethren, build an impressive piece of the kingdom. Other homeschool leaders have gone about things very differently. Rather than speaking to a large population that shares some powerful beliefs about community and authority, they have purveyed their cause to anyone who cares to listen. Rather than the explicitly Christian social movement Farris and his colleagues have created, other home schoolers have built a decidedly ecumenical home education. They have done so according to the rules and with the resources of "alternative" America—that fragile organizational network left after the ebb of liberal causes of the 1960s and 1970s. This is the world of alternative schools, progressive not-for-profits, food co-ops, and the occasional surviving commune that carry on the egalitarian ethos of the student movements and the counterculture. It is a small world now, short on cash, physical plants, and new blood, but still a hotly idealistic and quietly optimistic place. These home schoolers have met a rather different fate than conservative Protestants. Both groups have managed to create lively, talkative, durable causes, but one version of home education is larger and wealthier and more handily directs the national conversation on home schooling. This book addresses why homeschool history played out this way.

In the early 1990s, when I did the bulk of my homework for what follows, home education as a national cause was very much under construction. As I watched support groups, telephone trees, and national advocacy organizations get built, I saw that home schoolers often differed in what Elisabeth Clemens has called the "how" of organization: the characteristic ways in which they divide tasks, distribute authority, and define themselves as collective actors.[3] The difference proved decisive. When I finished my research in 1999, there were essentially two homeschool movements, one "Christian" and the other "inclusive." This book is about how that happened.

Despite their contentiousness, in the end what I found most remarkable about home schoolers was the big item on which they agreed. Time and again, parents told me that their children's self-development was worthy of virtually any sacrifice. Careers were suspended, incomes cut, houses left uncleaned or unfixed, adult social lives curtailed dramatically, and, sometimes, marriages strained, all in the interest of giving more to the kids. In doing their utmost for their children, home schoolers are much like all good parents, of course. Nevertheless, I found in home schoolers' extraordinary commitment a larger lesson about the meaning of childhood in our culture.

Homeschool parents will tell you that their kids are precocious and unpredictable. That they are uncomfortable in confining classrooms and rigid bureaucracies. That they don't like people behind big desks telling them what to do. That they learn best when they are given open spaces, breathing room. Can we hardly disagree? This talk, after all, is harmonious with the great American story, a story about freedom and possibility and skepticism of established authority. But there is something more there, too, something implicit about who we are not just as Americans but as moderns. At the heart of home schoolers' elaborate conversation about children is a faith that deep inside each of us is an essential, inviolable self, a little person distinctive from all others and, on the basis of that distinctiveness, worthy of extraordinarily specific care. Home schoolers remind us of how vivid that faith can be, and of how much it costs to put it in practice.

In what follows I have tried to do two things at once: to provide a studied account of a novel education movement, and to write an analytic essay about the relationship between cultural context and a social movement's form and message. In attempting to be a storyteller and an analyst simultaneously, I have almost certainly written a book that is both less lovely a narrative and less systematic an essay than it otherwise might have been. But such is the lot of a sociologist, and a discipline, simultaneously given to abstraction and specificity. My hope is that I have struck at least a few notes of harmony between these different scholarly tones.

Finally, I should offer a word on the structure of my effort here. I have tried to write a book that is informative to several kinds of readers. Sociologists, and others who are interested in the theoretical foundations of my analysis, will find in the footnotes some citations and commentary intended especially for them. Readers who are less concerned about the scholarly conversation that informs my thinking might decide to read the notes more lightly.

Here is an outline of what follows. Chapter 1 introduces the reader to the homeschool world and describes the nature and limitations of my inquiry. Chapter 2 examines classics of homeschooling literature and a sample of homeschool curricula, providing a sense of home schoolers' varied pedagogical approaches. It also listens to parents talk about the hows and whys of home schooling and begins to sketch the relationship between homeschool pedagogy and home schoolers' broader worldviews. Chapter 3 takes a closer look at mothers. Here I assess the scope of the work home schooling requires and the very different ways in which mothers make sense of that work. Leaving households, chapter 4 describes how home schoolers have worked to assemble themselves into a national constituency and examines the subtle ways in which different organizational sensibilities have had lasting consequences for the shape of the movement. Chapter 5 addresses how home schoolers go about their politics. It recounts a watershed event on Capitol Hill that both betrayed and solidified home schoolers' organizational divisions, and it proffers an explanation for why such leaders as Michael Farris have had such success in their endeavors. Finally, chapter 6 considers what home schoolers teach us about the nature of American childhood.

Inside Home Education

ONE OF THE FIRST THINGS home schoolers taught me is how central school is to the structure of modern life. Few parts of our biographies are untouched by the institution of schooling. People often choose where to live on the basis of school quality, and they typically pay for relative advantage in longer commutes and higher home prices. In households with children, the rhythm of daily routines is set largely by school schedules. State laws require all children to attend. Things like "summer jobs" and "winter vacation" only make sense in the context of school calendars. Government agencies at every level use schools to serve children with subsidized meals, health initiatives, and recreational programs. Employers and college admission officers use school grades to distribute opportunity. Social scientists, who often advise the lawmakers and the education officials and the employers, know much of what they do about children through information collected by schools and research conducted inside of them.[1] Leaving school makes you notice these things.

By the time I started noticing, I had fallen for home schoolers—for their talkativeness, for their evident commitment, and for the way that their dismissal of conventional schooling has made them open to far-reaching critiques of contemporary American life. This chapter outlines my effort to understand home schoolers. It reports information gleaned from other studies of home education, describes the contours of the homeschool world in the Chicago area, where I did much of my research, and introduces a few of the people who will help me tell what I learned.

SURVEYING THE HOMESCHOOL WORLD

Who are home schoolers, and how many of them are there? U.S. Department of Education policy analyst Patricia Lines estimated that as many as one million American children were homeschooled in the 1997–98 academic year, up from an estimated three hundred thousand in 1988 and fifteen thousand in the early 1970s.[2] A study conducted by Brian D. Ray and funded by the Home School Legal Defense Association (HSLDA), an advocacy group, put the numbers even higher: 1.23 million American children being homeschooled in 1996.[3] These figures are thoughtful approximations, not counts; nationally representative census and survey instruments have long failed to distinguish home education from public and private schooling, a statistical blind spot that is just beginning to be repaired.

Whether one takes the generous estimate or the conservative one, there is no question that home schooling is one of the most formidable educational causes of its time. Consider that the charter school movement, the darling reform of many in the education establishment that has received piles of positive press, currently encompasses about 350,000 students—perhaps a third the number of homeschooled kids.[4] Yet unlike charter schools, home education has grown without the imprimatur of groups like the National Education Association and through years of skeptical media coverage.[5] Perhaps because home schoolers challenge the expertise of school authorities, perhaps because so many homeschool families are deeply religious, or perhaps because homeschool parents are, almost by definition, little interested in school reform, their movement has rarely been given the scholarly attention it deserves.[6] Piecing together what we do know makes an impressionistic picture, but a useful one nevertheless.

In 1995, sociologist Maralee Mayberry and her colleagues released the best comprehensive statistical study of home educators to date.[7] The authors' fifty-six item questionnaire included measures of parental occupation, educational attainment, religious affiliation, household size and income, and divisions of domestic labor. Working with a sample of home-educating families in Nevada, Utah, and Washington (N = 1,497), the researchers painted a picture of a predominantly white, middle-class, and religious movement.[8] Ninety-eight percent of survey respondents were white; 1 percent were Asian American; the rest were a mix of African Americans, Native Americans, and Hispanics. Most parents were under forty, and the vast majority (97 percent) were married. Forty-three percent claimed at least some postsecondary education; an additional 33 percent were college graduates. Professional/technical and managerial/administrative occupations were heavily represented among the fathers; some were craft and service workers, and a few were farmers or ranchers. Fifty-seven percent of households surveyed reported incomes between $25,000 and $50,000; 26 percent reported less. In comparison with the general populations of the states in which they resided, respondents were better educated, slightly more affluent, and considerably more likely to be white.

The researchers found evidence that the work of home schooling is heavily gendered. Seventy-eight percent of mothers surveyed reported "homemaker/home educator" as their occupation, while nearly all the mothers who reported different occupations indicated that they worked at home. Whether as (for examples) bookkeepers, caterers, child care providers, or craftspeople, the working mothers surveyed stayed near their children. The researchers rightly wondered how these less than wealthy families compensate for the absence of a full-time female wage. Written responses to the surveys and follow-up interviews indicated that many women found home education "more important" than additional income. One mother reported that she was "highly invested in [my children's] well-being and am motivated by love, not by financial status."[9] Coping with the contradiction between paid work and family that is virtually inevitable for contemporary mothers, the women surveyed consistently chose family time over income.

The sample tapped a highly religious population. Ninety-one percent of respondents reported that religious commitment was "very important" to their lives (only 1 percent claimed it was "not important at all"). Seventy-eight percent reported attending church at least once a week. Respondents came closest to full consensus on the belief that God lives and is real: 97 percent agreed. Respondents also concurred on a number of measures of conservative religious orthodoxy. Eighty-four percent agreed that the Bible is the inspired word of God and literally true; 81 percent agreed that eternal life is a gift of God, predicated on belief in Jesus Christ; and 93 percent agreed that Satan is currently working in the world.[10] The researchers summarized the majority of religious home educators' orthodoxy as a belief "in the existence of an *external* authority, an authority that guides their moral decisions, including the decision to educate their children at home."[11] The survey figures suggest that a large majority of home educators place faith in a higher, Protestant Christian power.

But the story is more complicated than that. The researchers noted that 20 percent of survey respondents did not report a religious affiliation, while 12 percent did not complete the survey's scale of religious orthodoxy. Among those who did respond to the orthodoxy scale, a minority expressed commitment to a remarkably different religious orientation. In written responses, these parents described their affinity with a "new spirituality" in which, the researchers explained, "the ultimate source of authority lies within the individual, not with God."[12]

The picture painted by the work of Mayberry and her colleagues is not inconsistent with what few nationally representative data are available on home schoolers. In 1996, the National Center for Education Statistics administered a survey that distinguished home education from other kinds of schooling, a first in this field of study. On the basis of this survey, Notre

Dame sociologist David Sikkink found that home schooling was statistically associated with white, religious, two-parent households. Relative to the general population, homeschooling parents were in the paid labor force fewer hours per week—a hint about the amount of work home schooling itself requires. Homeschool households also were more likely to be found in western states and least likely to be Northeasterners.[13]

Since the early years of the homeschool movement, some researchers have tried to discern how homeschooled children fare academically. Available evidence indicates that these kids generally meet or exceed national averages on standardized tests. In the mid-1980s, for example, Jon Wartes examined the scores of home-educated children in Washington on the Standard Achievement Test series (SAT). His 1986, 1987, and 1988 samples exhibited overall median scores that hovered around the 66th percentile on national test norms.[14] The state of Oregon, which had test scores of 1,658 homeschooled students on record for the 1987–88 school year, reported that over 72 percent of the scores were at or above the 51st percentile on national percentile rankings.[15] In another study conducted by Brian Ray for HSLDA in 1992, the advocacy group provided an SAT testing service to 10,750 homeschooled children in kindergarten through twelfth grade; scores ranged from a low at the 56th percentile on national percentile rankings to a high at the 84th, with the majority of scores falling between the 70th and 79th percentiles.[16] Most recently, in 1999, educational researcher Lawrence Rudner released a study funded by HSLDA regarding home schoolers' academic achievement. Sample respondents performed exceptionally well on basic skills tests: remarkably, the home schoolers had higher median scores than the national norms for every subject in every grade. The study's stunning findings must be tempered by the fact that the research was built with a nonrandom convenience sample, financed by a highly interested advocacy organization, and has received criticism from both within and beyond the homeschool community.[17]

Indeed, even ten years after home schooling first made national headlines, methodologically rigorous statistical research on home schoolers remains scarce. The paucity of solid systematic data results largely from a lack of adequate sampling frames. Home education is legal throughout the United States, but states vary widely in the extent to which they require homeschool parents and their children to report to educational authorities. Even where formal accounting mechanisms are required, anecdotal evidence indicates notably less than full compliance.[18] Absent solid indices of homeschool populations, researchers have long been obliged to rely on convenience samples: enrollment lists of homeschool curriculum suppliers, test scores supplied by independent testing agencies, membership rosters in homeschooling organizations, and homeschool registration lists compiled by state officials and local school districts. Often, sample response rates have been low. Although it remains the most detailed demographic picture of home educators to date, the work of Mayberry and her colleagues is based on a survey with a response rate of 25 percent.

Despite the limitations of quantitative data, the existence of a lively and well-organized national movement is unquestionable. Previous observers have tended to overlook the fact that home schooling is a world of *organizations* as well as a population of parents and children. As early as 1988, one popular resource directory listed over forty correspondence schools and curriculum suppliers catering to homeschool families.[19] By the early 1990s, home schoolers could subscribe to half a dozen nationally circulated homeschooling magazines. A 1999 directory published by the pioneer periodical *Growing Without Schooling* listed literally hundreds of homeschool support organizations, in all fifty U.S. states and in ten other nations.[20] That same year *The Teaching Home*, a bimonthly publication targeted specifically to conservative Protestant home schoolers, provided contact information for expressly "Christian" homeschool organizations in every state, seven Canadian provinces, five other countries, and Puerto Rico.[21] In the United States the National Homeschool Association (NHA) and the Home School Legal Defense Association have long been politically active on behalf of home schoolers at the federal level.

Between 1985 and 1992, twenty-five states passed laws explicitly exempting homeschooled children from compulsory school attendance requirements. New state laws and judicial interpretation of older ones now make for wide variation in what state governments require of home schoolers, but despite local particularities home schooling is legal throughout the United States.[22] Bringing this to pass took years of work by scores of homeschool activists across the country, an effort that belies the myth that home schoolers are isolationists who have retreated from public life. As Sikkink and his colleagues have pointed out, a paradox about those who leave public schools is that they tend to be relatively *more* involved in civic life than their public-school neighbors.[23] In doing the political work that has made home schooling legal, in petitioning school boards for regulatory exemptions and more flexible services, and by serving as authors and speakers for their cause, home schoolers arguably are exemplars of effective, grassroots citizen activism.

My Research

When I began this project in 1990, I wanted to know, beyond the test scores and the head counts and the laws, who home schoolers are as people. What enables them to walk away from one of the most central institutions of modern life? What do they think about conventional schools, even the apparently good ones in affluent suburbs or with pricey tuitions, that render them second-best to home?

I wanted to know about the rhetorical frameworks that make home schooling reasonable. As a sociologist, I knew that people do not have convictions or even inklings in a vacuum. We inherit traditions of meaning that help define what we think and lend words to what we feel. I wanted to learn about the intellectual traditions from which home schooling had grown.

I wanted to know about the practical household decisions that make home schooling possible. I knew already that conventional parenting is a lot of work, and I suspected that home schooling is even more labor-intensive. I was interested in how people decided that they could afford the time, lost wages, and mental energy that home schooling costs. I also wanted to know how home schoolers assemble the help they need to get the job done. After all, conventional parenting is a collective project: babysitters, experienced neighbors, schoolteachers, and child development experts all are parts of the social machinery entailed in seeing children to maturity. I suspected that home schooling is a collective project, too, and I was interested also in how and with whom home schoolers cooperate.

Making such inquiries is important for several reasons. First, any legitimate interest in homeschooled children requires a parallel interest in their parents. Too often perhaps, the national media have only asked questions about the kids: how well they do academically or socially, whether they like home schooling, if they have enough friends, if they get into college. These questions are important, especially for policy makers, courts, and social service providers who work at the tender intersection of child welfare and domestic privacy. But an adequate understanding of any children requires that we know something about the architects and custodians of their life contexts. This book contributes to that kind of understanding.

Second, home schooling happens largely through women's labor. To be sure, fathers often are involved in the project, sometimes extensively. But as with conventional parenting and perhaps even more so, mothers assume a greatly disproportionate share of the homeschooling job. Further, these mothers are the backbone of the homeschool movement's impressive organizational system. Anyone interested in the fate of motherhood in contemporary America should take a closer look at home education—a movement peopled by women from many different walks of life who appear to have jumped headfirst into an elaborate domesticity.

Third, home schooling is an extraordinarily diverse social movement, and it has been built almost entirely since the end of the era called the Sixties. These two facts make it a good site for learning about the challenges of contemporary political activism. To political theorists with questions about how to build diverse political coalitions, home schooling is a rich case study. To scholars interested in the rise of the so-called Religious Right over the last two decades, home schooling provides a snapshot of the organizational sensibilities of conservative Protestant Christians. Finally, educators interested in improving parent-school relations will find much to consider, however disheartening, in these parents' tellingly simple critiques of conventional schooling.

Finally, home schooling provides another opportunity for the sociological imagination to demonstrate that even those behaviors that appear to be idiosyncratic, even "antisocial," are fundamentally collective. Like many of their fellow Americans, home schoolers like to think of themselves as individuals. They are system challengers, pioneers, a little bit alternative, not quite like other people. Yet to be so, home schoolers nurture relationships with other people who are "individuals" much like them. If skeptics have worried that home schooling represents an antisocial impulse, they have failed to see how much collective effort it has taken to make home education a provocative possibility for so many.

As is true with many ethnographic studies, a simple curiosity about home schooling preceded any of these headier concerns. A chance conversation with some friends of the family in 1989 blossomed into a ten-year project. "How are your children doing in school?" I asked innocently. I was told that the children were doing fine, but not in school. From there my questions multiplied quickly. Before I answered them to my satisfaction, I had interviewed parents from more than forty families, spoken informally with dozens more, visited ten nationally active homeschool organizations across the United States, and logged thousands of fieldwork miles throughout the upper Midwest.

The goal of ethnographic work is to learn about social life in an intimate way. The ethnographic vision presumes that an object of inquiry has an internal logic of its own, and that the world makes a different kind of sense to those involved in some activity than it does to everybody else. When I began this research in 1989, home schooling already had been given a certain kind of meaning by the popular media: home schoolers were quixotic idealists, bucking a great big system, engaged in an activity of questionable benefit to their children, a homespun anomaly in an increasingly rationalized world. I wanted to know something more and other than that: what home schooling means to the people who do it.[24]

I began this study at a random beginning point and followed home schoolers' webs of affiliation until I arrived at what sociologist Kathy Charmaz has called theoretical saturation, the point at which continued observations and interviews become predictably repetitive and yield little new insight.[25] In-depth interviews with parents provided my earliest lessons on home schooling and served as the spine of the research throughout the study. These interviews were conducted either with a single parent or with both parents at once, typically in their homes. The interviews were open-ended. I invariably encouraged parents to "begin wherever they thought the beginning was" and to recount their family's homeschool history. I asked them to talk through the schedule of a typical homeschooling day, to describe their curriculum, and to name which homeschool books, authors, and speakers they most revere. I asked what they liked best about what they were doing, about the hardest parts, and about the downsides of home education. I also asked about parents' own educational and work histories.[26]

Initially I sought out parents for interviews in "snowball" fashion, interviewing any who were willing to speak with me. Most of the home schoolers I met were white married couples, with at-home mothers and full-time breadwinner fathers.[27] In subsequent interviewing I sought out parents who did not fit this demographic pattern: nonwhite families, single parents, and working mothers. I also sought out variations in paternal occupation. In the end I had interviewed five black families, two unmarried couples, one single mother who worked full-time outside of her home, several married women who worked part-time or intermittently, and one father who was a full-time parent while his wife worked for pay. I also met people from a wide array of religious faiths. Fully half of the parents I interviewed indicated commitment to a Protestant evangelical faith, but I also visited Buddhist, Catholic, Orthodox Jewish, and avowed atheist households. In the end the contours of my sample were roughly consistent with what survey data and "insider" wisdom tell us about home schoolers: they are predominantly white and middle-class; many espouse conservative Protestant faiths; their households have full-time or nearly full-time moms; and

17

many of the families are large, not uncommonly with four or more children.

Home schoolers explain their work in rather different ways. All of them have much to say about the troubles with conventional schools, but their explanations differ subtly. Almost to a parent, they complain about the standardization of instruction in conventional schools. But those who describe themselves as Christians additionally lament secular curricula and the moral uncertainties of public-school peer groups. They often talk about home education in terms of divine will. They might say that home schooling is a fulfillment of God's command that parents take responsibility for their children's education in general, or of God's will for a particular mother to stay home.

Parents also opt to join rather different kinds of homeschool organizations. Some families participate in expressly "Christian" homeschool groups. These often include the word *Christian* in their names and provide newcomers with a *statement of faith* that stipulates core religious tenets of conservative Protestant Christianity. Some of these organizations make formal agreement with such statements a requisite of membership or of office-holding. Others participate in explicitly nonsectarian homeschool support groups. These purvey *nondiscrimination* or *inclusion* statements that formally welcome members regardless of religious preference or homeschooling philosophy.

There was a parallel, albeit a rough one, between homeschool philosophies and organizational affiliations. I was more likely to hear explicitly religious explanations for home schooling from those active in nominally Christian support groups. What initially appeared to be a simple and obvious correlation, however, turned out to be not so straightforward after all. I also met committed Christian parents who were active in nonsectarian groups and did not talk about home schooling in religious terms, and I met parents of varied religious commitments who had thought long and hard about what kind of homeschool organization to join.

In time I grew confident that, at least through the mid-1990s, this dual organizational system encompassed the majority of home schoolers in the Chicago metropolitan area. Even nominal membership in a local support group typically meant that parents were obliged to choose either "Christian" organizations or expressly "inclusive" ones. To be sure, as their numbers grew, parents were increasingly likely to find support options for more specialized colors in the homeschool rainbow. By 1995, a Network of Illinois Catholic Home Educators appeared, for example, and soon after the Jewish Homeschool Association of Greater Chicago. But these more specialized organizations came relatively late in the development of home schooling's organizational universe and in form are more akin to the inclusive side of the movement than the conservative Protestant one.[28] The organizational map was complicated, then, but it could appropriately be described as having two sides.

This organizational variation obliged me to find terms for the two sides, but I had trouble deciding what words to use. The conservative Protestants often call themselves and their organizations "Christian," but their *Christian* means something rather specific. It tends to be exclusive of non-Protestant Christianities and, as we will see, has important extrareligious functions. And more than a few home schoolers who are Protestant Christians are wary of the avowedly Christian homeschool organizations. I worried that such a polyvalent term would confuse rather than clarify. In the end I chose to call those religious who participate in avowedly Christian groups *believers*. This is a term native to conservative Protestantism, and one that also alludes to the spiritual convictions that many of these men and women bring to home schooling.[29]

The other side of home education is harder to encompass with a single term. Very likely the numerical minority of the homeschool population relative to the believers, this group encompasses an exceptional diversity of religious faiths. It includes Mormons, Muslims, Buddhists, Taoists, Catholics, Orthodox Jews, Jehovah's Witnesses, pagans, and atheists, as well as Protestants from many denominations and traditions. It encompasses people from a wide range of lifestyles. I met one family in their high-rise condominium with sweeping city views and other families who take pride in living far from the bright lights. Among them I met college professors and auto mechanics, practicing witches and devout evangelical Protestants. As a result of their differences and in contrast with the believers, these parents often have little in common with one another other than their shared interest in home schooling.[30]

I found also that the extent to which these home schoolers even thought of themselves as a "group," or wanted to be one, was very much an open question. In general the believers were comfortable talking about something called "Christian home schooling," or "the Christian homeschool movement," as if they could take for granted that such a thing existed. Those on the other side did not enjoy such cognitive luxuries. During the primary period of my research and for years afterward, these parents devoted considerable energy to discussing just who they were collectively, how they ought to work together, and who should be counted among them.

19

Ultimately I let my frustration with finding an adequate term teach me a lesson. I chose not to risk imposing order under the guise of describing it. In what follows I often refer simply to *some home schoolers* or, relative to the believers, *other home schoolers*. Occasionally I refer to *unschoolers*, using the name of a pedagogy favored by many of these families (and some of the believers!), but readers should understand my usage is a shorthand, provisional. Ultimately these home schoolers did find a name for themselves with which many were comfortable: *inclusives*. Near the end of the book I borrow their term.

Both camps of home schoolers in Illinois are linked with a national movement. In 1992, I began a series of trips throughout the United States to visit nationally active homeschooling organizations. Whenever possible on these visits, I interviewed people with a range of positions and statuses: the attorneys as well as their secretaries, the old hands and the new hires. In the interviews I typically focused on the practical details of people's work and, in many cases, their assessments of the organizational structure of home schooling as a whole. These trips gave me purchase on home schooling as a national phenomenon.[31]

As my understanding developed, I took the opportunity to have second and third conversations with some home schoolers whose knowledge and experience were particularly rich. I used these subsequent contacts to compare my emergent understanding with local experts. This ongoing checking process enabled me to revise, and sometimes discard, flawed or incomplete conclusions.[32]

Interviews were only a portion of the research. Throughout the study I was a participant observer at many homeschool events: support group meetings; regional and national home education conferences; book and curriculum fairs; camping and field trips; science club meetings; and "enrichment days" in which groups of homeschooled children took band lessons, played team sports, and did craft activities. Site visits to national movement organizations also provided occasions for participant observation and the generation of rich field notes.

Finally, I compiled an archive that constitutes a small portion of the wide stream of publications produced by the homeschool movement each year. Some of these texts are canonical among home schoolers, especially the book-length monographs that defend home education on academic, philosophical, and moral grounds. Books by John Holt, Raymond and Dorothy Moore, Mary Pride, David Guterson, and Chris Klicka fall into this category. Others are periodicals such as *The Teaching Home*, *Growing Without Schooling*, and *Home Education Magazine*. Then there are monthly and quarterly publications produced by local and regional support groups to inform their memberships of news and events. I obtained newsletters from groups in fourteen states, Canada, and Great Britain. Also in my files are curriculum samples and catalogs from many suppliers that serve home schoolers nationally. Materials from homeschool conferences also were useful sources of information. Conference planners often create elaborate packets for attendees that outline meeting schedules and sessions, provide names and counts of book fair vendors, and sometimes list the names and organizational affiliations of registrants. Additionally, I compiled a large stock of more ephemeral texts: flyers, brochures, and print advertisements in the general media, all put out by the homeschool world's vast array of entrepreneurs.

Any study of real people in a real world presents a scholar with important ethical questions. Mine concerned how to preserve people's privacy while maintaining the integrity of home schooling as a distinctive historical phenomenon. Some people spoke with me after I had assured them of anonymity in my published work, and I am eager to meet the spirit as well as the letter of those assurances. But I also interviewed many for whom, as public figures in an increasingly public movement, anonymity was entirely beside the point. I was faced with contradictory expectations from home schoolers, then, as well as a writer's obligation to make a reader's way smooth. In the interest of prosaic consistency, I have altered the identities of virtually all the people about whom I write with firsthand knowledge. I have given pseudonyms to all except the rare celebrities who are "household names" among home schoolers. In an additional effort to protect the privacy of those who appear in these pages, I have made only oblique reference to places of residence and occasionally have altered extraneous biographical information.[33]

In general I use the given names of homeschool organizations at the local, regional, and national levels.[34] I do this for two reasons. First, organizations typically are public actors. They choose names, and often clever ones, for the purpose of public recognition. Second, maintaining the given names of organizations lends historical veracity to my account of a movement that, as we shall see, has secured its own distinct niche in contemporary political history. My hope is that this writing strategy approximates high standards for both privacy and accuracy without unduly shortchanging either one.[35]

In addition to interviews and observational material, I also make many references to homeschool publications. All citations to texts in the public domain, and quotations from them, provide authors' actual names.

Like any inquiry, mine highlights some features of its object by leaving others in shadow. I have attempted an historically accurate sociological study of home schooling, not a comprehensive history. I here navigate the two broad currents of home schooling in America; in the process I have likely shortchanged other eddies in the river. Homeschool organizations that serve more specific constituencies—Islamic and Mormon home educators, or parents with special needs children, or home schoolers of color, for example—have received less attention here than a truly comprehensive account of home schooling would require. While I am confident that this book captures the general flow of home schooling nationally, the movement awaits a more thorough historian, one better positioned to name its heroes and less intent on asking specifically sociological questions.

Two other limitations of my work are worth noting here. First, in my effort to get to know their parents, I have given the perspectives of home-schooled children less attention. Ethnographic research shows that children's most significant social relationships and cultural points of reference often are at considerable remove from those of grown-ups, even when adults and children share the same physical space.[36] From my many interactions with homeschooled young people, and the witness of their impressive produce of art, literature, and journalism in many homeschool publications, I know that they have built social worlds meriting serious inquiry. There have been some such inquiries, but I have not done much of that work here.[37] Another limitation is that, as with many ethnographic studies, I cannot claim that my work is representative of the homeschool world in any systematic way. I have made every effort to confirm that my work correctly reflects my subject, but a mathematically defensible match between population and sample awaits better statistical information.

By the same token, I am confident that the kind of study I made provides insights that would be unattainable by any other means. An open itinerary is probably the most appropriate schedule for trips into uncharted territory. Home education was still very much under construction in the years I encountered it. I pursued a mode of inquiry that enabled me to alter my vision and my homework in accord with a dynamic phenomenon. Because I have worked inductively, I have been able to trail home schoolers toward some novel insights about the relationship between philosophy and organization and, more broadly, about the meaning of childhood in contemporary American culture.

In the end, home schoolers helped me to see that small differences in how people think about what they are doing can sum to big variation in organizational strength and political efficacy. They also vividly showed me how powerful, and costly, our beliefs about childhood can be.

HOME SCHOOLING IN ILLINOIS

"I'm fond of saying that I got dragged into home schooling backward, kicking and screaming," Deirdre Brown told me the first time I met her in 1991. When I asked how she became a home schooler, she took me back twenty years, to when her second son, Patrick, was just starting school. She remembers a kindergarten teacher scheduling a parent conference to discuss Patrick's attention span:

> [The teacher] said, "I just don't know what I'm going to do with your child. His attention span is just too long." I said, "Say that again please." She said, "Well his attention span is just too long. When I tell [the class] to draw a picture, Patrick has a half-hour picture in mind and the others will only sit still for about five minutes." And I said, "Well it sounds like *you* have a problem. I don't think *he* has a problem."[38]

Years later, Patrick's third-grade teacher literally "tied him in his desk" for reading the wrong books—C. S. Lewis instead of the class reader. On that occasion Deirdre met with the principal to request that Patrick be assigned to another teacher. She well remembers the principal's refusal.

> [He said], "Well, there's no way we can do that. If we move your child, we have to move everybody." Which is such a stupid argument. I hear it all the time. And it really is a blow to anybody's intelligence. Of course you can do it. If you're going to treat individual children individually, it isn't necessarily true that they'll each do well in the same classroom.

Dissatisfied, Deirdre moved Patrick outside the public school system. She found an amenable place for him, and for her own talents as an organizer, in the alternative schools appearing in Chicago and throughout the country in the 1970s.[39]

Patrick attended alternative schools for several years, and his mother found their democratic philosophies appealing. She had participated in the women's movement when her children were small, and much of the alternative schools' organizational blueprints were familiar from her earlier experiences.[40] One of Patrick's schools, for example, was run as a collective of parents, teachers, and students. Deirdre became an active parent, even an activist. Eventually she came to participate in the alternative school movement nationally, traveling to attend conferences of the National Coalition of Alternative Community Schools (NCACS).

In time, however, Deirdre became apprehensive that Patrick's academic potential was being stymied. She supported alternative schools in general,

23

but not any one for any child—especially her own. When the family moved to a new home in a different part of the city, the only alternative school available for Patrick didn't challenge him adequately. Deirdre pulled him out. "He ended up being at home," Deirdre said. "We didn't think of ourselves as 'home schoolers' necessarily, it was just that we didn't have any other choice."

Soon Deirdre found a language to describe what she was doing in the words of John Holt, a charismatic educational reformer who rose to national prominence with the publication of his first book, *How Children Fail*.[41] Holt had been a key player in the alternative school movement, and Deirdre befriended him during their mutual involvement in NCACS in the late 1970s. But at the end of that decade Holt began to urge parents to abandon schooling entirely. His argument came with a pedagogy, which he called "unschooling," that took place at home and required neither classrooms nor teachers. Holt published his own newsletter, *Growing Without Schooling*, that included addresses and phone numbers of the earliest unschoolers. Deirdre's name was among them, and in 1982 she got a call.

The voice on the other end of the line told Deirdre about a group of parents who knew each other through Lamaze childbirth classes and La Leche League.[42] They were considering home schooling their children. Could Deirdre help? A series of conversations culminated in an open house for interested parents in the spring of 1983. "We figured we'd have a dozen people," Deirdre said. "Forty people came. They couldn't all fit in the living room." The meeting became the nucleus for a new support organization, Home Oriented Unschooling Experience. "That's how the HOUSE network got started," Deirdre said.

Creating an organization required decisions about *how* to organize. "I've had a fair amount of experience in groups," Deirdre explained,

> and I said this group, with all of the different approaches [represented], this has to be a consensus group. There can't be somebody who's the boss and we aren't going to have officers, we're going to be taking turns because nobody's going to be the expert. We're so diverse, and we can't have anyone saying this is "the way" to do it. It just will not work. And generally speaking that's the way the HOUSE groups have run.

The mid-1980s were active years for HOUSE. The organization sponsored a lecture by John Holt in Chicago, shortly before his death in 1985.[43] HOUSE soon became a network of multiple chapters throughout the city and downstate. While HOUSE gained organizational momentum, one of its rules remained constant. According to Deirdre, "The one thing that the HOUSE network has insisted upon is that anyone can come no matter what their point of view is. No matter what their educational philosophy or their religious view or whatever, this is a group that's open to anybody who wants to come."[44] And come they did. By 1985, HOUSE members surmised sufficient interest in home schooling to sponsor a curriculum fair. Held at Chicago's Museum of Science and Industry, the fair signaled a turning point for home schooling in Illinois. "Things sort of took off after that," Deirdre said.

Not everyone found a home in HOUSE, however. From the earliest days of the organization there were Protestant Christians in HOUSE groups; some of them were happy there, but others were not quite comfortable with the parenting styles and teaching philosophies they found at HOUSE meetings. Theresa Marquette, a born-again Christian, was one of the HOUSE parents who sought support among others who shared her faith. Theresa was impressed with the organizational acumen of HOUSE in the early 1980s and, she says, grateful for the initial support she got from HOUSE groups. "But on a faith level, I struggled with it, the strong philosophy of unschooling among many of the people in HOUSE."[45] Part of the trouble, as I learned from many parents, was that unschooling's presumption about the inherent goodness of children did not sit well with conservative Protestants, who tended to balance their high regard for children's potential with a strong conviction about the inherent sinfulness of humankind.[46]

Theresa attended HOUSE meetings during her first year of home schooling in 1981; the following year, she inquired of HOUSE organizers whether she and a few other parents could start another group, under the HOUSE umbrella, specifically for born-again Christians. The group was to be called "His HOUSE," referencing both the connection to the parent organization and the satellite's commitment to their Heavenly Father. "Our intent was not to be exclusive," Theresa explained to me years later. "We had great respect for HOUSE. We were organizing kinds of people and we recognized that they had done a lot of good work. But we wanted support that was more in keeping with our faith."

HOUSE remained committed to its nonsectarianism. "People were of course welcome to start whatever kind of group they wanted. But they could not organize a Christian group and call it a HOUSE group," Deirdre Brown explained.[47] If a support group were to carry the HOUSE name, HOUSE organizers stipulated that it would have to welcome all comers and not be formally religious. While apparently there were no hard feelings on either side of the disagreement, Theresa Marquette and a handful of other believers left HOUSE and began to form their own support network specifically for conservative Protestants.

"My parents were both schoolteachers, and they told us as soon as we were starting to have children, they said, 'start saving your money now for private school.' And with that we were like, okay, private school. That's how we were thinking."[48] This is how Susan Jerome and her husband, Steve, explained the beginning of their own journey into home education. Like Deirdre Brown, they considered alternative schools before home schooling, but they had different alternatives in mind. For the Jeromes, Christian day schools were prime candidates. There were several such schools in the Chicago area when the Jeromes' children were small—local manifestations of the Christian day school movement that swept the country in the 1970s.[49]

But one day in the early 1980s, Steve and Susan heard about another option. James Dobson's syndicated *Focus on the Family* radio program, aired on religious stations nationally, carried a series of interviews with Dr. Raymond Moore. A Seventh-Day Adventist and education researcher, Moore had long advocated home instruction for young children. In his radio interviews with Dr. Moore in the early 1980s, Dobson went on record in support of home-based instruction, even carrying Dr. and Mrs. Moore's recent book, *Home Grown Kids*, in his mail-order service. "So that's where I first heard about it and I thought, 'I can do this!'" Susan said. "I got [the] book and read it and thought, 'Oh, this is it!'" Steve added that hearing about home schooling on *Focus* made it seem all the more plausible. "Dobson's endorsement really gave Dr. Moore some legitimacy. It gave home schooling legitimacy. I think it made a lot of difference for a lot of people, that Dobson supported it."

Soon the Jeromes sought out other people who were interested in home schooling.

When we started out, started to become interested in it, we heard about . . . a support group that was going to meet in one family's home. And we went. [I remember] the meeting was in the basement, there were ten couples. That was really the beginning for us. And after we had formed our group, we assembled information for other people, for other people who wanted to form support groups.

These early meetings were the nucleus of Illinois Christian Home Educators (ICHE), an organizational network that, over the next decade, would include virtually all Christian homeschool support groups statewide.

Susan explained how the basement group provided information that made things easier for families who came to home schooling in later years:

Initially you spent so much time looking up the law and figuring it out. I mean, back then there was no one you could call to just give you that information, like there is now. There were no experts. It was all uncharted territory. So we had to do the homework ourselves, actually go to the law books and look up what was pertinent to home education, and compile information about curriculum and all the rest. So after we started, we put together a big binder of information that included information about the law in Illinois, and all of the articles and literature that we had on home schooling, and we made it available to anyone else who was interested.

To their pleasure, these first families found that Illinois law was friendly to home schoolers. A 1950 state supreme court ruling had defined home schools as private schools under Illinois education statutes. Consequently, home schoolers in the state are required only to teach curriculum comparable to that used in public schools, in English, to their children between the ages of seven and sixteen.[50] The fortuitous court ruling, handed down decades before the contemporary movement began, gave the state one of the most favorable legal climates for home schooling in the country. But in the early 1980s, pertinent education law, like much else about home education, was unknown to many.

Many, however, were interested in home schooling. In 1984, ICHE sponsored its first statewide conference, with Raymond Moore himself as the keynote speaker. Moore cooperated with ICHE volunteers in coordinating the local event, supplying them with the Illinois entries on his national mailing list and giving them a share of convention revenues. Together with conservative family advocate Phyllis Schlafly, Moore appeared on the campus of Wheaton College, a prominent evangelical school in Chicago's western suburbs, on July 23, 1984. In the audience were 650 registered conferees. The event generated ICHE's first statewide mailing list, and $2,000 for its first checking account.[51]

As with the HOUSE curriculum fair, the ICHE conference was the beginning of several years of rapid growth for its sponsor. By the late 1980s, ICHE was holding annual statewide conferences. As Steve recalled, "There were a few years in there where the [registration] numbers just went up dramatically from year to year. I mean, [in] one year they doubled."

Unlike HOUSE, which had no formally appointed leaders—and, indeed, no formally written bylaws until 1992[52]—ICHE had adopted a

27

quasi-corporate structure by the late 1980s. It had secured 501(c)(3) tax-exempt status and was administered by an internally appointed board of directors; Steve and Susan Jerome were two of its first members. The board takes responsibility for producing ICHE's annual conferences and serves as a practical network hub for support groups statewide. ICHE became an organizational mechanism for linking local constituencies with one another and for defining local groups as expressly Christian; all groups in the network are obliged to formally concur with ICHE's "statement of faith," a document that lists basic tenets of conservative Protestant theology. Each local group, however, maintains a high level of autonomy. "We didn't tell [local support groups] how to run their groups, in fact we've never done that, and ICHE support groups still make their own decisions about how to run," Susan explained.[53]

Home schoolers' different life philosophies had some organizational consequences even in those early days. By the mid-1980s there were two somewhat distinct support networks, one nominally Christian and the other explicitly ecumenical, that operated according to somewhat different rules. But despite the emergent differences in organization, religious faith, and favored gurus, boundaries between the camps were fluid throughout the decade. Home schoolers of many different stripes often found themselves attending the same support groups, conferences, and curriculum fairs. Homeschool friendships linked those with a wide range of beliefs. In 1984 leaders from the two camps collaborated, forming the Ad Hoc Committee for Illinois Home Education Legal and Legislative Matters (Ad Hoc) to defend homeschooling freedoms before local school districts and at the state capitol in Springfield. Among the groups represented on Ad Hoc early on were HOUSE, ICHE, and Clonlara School, a Michigan-based, nonsectarian correspondence program that had many registered students in Illinois. Also represented was Christian Liberty Academy, another private school with a sizable correspondence program, headquartered in suburban Chicago.

Although home schoolers in Illinois enjoyed a favorable legal climate, their efforts still met with suspicions—especially in the early years—from some legislators, school authorities, and child welfare workers. Ad Hoc's mission was to talk back to such critics and, when necessary, to lobby in defense of basic homeschool freedoms. In 1987, for example, the committee lobbied against state legislation that would have required home-schooled children to be registered with the state; it presented an informational workshop on home schooling to staff of the state child welfare department; and it countered efforts by the Cook County regional school superintendent to regulate home schooling locally.[54]

Because its founders were aware of the wide range of beliefs and lifestyles represented in the budding cause, Ad Hoc adopted a consensual decision-making system whereby the organization could only pursue actions agreed upon by its entire membership. An early Ad Hoc flyer promised, "Due to the diverse nature of this group, all position papers must be agreed to word for word by all members. . . . Written correspondence must reflect the delicate balance of differing philosophies held by the Ad Hoc members." Ad Hoc's consensus rules included an all-or-nothing escape clause: "In the event that the committee is unable to establish a position agreeable to all members, it is understood that each [member] organization will take action consistent with their educational philosophy."[55]

In this ecumenical spirit, home schooling flourished in Illinois through the end of the decade. Numbers of recruits and support groups mushroomed in the 1980s, while some local advocates claim that the growth leveled off in the early 1990s. By 1994, Deirdre Brown estimated for the *Chicago Sun-Times* that there were ten thousand homeschooled children in the state, while other seasoned players in Illinois later told me they would put the number even higher.[56] HOUSE claimed nine local support group chapters statewide in 1993; by 1995, ICHE had over a hundred affiliated local organizations.

As its organizational network grew more elaborate, news about this little movement diffused through ever larger populations. As the years went by, more and more people had heard of home education. They had seen discussions of it on a talk show, heard about it on the radio, or knew someone at church, or down the street, who homeschooled her own kids. It was like anything new and provocative: the more people who got a little taste of it, the more there were who actually gave it a try.

From Parents to Teachers

MILES FROM THE office towers and leafy boulevards that postcards call Chicago, the modest buildings and simply landscaped yards on Tara Cook's block recall a middle-class, white ethnic north side. From the back porch where we are sitting, Tara keeps a subtle eye on her sons, Jonah and Trevor, playing more and less amicably in the narrow backyard. Jonah, the oldest and nearing six, has not yet been in school. Tara and I spend the better part of an afternoon discussing why.

"I have always been a little bit alternative," Tara tells me straightaway. Before having children, she worked as a nurse, most recently in the delivery room of a prestigious urban hospital. Back then she was "somewhat left-wing allopathic. . . . You know, I would be the one on the unit if people came in with birth plans and they wanted to not use monitors and drugs and all that kind of stuff, I would be one of the people who would say, 'Give that to me.'" Tara had some philosophical troubles with the work, though, critical as she was of conventional medical models of childbirth. Her own children were born either in birth centers or at home. Tara is now with her children virtually full-time, while also seeing counseling clients at her home a few hours a week. Her husband, Frank, a medical professional of less alternative stripe, maintains his office nearby.

"My interests have been children and child rearing, and all that kind of stuff, and reading a lot about it. So I used to just spend hours, whenever [my kids] were nursing or asleep, I would just read," she explained. "I had started reading articles in *Mothering*, and really enjoyed the concepts of home schooling. I really enjoyed the philosophies and the thoughts that went along with it, giving [children] more latitude. Also Raymond and Dorothy Moore's stuff." She spoke highly of John Holt's books: "I've read a couple of his. . . . *Learning All the Time* was the last one that I read, it was the one he was in the middle of writing when he died. And I just love it. I love it. I don't know what else to say."

Tara contrasted home schooling with her own educational biography, constrained as it was by the routines of conventional schools. "I'm a result of a Catholic grade school and then public high school and [a state college], and I feel like so much has been squelched. Creativity and enthusiasm for learning. It's been more like punishment and a burden a lot of times." She wants things to be different for her own children. "I want them to be able to learn, and create the space [for them] to learn out of heart and out of desire."[1]

An hour farther out, in the comfortable northern suburbs, Chicago and its famously troubled schools seem far away. But Eric and Marci Rayburn are still sufficiently wary of conventional schools that they have kept their daughter Carolyn, a personable second grader, at home. Unlike her infant sister, Sydney, who was asleep in the bedroom, Carolyn was never out of sight the evening I spoke to her parents. She spent much of her time sitting quietly between them on the sofa while they explained, in articulate detail, why they chose home schooling over public and private schools for their daughter. At times her parents asked Carolyn to tell me something about home schooling that she particularly liked: learning about forts and castles, making bricks from mud and straw, memorizing all the books of the Bible and then receiving her own Bible as a reward.

Eric and Marci had several reasons for keeping Carolyn home. One had to do with how conventional schools organize the learning process. "I realized that I wouldn't really have a choice over who my child's teachers would be, and over what kind of philosophy of life they would bring to my children every day," Marci said. A former public school teacher, she had been on the inside herself and did not like what she saw. "People are not loving toward children, you know, if the child has a problem and is disruptive in the classroom, it's not dealt with in love. It's dealt with [in a way that] I felt many times bordered on being inhuman." Eric complained about "the emphasis on competition in education, that the only way that you can be good is to have somebody else be not as good. That bothered us, that it wasn't a measure of self against your potential or your abilities but just, 'well, I got a better grade than you got'. . . . children were allowed to do that, and in some cases encouraged [to do that]." Some reading had helped the Rayburns make sense of their frustrations. "It was about the time this fellow was writing, Raymond Moore," Marci said, motioning to some books on the coffee table in front of her. They had set out some material to show me that evening. "We picked up a couple of these books and started reading them."[2]

Akin to Tara Cook and the Rayburns, all the parents I met had good reasons for home schooling: conventional classrooms that make learning a chore; inflexible or incoherent curricula; inhuman organizations that fail to discipline with love. Parents were eager to talk about their reasons. I had little reason to be surprised. People who do things unconventionally tend to become skilled at explaining themselves to critics.[3] Over the years, home schoolers' critics have been varied and numerous: school officials, grocery store checkout clerks, talk show hosts, and wary relatives.

This chapter is about how home schoolers defy the critics while learning to settle their own uncertainties. "I'm scared," another mother confided to me, "wondering whether I'm doing the right thing or not, whether I'm capable of doing it."[4] "I was scared, I was nervous. I didn't know if I could handle it, if this was the right thing," said another.[5] Home schooling *can* be scary. It requires that parents suspend faith in an entire education system. It brings the possibility that one's home work will be monitored by school authorities. Sometimes it means sacrificing a second family income and a significant margin of financial security. For those without formal training or experience as teachers, it requires that parents trust themselves to manage a range of tasks typically understood to be the purview of experts. And there is no student teaching, no trial run. As with conventional parenting and bicycle riding, one must learn by doing and suffer the scrapes as they come. But unlike with these more conventional skills, friends and relatives are much less likely to lend the empathy of experience. These sources of apprehension were especially formidable in the early years, through much of the 1980s, when the legal status of home schooling was more precarious, homeschool households few in number, and positive media coverage hard to find.

The transition from apprehension to commitment is made possible, in part, through parents' interactions with those who are already committed. Most of the home schoolers I met had participated in a support group at least in the early years of their effort. In support groups, "You kind of bump into people with similar philosophies or kids that have similar learning styles and things like that," said another mom.[6] Some parents participate in multiple groups. "I just really needed it for lots of reasons," said one mother of five who participated in two homeschool organizations for a time. "My children were all young and I needed the contact with other women who felt about the same way I did."[7] Support groups also prove to be good curatives for skeptics. As a mother of two explained: "I've tried to take [my husband] to some of the . . . meetings, which is an incredibly powerful thing. And I always put this in when I talk about it at all with people: 'Oh yes, I belong to a parent association of over 150 families. . . .' Well, it must be OK, because, after all, 150 families are doing it."[8] The numbers make the whole project seem more reasonable, less frightening.

The transition to commitment, then, is a meaningful one. To become committed to home schooling, people need to redefine "what everyone knows," namely, that there are good academic and developmental reasons for children to be in school. Commitment to home schooling is in significant part a rhetorical matter. It happens only when people can convince themselves that what they are up to is reasonable. To get a sense of how important the rhetorical element is, consider how unlikely it would be for a parent to consciously take any risk with his or her own child, *without a reason*.[9] Creating good arguments in favor of home schooling, then, was the first task of the nascent movement's entrepreneurs.

Making good arguments is complicated business. Good arguments are legitimate: they are built from premises that relevant parties already take as sound. This requires that their authors have considerable knowledge of the cultural context in which they are speaking. If the arguments are to change behavior, they should be innovative: what is given needs to be rendered problematic somehow. This requires intelligence, and at least a bit of savvy on the author's end. Finally, a measure of artfulness is useful. Arguments that are not overly complex and that make emotional as well as intellectual appeals are more likely to compel listeners.[10]

However implicitly, home education's earliest advocates understood all of this. They made their arguments legitimate by speaking in harmony with some resonant chords in American culture: our belief that all people are individuals, with rights; our suspicion that "experts" are not as trustworthy as common sense; and our worries that government is too intrusive and does not serve us very well. Homeschool advocates innovated on these notions by pitting them against a new target—school. And they often did so with elegant simplicity and gut-hitting emotion.

In one sense these arguments have many authors. They can be found at every support group and curriculum fair, in every homeschool periodical, and in a cacophony of Internet chat lines. But a handful of advocates assembled the basic features of homeschool rhetoric years ago. Their signal accomplishments were to fashion arguments strong enough to make people rethink conventional schooling and then to figure out how the arguments could be disseminated to the kinds of people who would find them compelling. Pulling it off required an enviable combination of intellectual and organizational skill.[11] These advocates did not create a social movement by themselves, of course, but they did much to establish the basic rhetoric through which home schooling is made reasonable even today.

The nature of that rhetoric has been important in two ways to the fate of home schooling as a social movement. On the one hand, its harmony with core tenets of the general culture has enabled home schoolers to convince consequential outsiders, and themselves, that home schooling is an acceptable thing to do. At the same time, the existence of incompatible,

33

even contradictory, arguments in favor of home schooling has made it easier for an always diverse homeschool movement to remain factionalized.

LIBERATING THE ESSENTIAL CHILD

Some cornerstones of homeschool pedagogy are outgrowths of the heady climate for school reform in the 1960s and 1970s. Part of the cultural percolation of those decades was a renewed political militancy among left-liberals regarding the role of education in creating social change. The authority challenges common on university campuses of the era had an echo among the educational intelligentsia, where a cadre of reformers spurred a grassroots movement with arguments for new schools independent of the educational establishment. A flurry of books called for progressive parents to "free the children" by "doing your own school." Author-activists such as Jonathan Kozol and Allen Graubard encouraged parents who "have despaired over the possibility of substantial changes within the public school system within a reasonable time" to start their own, autonomous institutions beyond the constraints of conventional school systems.[12]

Many reformers advocated dramatic change in conventional schools as well. Herbert Kohl, James Herndon, and others encouraged self-directed learning, doing away with desks, eliminating rigidly sequential curriculum and formal testing, and replacing all of these with more individualized and egalitarian approaches. These causes had an emancipatory tenor that harmonized well with the anti-Establishment rhetoric of the times. "Vietnam and the civil rights movement, counterculture—those had been the passwords," wrote James Herndon of this era of school reform. "We had sought alternatives . . . to what? Well, to everything, in the end, but especially to the mind-numbing public school classrooms."[13]

"For most American children there is essentially one public school system in the United States, and it is authoritarian and oppressive," lamented Herbert Kohl in his 1969 book, *The Open Classroom*. "Students everywhere are deprived of the right to make choices concerning their own destinies."[14] For Kohl, Herndon, and other advocates who were working to exemplify emancipatory pedagogies in "alternative" and "free" schools across the country, the problem was that the rigid authority hierarchies and lockstep curricula of conventional classrooms were designed to serve organizational objectives, not students. Schools were like factories or machines. They were bureaucracies, and bureaucracies were bad. They failed to allow children intellectual or emotional breathing room.

Invoking the rhetoric of personal experience, one of the hallmarks of other social movements of the era,[15] Kohl supported the ideas in *The Open Classroom* with his own frustrations as a fifth-grade teacher in a Harlem public school:

> I was having troubles with the curriculum, with my students, with bureaucratic details, with other teachers, and, most of all, with myself. I was bewildered and angered by what was expected of me, and overwhelmed by my contact with students. I was supposed to teach the fifth-grade curriculum, no matter who my students were or what they cared about. I was also supposed to take attendance; sign circulars . . . take my turn at yard duty, hall duty, and lunchroom duty. The demands were as frequent as they were senseless. Yet they were insignificant when compared with the pressure to fulfill the function considered most essential to a teacher's success—controlling the children.[16]

The tendency toward control was one of the progressive reformers' primary criticisms of conventional schools. These activists feared that schools were more likely to contain and process children rather than, as Kohl called it, "loving students as learners"[17] and "respecting the language and culture of the learner."[18] "My concern is not to improve 'education,'" proclaimed the reformer John Holt, "but to do away with it, to end the ugly and anti-human business of people-shaping and let people shape themselves."[19]

One of home schooling's earliest and most influential advocates, John Holt initially achieved prominence in the traffic of the progressive school reform movement. Holt's ideas were first widely disseminated in his 1964 collection of essays, *How Children Fail*. Beginning with this book, Holt's lifelong concern was that conventionally structured classrooms and curricula squelched children's natural inquisitiveness. He believed that all children had an inherent proclivity for learning, which schools routinely replaced with the anxieties of academic competition. Formal schools were less interested in making sure children learned than in making sure that their charges were graded and credentialed in some standard way. "Nobody starts out stupid," Holt wrote in an exposition on intelligence in *How Children Fail*. "You only have to watch babies and infants, to think seriously about what all of them learn and do, to see that, except for the most grossly retarded, they show a style of life, and a desire and ability to learn that in an older person we might well call genius. . . . But what happens, as we get older, to this extraordinary capacity for learning and intellectual growth?" Writing from his observations in a fifth-grade classroom, Holt

35

was seeking to understand the widely varied achievement levels of children. He answered his own question with a conclusion he would spend the rest of his life elaborating: it was not the different abilities of children that explained their varied achievement levels, but rather the competitive, judgmental environment of school. "What happens," he wrote,

> is that [this capacity for learning] is destroyed, and more than by any other thing, by the process we misname education. . . . We adults destroy most of the intellectual and creative capacity of children by the things we do to them or make them do. We destroy this capacity above all by making them afraid, afraid of not doing what other people want, of not pleasing, of making mistakes, of failing, of being *wrong*.[20]

It was school as a bureaucracy, requiring standardized ways of measuring achievement and distributing rewards, that Holt believed stifled children's inherent capacity for learning. "Children are by nature and from birth very curious about the world around them, and very energetic, resourceful, and competent in exploring it, finding out about it, and mastering it. . . . Babies are not blobs, but true scientists," he wrote in his 1981 book, *Teach Your Own*.[21] Holt long maintained that the innate intelligence and "love of learning in children, which is so strong when they are small," is destroyed by parents and teachers and the very structure of school organizations "encouraging and compelling [children] to work for petty and contemptible rewards—gold stars, or papers marked 100 and tacked to the wall, or *A*'s on report cards, or honor rolls, or dean's lists, or Phi Beta Kappa keys—in short, for the ignoble satisfaction of feeling that they are better than someone else."[22] For Holt, school's rigid, inherently competitive environment, rather than children's different abilities or opportunities, explained how children fail.

John Holt's prominence in the progressive school reform movement came not from formal credentials (he was famously elusive about his own educational background)[23] or from any formal research accomplishments but rather from his remarkable ability to meld an incisive institutional critique with a compelling philosophy of human potential. Testament to Holt's gift for impassioned prose and to the wide public interest in liberal school reform during the era, *How Children Fail* and the sequel, *How Children Learn*, eventually sold over a million and a half copies and were translated into several foreign languages.[24] Their author was heralded in the *New York Review of Books* as "in a class with Piaget."[25] But Holt would not long remain a school reformer. He soon abandoned hope of revamping schools according to his philosophy and began a crusade for a different kind of learning.

In his 1976 book, *Instead of Education*, Holt publicly proclaimed "the failure of school reform" and advocated what he believed a more philosophically defensible pedagogy. *Instead of Education* was an impassioned rationale for why formal instruction of virtually any sort is incapable of serving children's needs:

> Education, with its supporting system of compulsory and competitive schooling, all its carrots and sticks, its grades, diplomas, and credentials, now seems to me perhaps the most authoritarian and dangerous of all the social inventions of mankind. It is the deepest foundation of the modern and worldwide slave state, in which most people feel themselves to be nothing but producers, consumers, spectators, and "fans," driven more and more, in all parts of their lives, by greed, envy, and fear.[26]

Carrying the institutional-critical rhetoric of the school reform movement to dramatic proportions, Holt made an explicit connection between conventional schooling and an oppressive vision of the modern state. For Holt "education" now meant "learning cut off from active life and done under pressure of bribe or threat, greed and fear." He advocated instead a pedagogy of "*doing*—self-directed, purposeful, meaningful life and work."[27]

By the late 1970s, Holt had given this pedagogy a name. He argued that both children and their parents needed to be "unschooled"—stripped of their assumption that education was instruction and made to see that "true learning . . . has to do with our ability to think up important questions and then find ways to get useful answers. [It] is not a trick that can be taught, nor does it need to be. We are born with it, and if our other deep animal needs are fairly well satisfied, and we have reasonable access to the world around us, we will put it to work on that world."[28] Self-directed learning was the only kind one ought reasonably to expect of children. Holt even proclaimed this kind of learning an inalienable human right, "next to the right to life itself, the most fundamental of all human rights, . . . the right to control our own minds and thoughts."[29]

Before his untimely death from cancer in 1985, Holt had completed nine books, toured nationally and internationally for speaking engagements, and founded *Growing Without Schooling*, a magazine published out of Cambridge, Massachusetts, that both called for and helped solidify a nascent homeschool movement.[30] Through his prolific work Holt articulated core tenets of homeschooling philosophy: that children are unique individuals from the moment of birth, and that their essential beings are demeaned by conventional schools. Extending the American ideals of personal liberty and individualism to the earliest reaches of the life course, Holt maintained that children were individuals before they were ever social beings; he argued that disregarding or usurping this individuality was a kind of moral crime. Children as "do-ers"—self-directed learners— take on the status in Holt's pedagogy as fully autonomous beings: "The point is that it is the do-er, not someone else, who has decided what he will say, hear, read, write, or think or dream about. He is at the center or his own actions. He plans, directs, controls and judges them. He does them for his own purposes. . . . His actions are not ordered and controlled from outside. They belong to him and are a part of him."[31]

PROTECTING THE FRAGILE CHILD

During the same years that Holt developed his pedagogy, a husband-and-wife team carved out their own notoriety as educational reformers. Outside the cadre of progressive advocates in which Holt found his intellectual nourishment, Raymond and Dorothy Moore built notable careers as critics of conventional schooling. Seventh-Day Adventists by faith and educational researchers by training, the Moores developed a national reputation during the 1970s by deriding the conventional wisdom that early schooling was necessary or even appropriate for young children. Headquartered at Andrews University in Michigan, the Moores compiled results from child development research conducted at major universities throughout the country. Armed with a long bibliography, they conducted a public campaign that challenged the wisdom of sending children to school before they reached eight, nine, or even ten years of age. Like Holt, the Moores eventually abandoned the prospect of school reform; like Holt, they ultimately encouraged parents to pull their children out of school; and like Holt, their efforts created core rationales for a soon-to-blossom homeschool movement.

But the emphasis of the Moores' message was different. Holt sought to protect children's right to self-determination. The Moores sought, rather, to protect children from schools. In the Moores' pedagogical vision children are not autonomous beings. They require instruction—albeit careful instruction—from appropriate authorities. The Moores concurred with Holt and his circle that conventional schooling was detrimental to children, but not because it was authoritarian. For the Moores the problem was that the authorities ruled with methods ill suited to children's fragile natures. The distinction was subtle but significant, for it led them to advocate a pedagogy premised on hierarchical relationships quite unlike Holt's unschooling.[32]

The Moores used the language of child development to make their claims, drawing on research documenting the limits of young children's motor skills, vision and hearing capacities, and reasoning abilities. They argued that children were physically and developmentally ill equipped for formal classroom instruction until they achieved a point the Moores called their "integrated maturity level," or IML.[33] IML was the point in children's development when sight, hearing, motor skills, and reasoning capacities were sufficiently evolved and coordinated that children could be expected to function reasonably in a conventional classroom. Integrated maturity levels were highly individuated, the Moores cautioned. Each child reached his or her IML at a different time, and formal schooling was detrimental to the child who had not yet attained it. The Moores warned that vision impairment and a host of otherwise preventable learning disabilities were the risks of formal schooling before attainment of IML.[34]

The Moores' claims first entered the national media through a feature article in *Harper's* in 1972 and were elaborated in their books *Better Late Than Early* and *School Can Wait*. In the subsequent *Home Grown Kids* and *Home-Spun Schools*, the Moores explicitly linked their claims as researchers to the promise of home schooling.[35] To support their cause the Moores left academia and created their own organization. Their Hewitt-Moore Research Foundation in Washougal, Washington, provided advice, network connections, and curriculum services to families pursuing "home-based education," or home schooling.

In some ways the rationale for home-based education sounds like Holt's defense of unschooling. In a manner that unschooling's champion would have appreciated, the Moores use a rich metaphor to describe the mechanistic procedures of schools when they claim that many parents "are rethinking the idea of mass-produced education and are coming up with the notion that maybe 'custom-made' is not so elitist after all. Their youngsters are not manufactured toys; they are home-grown kids."[36] For the Moores as for Holt, schools are factory-like places, and their standardized procedures are what make otherwise good children into "problem" kids:

> The tendency for most schools and similar institutions is to make the child's program rigid. This is a necessary feature of mass production. The youngster's activity for much of the day is focused in a few square feet area around his desk, and timed out to the minute. As the years have rolled on, we have tightened the noose and piled on the studies, expecting the child nobly to respond with higher achievement. But it hasn't worked out that way. School records have dismally declined, with learning failure, delinquency, and

hyperactivity racing for first place in HEW statistics. Is this what we want for our children?[37]

In this folksy, readable prose, the Moores reiterate Holt's disdain for the bureaucratic elements of conventional schooling.

Unlike Holt, however, the Moores replace conventional schools with a more intimate school-at-home. Suspect bureaucrats are replaced with benevolent parents. "Mothers and fathers can provide deeper security, sheerer closeness, sharper instincts, longer continuity, warmer responses, more logical control and more natural example than the staff in the best care center or kindergarten," exclaim Raymond and Dorothy Moore in *Home Grown Kids*:

> Without ever ringing a school bell, monitoring a recess or opening a course-of-study manual or even knowing the inside of a college, their teaching and care in their home are for their children . . . easily superior to the most skilled professors outside it. And a combination of all parental advantages will instinctively or with simple and most modest help usually bring out children who excel academically, behaviorally, morally, and socially.[38]

The message is clear: schools cannot substitute for parent-child intimacy and the "instinctual" knowledge of parents.

By lending distinctive importance to the role of parents in appropriate instruction, the Moores invoke a hierarchical relationship between children and authority quite different from Holt's emancipatory pedagogy. Where Holt advocated children's liberation from instructional authorities of any kind, the Moores presume the legitimate authority of parents. Hierarchical relationships between children and their teachers are fine, so long as the teachers are the right ones. "The hand that rocks the cradle rules the world," the Moores remind parents. "Let's be sobered at the thought of loosening that grip." Throughout much of their work the Moores implied that more than sound research supports the appropriateness of parental authority. "Let us not forget that the God who designed the kids ordained the family to nest them. And let the school follow after."[39]

In many ways the claims of John Holt and the Moores sound familiar, coming as they do from old ideas about the nature of children and the parent-child relationship. Western culture has long regarded childhood as a special, even sacred, period of the life course. Much historical work suggests that the specialness and preciousness of childhood develops in tandem with the elaboration of modern individualism, a cultural product with a deep and complicated past. And American civil law has long lent sanctity to the parent-child relationship.[40] These reformers' arguments are not brand-new, then, but rather are innovative versions of established ideas. Making the arguments was a crucial beginning for a nascent homeschool movement because they created the general framework within which home schooling would be rendered comprehensible and compelling to parents, and defensible to consequential outsiders. The arguments had to be both old and new: old, so that they would sound familiar and even inevitable; new, so that they would spur a reassessment of the commonplace. Once assembled, the arguments enabled parents to do something unconventional with a bit more peace of mind. And they also made it possible for the newly committed to explain themselves to skeptical neighbors, spouses, and school officials. Thinking about homeschool rationales in this way gives us a clearer sense of the place of intellectual work in social movements more broadly. Coherent arguments alone may not change the world, but they do provide maps for behavioral innovation and elicit the convictions that propel people into action.

It would overstate their accomplishment, though, to contend that Holt and the Moores have done all of the intellectual work on their own. The claims that crystallized early on through their writings were subsequently elaborated by many other speakers and authors. Critiques of schools as mechanistic, detrimentally bureaucratic places pervade virtually every facet of homeschooling literature, from widely disseminated books and magazines to regional and local newsletters. "In efforts to increase productivity at minimal cost, schools have adopted a factory-like system of management," author Llewellyn B. Davis declares in a book-length defense of home education titled *Why So Many Christians Are Going Home to School*:

> Architecturally, they resemble factories and office buildings; administratively, they run like production lines. They have developed clear hierarchies of authority (student, teacher, principal, superintendent, school committee, etc.); and they have adopted standardized units of instruction. . . . Some authors call this educational approach modeled after corporate bureaucracy "The Research and Development Mentality," and have become concerned that it produces a distorted concept of reality and humanness.[41]

"Schools are not designed around the needs and desires of the individual," laments Donna Nichols-White, publisher of *The Drinking Gourd*, a nationally distributed newsletter for homeschooling families of color. "Children are not given the opportunity [in schools] to become self-directed and in-dependent." In contrast to the self-crushing routines of schools, Nichols-White concludes that "families who homeschool are in a position to tailor learning needs to their children. They are able to trust their children to learn."[42]

Parent-authors in another homeschool newsletter criticized the rigidity of formal schools with a bit more sarcasm. In a newsletter feature titled "60 Things Your Homeschoolers Might Be Doing If They Were in School Instead of 'Wasting Time' at Home," Pat and Lindy George provide an Orwellian picture of schools as inefficient, impersonal offices. Merely "waiting in line" receives six entries on their laundry list of time wasters, among them "waiting in line to have heads checked for lice," "waiting in line for the school nurse to record heights and weight as well as test eyes," and "waiting in line to use the restrooms."[43]

Homeschooling father and celebrated novelist David Guterson despairs in his polemical book, *Family Matters: Why Homeschooling Makes Sense*, that "school is about 'delivering instruction,' 'learner outcomes,' 'mastery of content,' and 'feedback and correction.' It is in many ways an abstraction and a weariness to the spirit. Children, in the majority of cases, adapt to it against their wills."[44] Like Holt and the Moores, Guterson sets up a con-trast between the nature of children and the nature of schools in which the latter evil threatens the former good:

> Life at school is a pyramid, and while all believe they have a chance to reach the top, most are systematically eliminated by examinations and grades. . . . The enormous competitive pressure placed on schoolchildren . . . inspires a variety of neuroses and anxieties. Children, of course, react against these pressures; their rebellion, delinquency, drug use, and identity crises are oft interpreted by psychologists and sociologists as likely responses to life at school.[45]

The "of course" is important. It obliges readers to agree with Guterson's assumptions about the nature of schools and children. Children's rebel-lion, delinquency, drug use, and identity crises are not, of course, kids' fault. They are, of course, the fault of schools. The architecture of Guterson's thinking is revealed a few pages later, in his very Holtian claim that

> every learner is unique. . . . No child conveniently bears out any theory or conforms to the model of learning put forward by any scientific camp. Nor does any child remain the same sort of learner year to year or even month to

month. Thus public-school teachers must contend with the fact that . . . the children before them are singular, complex, and ceaselessly changing, and there are anyway far more children in a given classroom than can be readily understood or significantly taught.

The inherent complexity and uniqueness of each child renders conventional schooling inadequate, as well as the philosophies behind it: "Teachers must throw out theory and begin with the child," Guterson writes, "and this they cannot easily do in a rigid, overcrowded institution."[46]

All these texts articulate the problems with schools and the nature of children reflexively, in ways that reiterate the critiques of John Holt and the Moores. Schools are bad because they do not treat children as individuals. Children have problems in school because schools do not serve their individual needs. Schools are like factories, but children are not like machines. Children are unique, but schools do not honor that uniqueness. These contrasts, repeated by many speakers in many kinds of texts and read by home schoolers time and again, forge a view of children as unique persons that conventional schools can never adequately serve. Once inside this literature, parents are encouraged by its litany of claims to lend the uniqueness of their children great importance. Distinctiveness is rendered too significant and too fragile to be entrusted to others.

In keeping with the Moores' early teachings, images that emphasize children's fragility are common. On their public Web site, the McKie family of South Carolina offers an essay called "The Green House Effect of Homeschooling." According to their greenhouse theory, "children are like tender young plants," and parents are the gardeners:

> The gardener plants the precious seed in special seed cups in his greenhouse. He provides just the right soil, lighting, moisture, and nutrition so that the seeds have the optimum environment in which to grow.
>
> As the seed begins to sprout, the gardener tends to it with love and care. . . . As the seedling grows, the gardener is able to transplant it into larger and larger containers to make room for its growth.
>
> The greenhouse allows the gardener to control all of the elements of the environment so that the plant grows into a sturdy, mature plant with deep, well anchored roots, and a strong supportive trunk. Then the gardener makes the final transplant. . . .
>
> This is a beautiful word picture of how we homeschoolers raise our children. Love is spelled T-I-M-E. We give ourselves to our children while they are young and need our instruction. . . . By the time they complete the high

school years they are firmly anchored in GOD'S WORD, and have learned to stand against the world.[47]

The Moores' claim that parents are children's best teachers is another common feature of homeschool literature. Educational experts are routinely derided, parental wisdom highlighted. Introducing her widely used guide to homeschool curriculum and support services, Christian author and publishing entrepreneur Mary Pride asserts that her book "is not another dreary tome by an 'educational expert' trying to awe you with her supposedly superior knowledge":

> We have experts enough already, scattered here and there like land mines in the field of education. The results of their expertise? Just look at the shattered lives of millions of schooled, yet uneducated, Americans. Each new crisis brings the experts out in swarms, recommending solutions that bring them more power and prestige—though they are the very people who caused the crisis in the first place!

Deriding the authority claims of the experts, Pride defends her own knowledge of home schooling on the basis of her own home learning: "You may be interested in what experience yours truly has with all these subjects about which I write. . . . Fair enough. I was favored with a home education myself!" She further invokes her work as a mother to ground her claims in home schoolers' favorite kind of authority, personal experience. "Bill and I are now teaching our own children, all of whom perform well above 'grade level.'"[48]

In support groups, such wisdom takes the form of practical advice that parents should trust their own abilities to teach their children. Common agenda items for support group meetings are rap sessions about such topics as choosing curricula, coordinating the learning of children of different ages, working with special-needs kids, and more open-ended troubleshooting exchanges. "You have to use your gut instincts," one father advised a new homeschool parent in a support group. "They'll tell you more than anything else." Another parent remarked in the same meeting: "I think it's very natural for the parent to be a teacher because even before I started home schooling I was teaching [my daughter], you know, about how to live . . . to do things in life. That's how it worked, and how it still works with us. It's a very natural way to learn, to teach and to learn."[49] Like the Moores, this mother uses the word *natural* to summarize the parental wisdom that, for her, is the secret ingredient that makes home education a success.

Encountered in homeschool literature and then nurtured in support groups and parent-to-parent conversations, home schooling's core rationales are sturdy enough to turn something scary—taking leave of conventional schools—into something sensible. Once that step has been taken, the ideas also invite distinctive educational practices, as parents and homeschool entrepreneurs work to put theory into practice.

Home schoolers variably emphasize the core arguments, for a number of reasons. First, home schoolers are an ideologically diverse lot. The heads of people like Tara Cook (who has always been a little bit alternative) are furnished with rather different ideas than those of evangelical Christians like the Rayburns, and because this is the case, different kinds of homeschool arguments fit comfortably into different mind-sets. Second, the arguments themselves contradict one another. Some homeschool gurus say that children rightly direct their own learning, while others say that authoritative instruction is an important part of a parent's job. Such contradictions mean that making a commitment to one set of arguments puts one in a certain critical relation to the others. Third, the arguments call for different kinds of practices: a relatively loose, unstructured pedagogy on the one hand, and a relatively scripted, parent-directed one on the other. As the different arguments get built in to particular household routines, parents tend to become more committed to one way of thinking—*their* way—than the others. Finally, because the arguments have rarely been free of the interests of their makers, homeschool advocates have often linked their particular arguments to particular organizations and products. They have been "entrepreneurial" in more than one way.

FOLLOWING THE CHILDREN

"Right now I'm just letting him do whatever he wants," Cathy Ericksen replied patly when I asked how she was going about homeschooling her son, Sam. "He had such a horrible experience in school that it seems important to just [let him] live for a while." Sam sat beside me in the restaurant booth, noshing on a plateful of Mexican food. He is a lanky, conversational eleven-year-old whose impressive vocabulary includes words like *ventilated, ability,* and *gender.* His mother tells me with more than a hint of pride that he had scored two to three years above grade level in all subjects the last time he took standardized achievement tests. Sam had been accepted into a magnet program for gifted and talented youngsters, but their recounting of that experience is a story filled with incapable teachers,

45

inappropriate discipline, late buses, and piles of unnecessary homework. As Cathy described it,

> We stayed up, doing this homework till eleven, twelve o'clock at night. In second grade! He was seven years old. Lots of writing. Lots and lots of work, work, work. Just line after line. Seven-year-old kids are physically not [prepared for] doing reams of paperwork with a pencil. Their little fingers just haven't developed the strength, or the agility to do that. And I would be sitting by him, holding his hand, saying, "Write, write," until, all of a sudden you realize, "I'm insane. I'm going to make him insane."

"I pulled him out. I took him right out of the classroom one day." She reports marching into her child's classroom in the middle class and saying, "'I want my kid now.' I was in tears." Following a subsequent year in a different public school, and another in a private religious day school, Cathy heard about a homeschool support group from a staff person at a local library, and by the time I first met them, she and Sam were both enjoying the end of their first year of home schooling. "I have no curriculum. I have no plan. We have no schedule," Cathy says. A fifty-one-year-old single mother, she works night shifts as a mechanic to be with her son during the day.

> If I'm tired in the morning, if I go to sleep, [I say,] "let me sleep, don't wake me up," because I've been up for maybe a day or two. But then I'll call him up and I'll say, "Sam, what do you want to do today? You want to go to the museum?" So we'll go to the Chicago Historical Society. We went back two or three days in a row, because we didn't finish it the first day.

For the Ericksens, home education is a series of excursions, clubs, and classes. "Everything we do is a lesson," Cathy explains. "On Fridays he does Boy Scouts. And 4-H Club every week. Plus hikes, and camp-overs. Plus Wilkes College," she adds, referring to a local community college where Sam takes karate and assists in the computer lab. Church and Sunday school are counted as part of the lessons ("I'm atheist," Cathy says, but adds that her son "has a right to choose his religion but he can't possibly make a choice if he's not informed"). Cathy sees little need for any more formal academic instruction. "If he's doing something, whatever it is, that's what he's interested in. He's doing something with his mind."

For the Ericksens the problems with schools were ones of inefficient organization, of ill-equipped or insensitive personnel: an incompetent teacher who favored boys over girls; a school administrator who refused repeated attempts for a parent conference; inadequate equipment; inhumane homework loads; two-hour waits for the school bus on cold winter mornings; the feeling that the system was not adequately serving their needs and was taking Sam's freedom and their family life together away. Cathy had placed her child in a magnet school in hopes of nurturing his intellectual talents, but she was sadly disappointed that "the teachers weren't as intelligent as the students." Excessive workloads were a drain on the rest of their lives. "The kids couldn't socialize after school. They were all working until way past bedtime, seven- or eight-year-old kids up at ten o'clock at night doing homework, and they've been doing it from the minute they walked in the house."[50] With home schooling, Cathy said she felt like she had her son again.

Cathy's eagerness to let Sam pursue his own interests and her broad conception of what counts as schooling are shared by many parents. Sally Norton is a former elementary school teacher and mother of two who thinks similarly. We spent a long summer evening talking theory and practice at Nortons' modest suburban home. Adam, Sally's youngest child, about kindergarten age, was playing with considerable industry in the backyard where we sat. Nine-year-old Jill was making french fries in the kitchen. Occasionally the children would touch base with their mom about their work and play. "That's how they learn . . . by actually being able to do things and giving them lots of things and trying to say yes as often as possible," Sally said to me, "I really work to not say no or just say let me think about it, so I can come up with a reasonable response."

She had been very unhappy with Jill's experience in kindergarten. She noticed the trouble each day after school: "She couldn't talk about school. She'd sit for an hour and a half, two hours, just blank, to mellow out from school before she could be part of the family. And when school was over it took her two weeks to come back to who she was as a person. I hadn't realized how changed she had been. I don't like that. That's terrible. She's not even herself." She began homeschooling Jill after her kindergarten year, and since then Sally has worked to unlearn the techniques she took for granted as a classroom teacher. "I had all the books, all the workbooks that I had bought. . . . I had all the charts and I had fill-in-the-blank and all [that]. Do you know what I learned? I didn't need all that stuff." Instead, Sally likens home schooling to a tutoring relationship, in which "you know where you're going to start at the beginning of the year, and you know where you're going to end up, where you're aiming for as far as skills. And you just go. And when they don't get it, you know. And you correct that and let them know. You correct how you teach it, you don't correct the child." Rather than the orderly lessons and lesson plans of schoolteaching, Sally praises a more flexible homeschooling approach.

Now, all sorts of daily activities count as learning.

> Last year [Jill] let me know she wanted to learn to cook. So [we] did. That's how she learned a lot of her math, a lot of her fractions. . . . A lot of her reading she learned because she wanted to read those recipes. And she'd go, "What's this word?" And I'd tell her, and I would tell her the parts of it, and she'd go, "OK, fine."

Building an addition to their home was another educational opportunity. "This has been a learning experience," Sally said of the project, a new garage.

> We were out here all the time, and I had Jill out here, on how you dig a foundation. How you place everything. What is cement, what strength is cement. Why it's deep in certain corners, why it's less in the middle, why do you have wire covering it, why is there a drain hole. . . . Now you can read about this stuff in a book. But, we learn three different ways. We learn by sight, touch, and actually doing.[51]

The flexibility of what counts as "school" in some homeschool families can be an adjustment for children as well was their parents. Penny Turner, a mother of three, explained that her son had trouble with the transition:

> One thing I noticed about Jeffrey when we first started home schooling, he constantly needed me to tell him what to do, and I said, Jeffrey, one of the reasons we're trying to do home schooling is so that you don't have to have someone tell you what to do all the time. And it took almost a year before we finally got out of that, and now he pretty much does what he wants to do. . . . We try and set some parameters on things, but for the most part, you know, when he feels like reading he reads, or writing, or whatever he's going to do.

Despite her son's initial wishes, they committed to a flexible pedagogy.

> We started out more structured. I think almost everyone I talk to who takes them out of school does that, just because they're so used to the school routines, but it just didn't last very long because it seems like that doesn't work real well in the home. At least it didn't in ours. . . . And it was kind of a battle for a while. He'd ask me, what should I do? [I'd say], well what do you want to do? What are your interests?

The Turners wanted a home education tailored to their children's desires, but like many parents they also were concerned about what skeptical outsiders might think. Some states and local school districts require that homeschool families keep formal records of their work and teach certain amounts of particular subjects; some suggest testing children for academic achievement. Given such requirements and initial hesitations about the utter freedom an unschooling philosophy affords, many parents seek the help of correspondence school programs to satisfy school officials with necessary documentation and to assure themselves that their children are on track with their learning.

"We purposely stayed with Clonlara, so that we could have the transcript," Gerald Turner told me.[52] The purveyors of this correspondence program share Penny and Gerald's commitment to individualized instruction and their skepticism of formal academic structure. Founded in Ann Arbor, Michigan, in 1967, in the midst of the alternative school movement, Clonlara School now provides a popular correspondence program designed specifically to meet the needs of homeschooling families. Clonlara's product lends an institutional face to individual homeschooling projects, keeping transcripts and grade-level designations for its students upon request. Clonlara frames its services as a means by which parents can dispense with the tedium of record keeping and be kept free for more important work with their children. "By enrolling in Clonlara School . . . you have given Pat Montgomery, Director, the duty of handling all the administrative tasks associated with your home educating," the program's enrollment material explains: "The idea behind this, naturally, is that you will have your hands full educating your child(ren). Answering telephone calls, writing letters, filling out forms, etc. definitely would get in the way of that; so, your Director accepts the responsibility of taking care of those matters with and for you." Clonlara takes pains to put children's and parents' desires first, providing only a skeletal order within which each family can place its own textbooks, learning activities, and daily schedules. Enrollees are required to submit regular reports of their children's work to the school offices in Ann Arbor, where a file is maintained for each enrolled child, but the format of such reports is left up to individual families. Clonlara's curriculum literature explains that "it's wise to keep some form of time record" and provides grid sheets for families to log in hours spent on various subjects. "If this format becomes too much of a chore," it continues, "you might decide to keep a journal (diary) instead. We don't care *how* you record your home school time. Just let us know what form of record keeping you choose." Clonlara is flexible on what it calls "home school time," encouraging families to see a wide range of daily activities as learning experiences: "If you do use . . . monthly record forms, be sure to list *all* of your student(s)' activities. Bike riding, taking walks, swimming are all physical education. Cooking is Home Economics, measuring ingredients is Arithmetic, reading recipes is—of course—reading. Everything counts as 'schooling' in the home educating family."[53] Clonlara's home-based program for high school is a bit more structured, requiring more rigorous instructional hours in order to accumulate credits toward a diploma, along with three hundred hours of "community service" work. Still, the program is designed primarily to lend an administrative logic to home schoolers' own routines rather than to make those routines conform to some extrinsic, schoollike order.[54]

Since following the lead of their children, rather than the constraints of any learning program, is the primary objective of many home schoolers, some of them find even this minimal degree of rationalization out of sync with the rhythms of their children's lives. Helen Lofton, a mother of three, told me that her children are enrolled with Clonlara, but said she was "really surprised because I'm not as structured as I expected to be." A former schoolteacher herself, Helen has come to appreciate the wide flexibility Clonlara affords. "The first month we did use the grid and, you know, wrote out everything that we had done," referring to Clonlara's record sheets:

> But what's been happening the last couple of months is that the kids have been doing so much on their own that we've been kind of stepping back. Ted is involved real heavily in a train set, building it in the attic, including the electrical [work], and so he's been doing a lot of reading. We got a couple of extra books just yesterday in the mail, in fact, on layouts and that type of thing. We have three computers in this house at this point, and one of the things that they have been really into lately is [some math games software]. It's a really wonderful program. Right now they've just been on the addition and subtraction. Adam [has] gone into multiplication and division, too. A lot of hands-on stuff. And we've been doing a lot of field trips.

Her talk quickly moves from curriculum and record sheets to Ted's train set, Adam's computer software, family field trips. Her children have been so involved with their own interests that she and her husband are allowing them as much independence as possible. "The only structured thing we had is [that] there's no TV during the day. That's the only structured thing," she continues, clearly happy with the way her children have handled the freedom. She noted with pleasure that one of her sons "read a book in a day and a half, because he could sit down and read a book for the day without being interrupted."[55]

Finding ways to think of their children's daily activities as legitimate forms of learning, many home schoolers become convinced of the value of letting their children take the lead. Echoing and innovating on the claims they find in books, newsletters, curricula, and support groups, they become convinced that their children's own ways are ideal ways.

TRAINING CHILDREN IN THE WAY THEY SHOULD GO

"You know, Mitchell, there's a commandment in Deuteronomy," Eric Rayburn said. "'But this you shall teach your children, when you walk by the way, when you're sitting in your home,' and it's very difficult to integrate Christianity into a child's life if you're not a part of their life. And what we do in many cases is turn our children over to non-Christians for a great portion of their day, and expect that they're going to learn how to integrate Christ—"

"Into their life," Marci said, finishing her husband's thought. As we talked that evening, it became clear that the Rayburns had a second reason for home schooling, namely, a concern about the content of what children learn in school. Like many evangelical and fundamentalist Christians who homeschool, Eric and Marci's project is not just about honoring children's individual needs but also about raising their children in a distinctively Christian way.

"There are many positive reasons why parents decide to teach their own children at home. But one of the most important benefits we receive from home schooling is simply avoiding the negative influences of our present-day public school system." Thus begins an article titled "What Really Happens in Public Schools," from a newsletter called *The Basic Educator*. The mailing is produced by Basic Christian Education, a Michigan concern that purveys a homeschool curriculum. The article enumerates a score of problems that apparently are pervasive in American classrooms. The list covers a wide swath: "50 percent of the girls will become pregnant out of wedlock before graduation day. 70 percent of the boys will become sexually active before they leave high school"; children will "be exposed to violence, crime, lack of discipline, and, of course, drugs of every kind"; "Communism and socialism may be presented in the best possible light and capitalism taught as a greed-motivated economic system"; "Many [children] will be exposed to New Age philosophies, Yoga, Transcendental Meditation, witchcraft demonstrations, and Eastern religions." [56]

Such problems are of particular concern because impressionable children are ill equipped to combat them. "Their minds are pliable, receptive, easily influenced," explains an author in another homeschool tabloid, *The Christian Educator*, published by a different curriculum supplier: "The Lord has made them that way—long on imagination but short on

51

reasoning power. They can't even see, to say nothing of bringing home for you to answer, the godless, secular view of life that in subtle ways is constantly handed down to them in the schoolroom."[57]

In much of the believers' literature, peer influence is also a serious concern. Schools are dangerous places because they expose children to a wide population of peers over which parents have little control. Countering the common criticism that home schooling deprives children of adequate "socialization" experiences, believers argue that sustained interaction with unchosen peers is detrimental to the minds and morals of children. "What about socialization?" ask Sue Welch and Cindy Short, editors of *The Teaching Home* magazine, in a frequently reprinted feature called "Home-School Questions and Answers." "Popular opinion assumes that children need long periods of interaction with a large group of peers to acquire social skills." The authors retort, "Some child-rearing authorities, however, believe extensive peer contact at an early age causes undesirable peer dependency."[58]

"When parents try to explain why children should not say certain words or eat certain things, they may not understand, for they are not 'cognitively ready'—they do not understand fully the 'why' of mother's or daddy's explanation," explain Raymond and Dorothy Moore, again invoking a child-development language to frame their admonition about peer socialization. "And since 'All the kids are doing it,' they give the backs of their little hands to their parents' cherished values, and become dependent upon their peers for their value systems." The believers fear the loss of their children's minds and hearts in the tide of peer culture. "Step by step parents lose control, their authority usurped by the school authorities to whom they delegated responsibility for their children," warn the Moores. "Authority and responsibility usually must be commensurate, so when one is given up the other usually follows." Such an eclipse of parental authority is a danger that goes far beyond academic concerns. "Much learning failure can with expert care be corrected," the Moores note, "but with rare exception, when a child loses a sound value system, it is never regained. So peer dependency is a kind of social cancer. Humanly speaking, to try to heal it is like putting a Band-aid on a burned roast."[59]

"When a child is peer-dependent, he receives his sense of identity from the children around him," cautions Llewellyn B. Davis in *Why So Many Christians Are Going Home to School*.

He adopts the values of his peers and rejects those of his parents; becomes a victim of "social contagion" in which he assumes the dress, language, behavior, and interests of his peer group; is unable to stand up for his own convictions in the face of peer group opposition, even if he knows he will be punished for his actions; [and] forms his sense of personal worth from his peers' opinions of him.[60]

Invoking a rhetoric of illness ("cancer," "contagion") to describe the dangers of uncontrolled peer interaction, believers frame the child-world of school as a kind of jungle where parents send their kids only at risk of infection. The solution: keep them at home, away from that environment altogether. The rhetoric has a physical counterpart as well. In an article in *The Christian Educator* listing seventeen "Advantages of Home Schooling," the following is given as number fifteen: "Home schooled children have health advantages. . . . [They] are less apt to catch communicable diseases and colds from exposure to inclement weather. They will be more apt to eat nutritious lunches since schools tend to serve high-starch, low-protein meals."[61] And they are more likely to stay "clean" in general. As Kate Wilson, a mother of two, explained to me, "Schools are dirty. With all those kids, it's a lot of dirt." At home, her children "didn't get as dirty, and they didn't wear their clothes out so much."[62]

For believers, home schooling is partly about saving children from multiple contaminants. These parents concur that children need individualized instruction, but they add that children need to be kept from various social contagions and educated carefully if they are to become moral adults. The cause often warrants biblical allusion. "What would happen if our children were allowed to run around unsupervised with . . . other children? The companion of fools would suffer harm," preaches homeschool leader Gregg Harris, invoking an edict from the book of Proverbs. "The more that our children have the opportunity to be the companions of foolish children, the more impervious they are to our counsel. And the more they resist the experiences that we've had, the more things we can offer to help them avoid so much trouble."[63]

"I think that it's really important to control [my children's] peer interactions when they're younger, and let them develop a good basis for how to handle various situations before they're put out into a large group, and affected by a lot of different kids who . . . make their decisions based on what other kids are thinking," explained Kate Wilson about her own incentives to keep her children home. "I don't think I'm making that real clear," she continued. "Moral decisions, what's right and what's wrong, things like that. They're too much influenced by their peers, who don't know any more than they do [about] what's right and what's wrong."[64]

Parents need not do all this work on their own. In addition to the vital parent-to-parent assistance home schoolers get through local support groups, the homeschool world supplies them with a wealth of printed curriculum programs, how-to manuals and seminars, and teacher-assistance hotlines. The growth of home schooling in recent decades has spawned a veritable industry of religious curriculum services. Parents learn of these services from one another, from direct-mail campaigns, and through advertisements in homeschool periodicals. They can peruse the wares directly at homeschool curriculum fairs. In recent years the number of curriculum and related-product suppliers has gotten so large that many parents report being overwhelmed by the options and even suspicious that home schooling has become big business. Nevertheless, the industry has grown apace with the homeschool movement. A 1993 curriculum fair in the Chicago area, sponsored by Illinois Christian Home Educators, boasted over 70 exhibitors; a similar event in upstate New York in 2000 had registered close to 100 booths. Exhibitors invariably have a product to sell, a homeschool-related "ministry" to share, or both. *The Teaching Home*, an expressly Christian periodical, and *Home Education Magazine*, a nonsectarian one, regularly carry advertisements for dozens of homeschool learning aids.

Evangelical and fundamentalist Christians have the most to choose from when shopping for homeschool curricula. Since the earliest days of the contemporary movement, Christian schools and religious publishers have been quick to supply believers with published materials to augment their household routines. Continuing a long tradition of separatist education,[65] religious publishing houses, colleges, and upstart organizations have produced a large body of educational materials that relate the wide contours of believers' worldviews with the day-to-day tasks of home learning. Providing parents with systematic instruction plans for lessons in mathematics, language arts, science, and social studies along with Bible lessons and primers for spiritual growth, these curricula often ingeniously meld the teaching of the faith with more conventional academic subjects.

The A Beka Book curriculum program, for example, popular among believers, provides integrated learning materials for children of nursery school through high school age. Parents may choose to formally enroll their children in the A Beka Correspondence School, operated from the organization's home base in Pensacola, Florida, or order individual texts to augment other academic routines. The Correspondence School provides parents with day-to-day instruction programs, texts, "class and homework assignments, and tests"[66] and establishes a permanent academic record for each of its enrollees. Homeschooled children can receive report cards and transcripts and can elect to earn a high school diploma. Produced by A

Beka Book, an affiliate of Pensacola Christian College, A Beka's texts for home schoolers lend academic and philosophical coherence to individual families' schooling routines.

Beginning with a nursery school program featuring introductions to numbers, letters, Bible study, and health for two- and three-year-olds and culminating in high school courses that include instruction in biology, physics, sex education, and foreign languages, the curriculum orders the learning process while weaving Christian teachings into virtually every subject and lesson. In addition to a comprehensive, pre-kindergarten to twelfth-grade Bible program (young children learn with Bible story flannelgraphs, at age five begin a complete "Bible Curriculum," and in their teens study texts with titles such as *Bible Doctrines for Today* and *Managing Your Life under God*), the texts integrate Christianity into subjects as diverse as mathematics, biology, and health. An A Beka math text for seventh and eighth graders features lessons on planning a budget that include a budget line for the family tithe alongside expenses for housing, clothing, medical costs, and food. A Beka's *God's World* science book series for elementary-aged children assumes the literal validity of the Genesis account of Creation, deriding evolutionary conceptions of world origin. A health text for young children includes a lesson on how to "think right thoughts," claiming that "right thoughts can help you to have good health" while "wrong thoughts can make you feel unhappy, fearful, or grouchy." Discerning between right and wrong is framed as a theological problem, answerable by deference to the Bible. The high school health curriculum encourages children to, literally, "Say 'no' to drugs" and to get their "sex education from the bible."[67]

Hardly alone in its offerings, A Beka stands alongside curriculum publishers such as Bob Jones University Press, Christian Liberty Academy, Alpha Omega Publications, KONOS, the Weaver Curriculum Series, and Advanced Training Institute International (ATI), among others, that provide religiously oriented learning systems to the homeschool market. Different publishers offer different strategies for ordering the learning process. The Weaver Curriculum, which the Rayburns chose for their daughter Carolyn, is organized around a sequential journey through the Bible rather than conventional school subject designations, while KONOS orders learning around "character trait" themes such as "Attentiveness," "Obedience," "Orderliness" and "Stewardship." Despite their particularities, these curricula are similar in several ways. They meld training in the Bible and in Christian living into the fabric of academic instruction. They provide alternative sources of knowledge for parents and children that is consonant with believers' broader worldviews. And many of them mimic the orderliness of conventional schools, with their emphasis on sequential learning and formal lessons.

"As a parent you can create a schoolroom around the kitchen table," promises informational literature from Christian Liberty Academy Satellite Schools, a large correspondence program for home educators based in Arlington Heights, Illinois. "You can provide desks and chairs inside a spare bedroom, or call class from the family den or library. As a parent you can become a teacher within one of the largest school systems in the United States." Christian Liberty Academy (CLA) purveys a religiously oriented school-at-home, complete with text and workbooks, tests, grades, and high school diplomas.[68]

Although he was careful to add assurance that the materials "are custom-designed to meet the needs of the student," a CLA administrator made clear to me that the program is decidedly "traditional": "We handle a traditional curriculum, kindergarten through twelfth grade. The books you get are the type of books which you'd see in a day school. So what you're doing is you're setting up kind of a day school operation on a personal basis, a very personal basis in your home."[69] Similarly, CLA's promotional literature promises, "Although our student and teacher materials are individualized, they are not set up in a 'self-taught' format. Our school program does require normal teaching responsibilities."

While CLA encourages parents to think of themselves as teachers and their homes as schools, A Beka offers them the requisite classroom accessories: the American and the Christian flags (and hardware "for mounting classroom flags on the wall"), "motivation buttons" with captions such as "handwriting expert," "math whiz," and "I did my BEST today," and award certificates proclaiming students' "perfect attendance" or "superior work."[70] For additional fees, parents can enroll their children in the A Beka Video Home School, a videocassette series that "features the master teachers of Pensacola Christian School in a traditional classroom setting for the instruction of your child at home." Informational literature for the video program warns that "no alterations may be made to a course; each is a complete unit." As in conventional schools, "total class time is 5–6 hours per day" for the elementary program, "including 3–3½ hours of video instruction."[71]

While relatively few believers go so far as to establish video classrooms in their homes, many of them emphasize the importance of school-like order for their learning routines. These parents more often use a school vernacular to talk about their work at home. "I have a reading program that uses the chalkboard, and oral work," Kate Wilson explained to me in her home one afternoon, pointing to a corner of the family room where a chalkboard had been placed. "So I take our kitchen chairs every day, and set it up here," she said, motioning to a section of the room where she is "in school" with her youngest son on weekday mornings.[72] When they talked about how Carolyn was progressing with her academics, Eric and Marci Rayburn used the language of sequential grading to describe their daughter's academic progress, talking about her work in "first grade" and contrasting it with "second grade" work.

Explaining that she and Robert had initially set up a "classroom," complete with secondhand school desks, in the basement for their five children, Martha Edwards remarked in 1989 that their level of school-like structure had relaxed quite a bit over several years of teaching at home. Still, she insisted, "We have a schedule. I try to keep it very consistent. There's a wake-up time, and there's a breakfast time and there's a cleanup time. There's chore time, there's this time, there's that time. We do have routine. Otherwise there would be, disorder," she said. "Chaos."[73]

Curriculum programs do much to keep chaos at bay. While lending predictability and sequence to family routines and providing parents and college admission boards with transcripts and grades, they also bring a cosmic order to what is learned. With the aid of curricula that frame instruction in virtually all subject areas in biblical terms, the lines between academic and religious learning blur.

Eric Rayburn explained that he wanted his daughter Carolyn to gain knowledge that was integrated and coherent—"integration of all of life and learning," he called it, "as opposed to studying geography and studying English . . . we didn't want Carolyn and Sydney to learn in those little hunks and think they were all separate and had no relationship to each other."

To help them pull it all together, the Rayburns use The Weaver, a curriculum that relates many of Carolyn's lessons to a sequential reading of the Bible. "You start with your Bible lesson, and a theme is chosen from that, and all subject areas are related to that," Marci explained, "except math and reading. You supplement with a math program and a reading program."

"This tends to be more social studies," Eric said.

"Science . . ."

"Bible, science . . ."

"Language arts. And it's multi–grade level so that if you have children at different levels you can all be basically studying the same thing. But each

child might have a different project," Marci continued. In addition to regular daily lessons in these subject areas, the curriculum includes ideas for
special projects. Carolyn's brick-making project had been part of a study of
the Tower of Babel. Old Testament genealogies had prompted a study of
family history in which Carolyn wrote a grandparent with inquiries about
her own family tree. This kind of integrated learning is one of the
Rayburns' major homeschooling goals. They want to give Carolyn not just
knowledge and the means to acquire more but also a system for making
sense of all she learns, something "that she'll be able to use to fit other
things into rather than the other way around," Eric said. "I don't think it's
all knit yet for Carolyn, but I think in a couple more years there's going to
be large portions of that fabric in place."[74]

Sitting in the basement living area adjacent to where their children's
secondhand school desks had once been, Robert and Martha enthusiastically described the curriculum they had chosen for their children. Published by Advanced Training Institute International, based in Oak Brook,
Illinois, the program provides lessons in science, history, mathematics, social studies, and reading from a decidedly religious perspective. "It takes
the Sermon on the Mount, verse by verse," Martha explained. "You start
from the first verse, that's the first [curriculum] booklet. And you spend
three or four weeks on it":

> And the first verse of the Sermon on the Mount is, "Now, when he saw the
> multitudes he went up on the mountainside and sat down." So, this first
> booklet took those words, that thought, that meaning, of scripture, and went
> into medicine with it. And went into geography with it. And went into law
> with it. Went into math with it. And character. [That one] was "alert-
> ness," "seeing that there were multitudes." Eyesight we talked about—near-
> sighted, farsighted. And the thing is, depending on the age of the child, you
> can go as deep as you want. How deep do you want to go in explaining the
> muscles of the eye and how the lens distorts and, why, if someone is near-
> sighted, farsighted, astigmatism, whatever. It goes into all these things for
> us.[75]

By creative elaboration, curriculum authors spin out a wide range of lessons from biblical passages. Every word and phrase can be a metaphor for
a revered character trait, a starting point for a science lesson. In this instance the first line of the first verse of the Sermon on the Mount, "Seeing
the crowds, he went up on the mountain,"[76] commences science lessons on
sight, light, and the biological structure of the eye, as well as character
studies on the virtues of "alertness." Martha noted that her children's

"entire curriculum will be Matthew 5, 6, and 7. Through high school." Detailed lesson plans provide project descriptions and learning guides for children of various ages, so that the whole family can do the same lesson at once. "Our part in this," Martha explained, "is to read through this booklet."

> Digest it ourselves. And then give to [our children], depending on where they are, how old they are, what they can handle, what we're looking at in their lives the most. We go through the booklet, accenting what *we* think is important. They don't tell us from the headquarters, "You have to teach everything that's in here," "This is what the eleven-year-old needs to know," and "This is what the ten-year-old needs to know." They are really giving us the freedom to teach what we need to and then [they] give us tons of project ideas, different object lessons and things that will make this [material] come alive.[77]

Thus publishers and parents become partners in children's training. Publishers create texts and provide a format for standardizing the learning process, while parents do the work of personalizing the material for their children's interests and needs.

Robert lamented that in school "there's so much insecurity, and a desire to gain approval, whether it's [from] the teacher or peers." Understanding children as fragile, susceptible to the questionable influences of secular teaching and unsavory peers, he fears that his children might be led astray. In conventional schools the problem is that children "end up spending prime time with kids [their] same age, who have no more to offer [them] than [they] already have." Differing sharply from John Holt's faith in children's individual choices, Robert is wary of placing his children somewhere beyond the pale of parental control. "What do little kids know?" he says, "I think especially in a day like we live in today, where so many children in the schools are coming from broken homes, there's just so much room for improper influence, wrong thinking. There's nothing to be shared that is solid."[78]

For the believers, this search for solidity invariably ends in biblical principles they hold dear. Often, they use formal curriculum programs to help integrate those principles into every facet of their children's education and to coalesce the world's various little hunks of knowledge, as Eric Rayburn called them, into a coherent worldview.

An often-cited verse among Christian parents is Proverbs 22:6: "Train up a child in the way he should go, and when he is old he will not depart from it." Many believers are quite comfortable with the notions of training and teaching, and the hierarchical relationships between learner and teacher that those notions imply. "If you're wanting to train a horse, you're not going to try to do that in a stall," says homeschool advocate Gregg Harris, invoking a livery metaphor to describe the central lesson of his videotaped lecture "Child Training, God's Way":

> There's not enough freedom there, not enough room. At the same time you wouldn't want to just take the horse out into an open field . . . because the horse would have too much freedom. You could not control him within that larger setting. And so what those who train horses have discovered is very useful is a thing called a corral. In a corral the horse has just enough freedom to do what's right, but nothing more.

"The corrals," Harris continues, "or training grounds that we have to use with our children in the home show up in many different ways."[79] Harris goes on to elaborate on specific examples of how Christian parents can appropriately train their children: teaching by example of godly living; dealing with household conflicts as they emerge in daily life; entrusting children with financial responsibility through their own small businesses; and establishing explicit "house rules" to clearly demarcate appropriate and inappropriate behaviors.

One consequence of this emphasis on child training, then, is that it makes the use of formal curriculum much more sensible. The Holtian faith in children's own learning choices means that parents must structure learning as they go, but the believers' convictions about child training encourage them to think in terms of lessons and instruction. For many believers the project is less about children's own desires and proclivities than about what children need to be taught. This instructional orientation is advantageous to product suppliers because it nourishes demand for school-like materials at home. Workbooks, lesson plans, merit badges, even videotapes of schoolteachers in classrooms are things that parents, as "teachers" in homeschool "classrooms" appropriately need. Home schoolers like Sally Norton, Penny Turner, Helen Lofton, and others, who boast about leaving school ways behind them, might disagree.

THEORY AND PRACTICE

How closely do home schoolers follow the terms of their favored advocates and curriculum plans? After all, conventional schools are notorious for slippage between theory and practice: organizational rules, curricula, and in-service workshops are often designed as much to please outsiders as to change teachers or classrooms.[80] And any parent might wonder if either the household democracy of the unschoolers or the tidy curriculum programs favored by some believers actually work with real live children.

In fact homeschool reality is mixed. Parents who use formal curricula often note that their home work doesn't look as much like school as their textbooks and scope-and-sequence charts might suggest. Heather Hughes, a mother of two young children, put it this way:

> Since last year was our first year, you get in your curriculum and you try to do everything by the book. But what you have is a classic classroom situation in that case. And I found that I lost [my son's] attention so much, trying to do it very formally. But when you're first starting out, "this is the way you're supposed to do it." It's the way you and I have always done it in school. So yeah, we did change the format a little bit. We relaxed a lot more as the year went on, because it was just too frustrating trying to do it this way. And too many things pop up. If the phone rings, or somebody comes to the door. You just have to go out and get groceries, you're totally out. There's other things, your life is kinda like going, you can't stop life, because you're here teaching. So we had to get much more flexible. Also [my son] learned a lot better if I just sat down and talked to him regular rather than stand up in front and be a teacher. I reevaluated when I thought, well I taught him how to talk, and how to walk, and how to use the bathroom, how to make his bed, and brush his teeth. [And] it wasn't done on, "OK, step one, put the toothpaste on the toothbrush." It was done, you know basically, you just say this is how you do it. It works wonderful. . . . It's just a more natural way of learning anything.[81]

Robert and Martha Edwards use ATI, one of the more elaborately organized curriculum programs on the market. But they concur that home schooling is a lot more than following the guidelines.

> ROBERT: There is this whole idea of "home schooling" and "home education." And it's words but I think there's a big difference. Because I think a lot of people think that [we] are just doing what they do in school here at home. And we're not bringing the school here. It's different. It's not sitting at desks. It's not school as you and I know it. You can call it home education. But it's the school of life. You are throwing in academics. They're important.
>
> MARTHA: They're not the focus. They're doing [the academics]. There has to be some structure. But it's an organism more than it is an

organization. I often find myself [thinking,] "Lord, help me to get off of these details of the way I grew up, and the way I think about school, and get away and see the bigger picture!"[82]

It is also true that parents who favor less structured approaches sometimes think about their efforts in professionalist terms ("Educationese," as Robert Edwards once called it). Tara Cook, a big fan of John Holt, is a good example. When I first met her, she was not using a curriculum, but she was keeping careful tabs on what her children were up to. "Now, every day in the computer I'm logging what I see, five days a week. I'm basically just saying either 'math,' 'science,' 'sociodramatic play,' what categories I observe and just put them down." Tara is committed to a free-form home education, but she nevertheless keeps track of her efforts in categorical terms.[83]

It is also the case that there is real variation in parent strategies. People who talk differently about home schooling tend to work differently as well. Simply by choosing a curriculum program for their kids, or books for their own edification, parents enact a tendency toward structure or freedom. Home schoolers know this. At any gathering of homeschooling strangers, talk will be peppered with comments like "We're an ATI family" or "I take an unschooling approach." Curriculum fairs create physical manifestations of this kind of discretion as well: parents literally shop for materials that are in alignment with their own preferences.

Other indicators that home schoolers take their theories seriously are subtle differences in how they manage their children in public gatherings. Whenever I attended the meetings of Tara Cook's HOUSE chapter, noise from children's voices and children's play virtually dominated the proceeding of meetings. Toddlers would tug at mothers' knees in subtle requests to nurse; they were often obliged on the spot. Older children would walk into the circle of adults to make announcements about play developments in an adjacent room. Overheard argumentative voices or tears were quickly assessed by grown-ups. Some considered the group's child-friendly environment an asset. "I like it that there are so many children at the meetings, that we don't regulate them," Tara Cook once said to me. It was only with reluctance that the group eventually decided to discourage children from loud play or undue interruptions during meetings. "It was so hard to get anything accomplished, with all the noise," another HOUSE member said.[84] Still, children did interrupt. Babies cried, mothers nursed, and business proceeded more or less at its noisy usual.

Not all meetings are run like this. Susan and Steve Jerome, ATI parents and early organizers of Illinois Christian Home Educators (ICHE), talked about differences in how support groups manage children:

STEVE: We made the decision early on not to have children come to our [local] support group meetings.

SUSAN: Yes, because we felt that the meetings were for support for parents. And so how could you talk, for example, about the difficulties you were having homeschooling with your children if your children were there? So we just had a different idea of what a support group was than some of the other groups, like the HOUSE groups where, I've never been to one myself, but I'm told they run very differently, you know, the children are there and there's a different atmosphere.[85]

This difference in organizational sensibility shows up as well at the state conferences of Illinois Christian Home Educators. The brochure for the 1993 meeting encouraged parents to "please use [the conference] as an opportunity to educate yourself. We just don't have enough space for children and adults. So leave your children under 14 with a sitter." Young people aged fourteen to nineteen were welcome to enjoy a specially planned "Teen Schedule," but only if they had been "homeschooled no less than one year." "Please, no exceptions," the brochure added in bold-face. A special section of the auditorium was also reserved for teens during the conference's main session.

Parents were subject to some rules regarding their children as well. Conference literature advised that they "please remove crying or noisy infants from workshops or sessions."[86] During the morning session, Steve Jerome, an ICHE board officer at the time, made some introductory re-marks. Among them was a reminder that a special room had been reserved for mothers with nursing infants. The space was equipped with a sound system so that the mothers could follow the proceedings. After the keynote speaker concluded her presentation, Steve returned to the podium to give some closing announcements, one of them about breast-feeding. "Moth-ers, you get about a C– for your use of the nursing room during this first session. I heard lots of cries out there during the presentation, and it really isn't fair to the rest of the audience. So please, use the nursing room for your infants during the rest of the sessions today."[87] The comment indi-cated that Steve took for granted that his audience could use a little more discipline. And though he used the "C–" metaphorically (it was met with a few chuckles from the crowd), the fact that grading could be funny rather than unsavory was another little clue about which side of the homeschool world I was sitting in that day.

Even if practices don't precisely mirror what the books say, then, behavior parallels philosophy. The believers are more cautious about the liberties they extend to their children and are more willing to stipulate how things will be done. Those who favor hands-off approaches are more hesitant about this kind of administration, both within their families and beyond them.

Over time I learned that this difference reflects a deeper division among home schoolers, one that has to do with how childhood and, by extension, human nature are understood. For many believers children are not pedagogical free agents but subjects of parental authority, and appropriately so, since their fragile selves require strong hands to keep a questionable world at bay. Children need to be trained because they are, like all persons, prone to sin. Like all persons, children must be directed by wiser elders to keep them from error. This core belief, that people might make the wrong choices if they are left to choose on their own, legitimates believers' efforts to direct the choices of their children. Replacing the unschooling ethos of child autonomy with more hierarchical notions of direction, guidance, and training, the believers nurture a conception of human nature that lends certain persons authority over certain others. This hierarchical logic is perhaps most subtle in the believers' conception of the parent-child relationship, since here their conception of children's needs parallels a notion that many people take for granted: children need to be trained. Still, the relative emphasis given to hierarchical household relations versus children's independence distinguishes the believers from other home schoolers and gives evidence of the believers' location in a distinctive cultural system.

The believers' ideas about how best to homeschool are in keeping with a broader feature of the conservative Protestant worldview that Kenneth Wald and his colleagues have termed "authority-mindedness."[88] Many scholars have noted that concern with maintaining appropriate authority relations is an important feature of conservative Protestant thinking about how best to organize homes, schools, and churches.[89] Believers' authority-mindedness is also evident in their beliefs about child discipline. Sociologist Christopher Ellison and his colleagues found through survey research that conservative Protestants are significantly more likely than other parents to condone the use of corporal punishment and to use physical means of disciplining their children.[90] In a related study of child-rearing advice manuals, Ellison and John Bartkowski show that conservative Protestant authors counsel parents rather differently than "mainstream" ones. While mainstream child-rearing experts tend to write from the premise that democratic and egalitarian principles ideally govern family life, conservative Protestant advice givers are considerably more likely to depict the ideal family as a hierarchy, with parents appropriately directing and disciplining their children.[91]

This relative emphasis on child discipline and parental authority is in keeping with conservative Protestant beliefs about human nature. In conservative Protestant theology, human beings are essentially sinful (". . . all have sinned and fall short of the glory of God" [Romans 3:23]), a belief that implies a clear standard against which persons are appropriately judged. As Bartkowski and Ellison point out, such a conception of the human condition is a foundational feature of conservative Protestant ideas about parent-child relations. In light of human sinfulness and divine expectations, parents are admonished both to train children in righteousness and to model for their children the authority of the Heavenly Father, children's ultimate master and judge.

However, it would misrepresent conservative Protestant theology, and conservative Protestant parenting, to emphasize only the authoritarian dimension. "For God so loved the world . . . , " begins a verse often repeated by born-again Christians (John 3:16). The God who judges is also the God of Creation, who made humankind in his own image and who loves his creatures enough to forgive them of their sinfulness. Thus conservative Protestant theology posits a dualistic human nature: we are essentially sinful, in need of discipline; and we are essentially good, worthy of love. Or as one slogan, popular fodder for posters and refrigerator magnets, puts it: "I'm OK—God doesn't make junk!"

This other side of human nature is evident in conservative Protestant parenting. While these mothers and fathers may discipline more forcefully, they may also love more expressively. Working with data from the same survey studied by Ellison and his colleagues, W. Bradford Wilcox found that conservative Protestants are considerably more likely than others to report that they regularly praise and hug their children. In an accompanying analysis of child-rearing manuals, Wilcox argues that "while some conservative Protestant experts stress the sinful nature of children and the need for discipline," most of these authors encourage Christian parents to strike a balance between expressions of discipline and love.[92]

Parents who homeschool as believers raise their children in a cultural tradition that preaches both the sinfulness and the value of all persons. This dualism informs how believers think about their own children and how they organize their work. Well-chosen metaphors naturalize the dualism and perhaps make it easier to comprehend. In a column for *Homeschooling Today*, a periodical targeted specifically to believers, author Debbie Strayer likens children's educational interests to "sparks"—little lights, powerful but dangerous:

> As teaching parents, we are presented with a huge array of educationally important things to serve our children. Many things are considered essential, such as phonics and math. Many are deemed very important, such as writing and science, with our study of the Bible as the central diet. As we consider the many things our children simply *must* have, we tend to eliminate those things that are cumbersome and difficult to schedule. . . .
>
> Often, what is regrettably laid aside is the fanning of sparks. You have all seen them—looks of excitement or understanding that appear on your child's face unexpectedly.

Strayer notes how many of her readers may think of the spark as dangerous: "As homeschoolers, we fear wildfires. The thought of allowing the sparks to be fanned at all can conjure images of out-of-control flames indiscriminately ruining everything in your child's academic path, so we throw water on the sparks. . . . 'That's nice dear, but let's get back to work.'" The column is a bid for balance between honoring children's God-given curiosity and a heavenly ordained discipline: "Clearly, it's alright to have a plan . . . the order and peace that result from planning and routine are much needed by homeschoolers. Our diligence and pursuit of God's plan for our homeschooling provide the fireplace; a safe environment for sparks to ignite, be satisfied and naturally diminish."[93] This imagery of home schooling echoes and extends conservative Protestants' two-sided conception of human nature. Our children are divine lights, but they should not be allowed to burn uncontrolled.

Seeing that the believers' conception of children is dual also illuminates how parents from such varied philosophical and lifestyle backgrounds might find a common interest in home schooling. Although they said so in different ways, all the parents I met concur that their children have sparks that get squelched in conventional schools. This is the common ground on which John Holt, Raymond Moore, and a wide array of parents and advocates come together. They part ways on the question of whether and how to manage the fires. On this issue the liberation ethos encapsulated in John Holt's writings leads to very different answers than believer theology.

Given that home education inherits such different cultural traditions, it is not surprising that many home schoolers have hybrid ideas about what they are up to. Sally Norton, who told me she "had read but wasn't real crazy about . . . John Holt's books," takes an approach to home schooling very much in keeping with the logic of unschooling. When I met her, she was not using a formal curriculum, even after two years of home schooling Jill. Her conception of schooling was broad enough to include observing construction work and making french fries (while Jill cooked up a batch during our interview, Sally pointed it out as an example of learning by doing). And Sally realizes that she does things differently than many of the other parents in her Christian support group. "You know, the Christian Liberty Academy type person . . . they do all the workbooks, they do exactly what they are told and the day they are told to do it. I'm not that kind of person. I'm not happy that way. So we don't do it that way." Still, Sally concurs with other believers that she homeschools partly in response to heavenly command:

> I was one of the people that worked backward on the commitment to God. Some people, their commitment to God and raising their children was first. I kind of went backward with that, and all these other things, and then thought, boy that's true. God has given me this main responsibility, it is mine. And yes, this is a religious conviction. And it's become very very strong. I don't know that I'm able to verbalize that real well. Other people are much better verbalizing that Christian commitment part of it, but I feel very strongly about it.[94]

Cheryl Marcus is another mother who has an unstructured approach that gives lots of leeway to her daughter's wishes. But she also has concerns about moral upbringing that sound very similar to those of the believers: "I don't like the way the schools are going. . . . What's wrong with Christianity all of a sudden? You know? This country was founded on Christian, on religious principles. [People] came over here for religious freedom, and now all of a sudden all religious references seem to be stricken out of the public school, and I don't like that at all." Unlike Sally, though, Cheryl felt out of place in a Christian support group that she attended a couple of times:

> They were people [who] did not believe in fantasy. And they don't believe in Halloween and things like that. My daughter likes ghost stories; she couldn't talk to these people about ghost stories. These people had *workbooks*, I swear, that said things like—they would have a Bible verse in their math book, [and]

things like "One Pharisee plus two Pharisees equals how many Pharisees?" This was too much for me. I mean, I believe in live and let live, but I wasn't going to spend all afternoon with these people.[95]

Cheryl concurs with the believers that the Bible is a good sourcebook for the teaching of moral principles, but she seems to think that such things can be carried to an extreme.

Sally and Cheryl found support for what they were doing in an emerging homeschool world whose organizational system only roughly echoed the philosophical diversity of homeschool parents. There were thousands of homeschooled children in Illinois by the middle of the 1990s and perhaps 150 support groups.[96] Organizations serve multiple parties by definition, and in so doing they must make choices about whose points of view, whose interests, they will accommodate most fully. Sally participates in a support group with a decidedly Christian character; membership is open to anybody who wants to join, but parents are obliged to express agreement with a statement of faith in order to hold office. Cheryl Marcus participates in a HOUSE-affiliated group that has a different philosophical cast. In the early 1990s, HOUSE's statement of purpose read, in part, "Because of the diversity of the families we serve, HOUSE does not support any one religious or philosophical outlook."[97]

Choices made on the basis of philosophy—about how to assemble a support group, or about which one to attend—ultimately have consequences for the shape of home schooling as a social movement. When they began homeschooling in the mid-1980s, Robert and Martha Edwards initially attended a HOUSE group, but they were unimpressed with the teaching philosophies they found there. "It was a good group for support," Martha explained, "but we pretty much knew right away that there were all sorts of different philosophies in that group. So it was good for general support about home schooling, but it wasn't exactly for us, philosophically." When Deirdre Brown worked through HOUSE to bring John Holt to speak in Chicago in mid-1980s, the Edwardses attended but were similarly unimpressed with Holt's message. As Martha said it, "I remember going to that and hearing him speak and thinking, this really is not how we think about it at all. The idea of the virtuous, good child and letting them develop. It just doesn't go with, I mean, as Christians we see that children have sin natures too, that's part of what we are as human beings. And we just can't ignore that part of it." Ultimately the Edwardses left HOUSE to form their own, Christian group, which eventually affiliated with the statewide Christian network, ICHE.[98]

John Holt and the Edwardses certainly disagree on some things, but in one way the movement Edward and Martha helped to build has matured in a manner that would have pleased its most famous secular proponent. Holt envisioned a movement characterized by a broad pluralism of learning styles and strategies, tailored to meet personal needs. In Illinois and throughout the country, home schoolers have created an impressive array of organizations that bear the marks of such diversity. And over the years home schooling has accrued a long list of rationales that bear the marks of an ecumenical intellectual pedigree.

Still, it is hard to imagine that Holt would be comfortable with Gregg Harris's corral model of child training, or with any of the believers' learning strategies that, like Christian Liberty Academy's, resemble "setting up a kind of day school operation in your home." Indeed Holt was so adamant in his derision of formal models of learning that he was even uncomfortable with the terms *teaching*, *schooling*, and *home schooling*, and tried in much of his work to remove them from his own vocabulary. The title of his flagship publication, *Growing Without Schooling*, summarized a pedagogy that had little room for formal instruction or training of any kind. Rather, Holt believed that both children and their parents needed to learn to be "unschooled," freeing themselves from conventional understandings of what education is all about.

If unschooling lost out to phrases such as *home schooling* and *home education* as the preeminent descriptors of the cause, it is in part because so many of those drawn to it are not interested in leveling relationships between children and authorities. Intent on retaining the hierarchical relationship between teacher and learner, many believers have held on to the notion of "school." In this sense they are less the heirs of Holt than of Raymond and Dorothy Moore, whose version of home education balanced parental authority with the individualism that all home schoolers cherish.

In the end, what may be most remarkable is not the differences between these pedagogies but what they have in common—with one another, and with mainstream understandings of childhood more generally. All home schoolers are passionately committed to the notion that their children have distinctive selves that need to be nurtured by individualized care. But the idea that each child's idiosyncratic needs are of paramount importance has become widely taken for granted in our culture, at least among the white middle classes from which most homeschool families come. In her recent study of how contemporary mothers put conventional child-rearing advice into practice, sociologist Sharon Hays argues that parents tend to assume that good parenting is largely a matter of honoring children's own needs and choices. Hays quotes one mother as saying:

> I think listening to your kids; not making assumptions about how they're feeling, what they're doing—really just taking the time to listen to them and let them talk and let them let you know what's going on. Kids need to learn to trust what they're thinking and feeling, and learn to identify what they're thinking and feeling. You [need to] take the time to sit down and help them to figure out what they need figuring out.

Another of Hays's mothers says of relationships with her kids, "I let them establish their own schedule. I respect the individuality of children and I respect children as people and I think they know who they are and they know what they need." As a third put it, good parenting means that "you learn your kid."[99] Such claims are not far afield from Tara Cook's home-school philosophy, which involves "taking my adult concerns and trying to let them go. Entering [my son's] space, the way he is operating, just being there, and listening." They are not much different in principle from Debbie Strayer's encouragement that Christian parents fan their kids' "sparks," those promising, unexpected cues children give about what *they* want to learn. What distinguishes home schoolers from other parents is not their basic understanding of childhood, then, but rather the exceptional extent to which home schoolers have elaborated that understanding and put it into practice.

The philosophical proximity of home schoolers and the rest of us suggests that this little movement teaches larger lessons. Tara Cook and the Rayburns, for example, talk differently about the troubles with schools, and their lists of complaints vary. Tara is most concerned with nurturing her children's creativity and desire for learning, while Eric and Marci spoke at greater length about unloving teachers, academic coherence, and a Christian worldview. But they all agree that public schools are a weak option for their own kids. The relative academic quality of their local schools may be beside the point: "[Our town] is considered one of the best suburbs, school-wise," Marci Rayburn told me.

For Marci and Eric, as for most home schoolers I met, the troubles with schools are chronic and structural. They have to do with the difficulty of accommodating individual differences inside of bureaucratic organizations, with the tensions inherent in teaching standardized curricula in intellectually and spiritually diverse communities, and with the disjuncture between parents' singular interest in their own children and schools' general interest in whole cohorts of kids. And the problems have to do not only with schools but also with those who claim to know much about them. Recall Mary Pride's reference to the educational "experts" of whom we have "enough already, scattered here and there like land mines in the field of education." If the schools are misguided, so, too, are those who have made professional commitments to understanding and improving them. That such sensible parents share this utter lack of faith in public schools and their keepers signals an educational legitimacy crisis whose breadth and depth have yet to be fully measured.

Natural Mothers, Godly Women

THE ARGUMENTS that support home schooling concern children's needs, but putting those arguments into practice has had significant consequences for grown-ups. In individual families, someone has to do the work of making home replace school. Beyond the household, many hands have been needed to build the durable support system that makes home schooling less frightening, less burdensome, and more fun.

In households and in the broader movement, the great majority of this work has been done by women. While on the surface this division of labor might seem troubling in a postfeminist world, in fact it has some remarkable utilities for the women who do it. Through home schooling, women have created novel ways of being working mothers and garnering significant amounts of household power. Not coincidentally, conservative Protestant ideologues have found in home schooling an effective means of updating the so-called traditional family so that it better conforms to contemporary understandings of ideal womanhood.

But first, let us have one thing clear: home schooling is a lot of work. Consider a typical day in Pamela Eckard's household. Pamela and her husband have three boys: Micah, age 8; Seth, 6; and Brandon, 3½. Pamela is up by 6:15 each morning, "so that I can get time for myself or, you know, I like to have the table set when the boys get down so they can get up and eat breakfast right away." Breakfast is at 7:15. Sometimes her husband, Gene, a furniture restorer, joins them for the meal before he leaves for work, but a morning exercise schedule often keeps him away from the table. School starts at 8:45, but "before school starts [the boys] are expected to be dressed, have their pajamas put away, their beds made, and their teeth brushed, and they do a fair job of that." There are also morning chores. Pam set up a rotating work schedule for the boys to help with housework, "and that sort of means they're helpers." I notice that in explaining the boys' jobs, Pam implies that she is often involved somehow. "Hanging up clothes . . . [they] used to just get the pile of clothespins and hand them to me. . . . The boy who is the kitchen helper gets to plan meals with me. . . . Cleaning . . . when it's Micah's job, I usually expect him to do all the vacuuming, Brandon I maybe expect him to shake the rugs."

Pam tries to keep the time between 8:45 and 11:30 sacred. "I do as much housework as a I can before that, but during that time I am available to the boys." Devotions are the first activity. "They work on memorizing their Bible verse from Sunday school, and . . . I have a couple of different devotional books that I use." KONOS, the curriculum Pam has chosen, includes Bible verses in its unit studies, which sometimes get folded into family devotions. Listening time usually comes next. "They each pick a story and we read for probably thirty to forty-five minutes. We've read novel-type books, we've read the whole *Little House on the Prairie* series." Like many home schoolers, the Eckards are frequent library patrons. The house has two shelves full of library books on the day of my visit. After reading time it's down to the basement, where Pam keeps most of the school materials. There, for about two hours, "they're kind of on their own and they can choose," with some caveats. Math work and some sort of reading activity are requirements. But "they can pretty much just go and pick something that they want to do. And then if they need someone to do it with . . . I'm available."

KONOS provides many suggestions for learning activities based around unit studies of character traits. At the time of my visit the boys were studying "attentiveness." Pam had brought home library books about eyes and ears. "We study the ear because being attentive means listening . . . under attentiveness you study ears, sound, music, eyes, seeing, other senses. . . . You just go through and pick the ideas that you want to use for the kids, and so it gives you great freedom in tailoring it to the need of your child." KONOS recommends that parents supplement the curriculum with phonics and math programs. Pam did this, but then she pulled back on the phonics with Micah when she hit a wall. "He made a comment to Gene one night when he was praying, something like 'Dear Lord, help Mom to stop pushing,' and he went from being an occasional bed wetter to a full-time bed wetter." She implies that this was the decisive clue that made her change tack. A former schoolteacher, Pam supplements the formal programs with a lot of her own materials in any case. "And I resist workbooks, period, for kids." A math course she took the previous summer gave her lots of ideas, as did some tutoring she did recently.

After basement cleanup it's writing time, which Pam confesses isn't going very well. "I would like them to write letters to their grandparents and things and that just isn't happening." Still, she wants fifteen minutes of writing activity each day. Often she takes dictation, writing down stories that the boys tell to her. Pam has been impressed by the clarity of the boys' sentences. The morning ends with fifteen minutes of silent reading. In a pattern common to many homeschool households, where tutoring virtually replaces child management as the instructor's main job, formal school time in the Eckard household is less than three hours a day.

But a mother's work is never done. In addition to tending her own three children, Pam cares for an infant in her home several days a week and an older child after school in the afternoons. She talks confidently about absorbing the extra child care. "Fortunately, [the baby's] at an age where she does a fair amount of sleeping, so that makes it easier," and the older one "is no big deal because that just gives Micah someone to play with." Nevertheless, the Eckards' home is a kid-busy place. Field trips through Pam's local support group, weekly academic and play sessions with another homeschooling family, and fortnightly visits to Grandma's enrich and complicate the daily schedule.

Pam shoots for 5:30 for dinner. By 6:30 the kids are heading to bed, and one more lesson. "I always try to read a bedtime story, but it doesn't always work. . . . I would say probably 80 percent of the time they each get a bedtime story." The oldest is in bed by 8:15, and then Pam and her husband have a bit of time for themselves.

Dad helps. "He finishes work at a quarter to five. He often goes to the library after work and brings home more books for the boys to read." Gene also does what Pam calls "impromptu stuff." For example, "We were driving to my sister's house last summer, and the kids were looking at the stars and all of a sudden he started talking all about the constellations and all this stuff came out, and I was just amazed. . . . He has a lot of input like that." And Gene worried, at first, that home schooling would be too much work for Pamela. "He somehow had a picture of me sitting down and teaching Micah for five hours a day," she said. To counter his apprehensions, Pam taped one of Raymond Moore's appearances on *Focus on the Family* and had Gene listen to it. "Then he made a 180-degree turn and became very much in favor of it. . . . He probably isn't as excited about it as I am, but at least I feel that he's on my side and he can really see a lot of the benefits of home schooling."

Home schoolers like to say that none of their households are typical, but the Eckards' is typical at least in its division of homeschooling responsibility. Mom does most. Of course, mothers doing more work with children than fathers is not in itself exceptional. In U.S. households generally, women perform a greatly disproportionate share of child care, doing more of the practical work of feeding, washing, supervising, and interacting with their children.[1] Women also perform much of the thinking work of parenting. Research has shown that mothers are more likely than fathers to keep tabs on the details of their children's lives: remembering past behaviors, for example, when making decisions about medical care in the present, or keeping track of children's current preferences and dislikes.[2] Mothers simply do a lot more parenting than fathers, and this is true even when both parents work outside the home and regardless of whether parents hire in-home help.[3] Homeschool households are not exceptional in the way parenting is divided, but they are distinctive in the sheer amount of it that gets done and in how it is understood.

Understanding how home schoolers make sense of their work leads us quickly to broader issues of gender and parenting in contemporary America. For whether they like it or not (and I met parents with both points of view), home schoolers live in a broader culture shaped significantly by a generation of liberal feminism. Beyond the expanded legal protections and more gender-equitable workplace rules it has won for women, the feminist movement also has changed the cultural model of ideal womanhood. Unlike her post–World War II era counterpart, today's ideal woman may have children, but she works outside her home as well. She is financially independent, or at least potentially so. She enjoys and defends a measure of emotional autonomy from her spouse and children. She is "her own person." If she is married, she wants an equitable relationship with her husband, including equity in caring for children.[4] In this cultural context, homeschooling mothers' elaborate obligations to their children appear anomalous. As with the act of home schooling itself, these mothers occasionally find that they need to do some explaining to friends, family, and sometimes even themselves.

But the broader culture contains contradictory messages about the relative importance of paid work and mothering. Out there on television, in glossy magazines and in parenting sections of bookstores, Mother vies with Woman for attention. Even while women are increasingly expected to think in the first person about their lives, contemporary standards of motherhood have become extraordinarily labor-intensive. To be an adequate mother, according to the child development experts, requires careful attention to the minute idiosyncrasies that make children individuals; constant nurturing of a child's physical and cognitive development; and the consistent elevation of children's needs above virtually all other of life's demands.[5] Prioritize your own needs, but be heroically committed to your child's needs as well—a philosophical problem and then some. As many mothers know from experience, the contradiction is at bottom unfixable. Since the tension cannot be resolved, it must be struggled through instead.

Homeschooling women may appear to make their peace with the dilemma by coming down squarely on the side of motherhood. But a closer look reveals that their choice is more nuanced than that. These women are full-time mothers, but they also are engines of elaborate family projects and the brick and mortar of an impressive social movement infrastructure. While it may look traditional at first blush, home schooling's dramatically expanded motherhood is also subtly in keeping with liberal feminist demands that contemporary women be more than "just" housewives.

The great majority of the couples I met are able to homeschool because of the commitment of a full-time mom. They differ markedly, however, in the extent to which they recognize motherhood as a social role distinct from the women who perform it and the children to whom it is obliged. As with their approaches to teaching, home schoolers' approaches to motherhood fall into two broad categories. Some home schoolers tend not to talk very much about mothers, lending most of their attention to the kids. This creates a cognitive dilemma for some homeschool mothers, who find themselves doing a lot of work that they have a hard time explaining. Believers, on the other hand, have a lot to say about mothers. In fact, many of the believers' most prominent homeschool advocates devote considerable energy to making sense of motherhood as a social category, independent of the particular women who do the job. Part of a larger script of idealized family relations, motherhood is a lead role in God's plan for believers.

These different ways of making sense of motherhood teach some important lessons about the current fate of mothering in American culture beyond the homeschool movement. First, the absence of talk about mothers among some home schoolers, despite all their talk about kids, reveals that our conceptions of children have costly, if sometimes invisible, consequences for moms. Second, the believers' elaborate talk about mothers as well as their children demonstrates the remarkable extent to which conservative Protestants have gone to envision a social system more amenable to full-time domesticity.

Motherhood and Then Some

In all but one of the homeschool families I met, mothers were the primary caregivers and educators in their homes. Mothers take primary responsibility for supervising their children all day. They keep track of sometimes hectic schedules that may include music lessons, part-time jobs, athletic practices, and club meetings for minivans full of youngsters. Parents typically report that mothers are the ones who keep academic records, organize lesson plans, and do most of the instructional work. Fathers often give some of the lessons (science and math are common purviews of dads), but their teaching roles are supplementary. Mothers do most of the work and most of the organizing of the global project, while fathers have the luxury of being responsible for more discrete tasks.[6]

Like Pamela Eckard, Jennifer Kullom does most of the teaching with her three children. School time is from 8:00 to 11:00 in the morning at the Kullom house. Jerry works night shifts, so he is home during this time, and he does the schooling "at least once a month, so that I can go to Bible study," Jennifer explained. Jerry assured me that he does "other things" with the children: "I do current events, we talk about what's in the newspaper, what's on the news, what's going on. We have a big map and globe downstairs, we talk about geography and where certain countries are, what's going on in certain countries, things like that."

"And devotions," Jennifer added. In a pattern common among believers, Dad plays a broad ministerial and supervisory role. As Jerry put it: "I think that a lot of the key factors for dads, which helps make a lot of it work, is not necessarily having to be there, but the children having to be accountable to them for what they learn. Children are accountable to their mothers, . . . but you know, Dad comes home, we better know this or we better have this down. . . . So I think dads play an administrative role." Jennifer seemed to concur with this assessment. Husbands "can declare holidays if their wives are overworked," she added with a chuckle.[7]

Jacob Maxwell told me that home schooling is largely his wife's responsibility. "Of course, mostly, I think the impetus for all this is Diana's, because the major burden of it falls on her . . . it was something she really wanted to do." A physician with a busy private practice, Jacob says he was unable to consider doing things any other way. Still, he likes to participate where he can:

I have every Wednesday off, every other weekend off, and so we can spend that time doing things with the kids and trying to make educational time. It's a little easier for me to think about it when we're interacting . . . to make everything an educational experience. [For example,] . . . the kids were talking about playing the game Sorry. . . . There's a card in there that's number seven and you can split your sevens so that you can move two pieces so that they add up to seven, so they learn addition and subtraction that way.[8]

From idea to execution, home schooling has been Diana's project, but Jacob enthusiastically plays along.

This division of labor emerged not only in parents' explicit recounting to me of who did what, but also in subtle divisions of conversational labor during my interviews. When I called to schedule interviews, parents invariably assumed that I would want to speak with the mom; sometimes a woman would ask if I would like to speak with her husband, too. When I interviewed mothers and fathers simultaneously, I found that in general parents participated roughly equally but that they tended to talk about different things. Fathers had a lot to say about the "whys" of home schooling: why it is good for the children and why conventional schooling is less good; why Christians especially should care about it. But they often had less to say about the details of the work: the schedule of piano or horseback lessons, the math manipulative that worked particularly well, the phonics program that utterly failed. Such topics were more likely to be the mothers' purview.

Since home schooling fills days and nights with so many new tasks, mothers often mentioned that they had to reevaluate old household priorities. "I had to learn to let my house be messy," Kate Wilson told me,

> because there wasn't time to make it perfect anymore. When your work quadruples like that, . . . and I suppose that happens to people who work outside the home too, but I learned it through home schooling. And then having your kids home all day too it gets messier [both of us chuckle]. And having school books all over . . . I've got boxes of books I don't have anyplace to put, but that's the way it is in our house.[9]

Pamela Eckard said proudly of her first busy year of home schooling: "My house was dirty, but my kids have watched very little television."[10] Martha Edwards told me that "everybody pitches in":

> Everybody has to help. Because I cannot go around like a woman who sends her kids to school, and go around the house and clean the house all day. I don't do that kind of thing. I don't have the time. I have to plan lessons. I have to take care of everyone. I have to just know what's going on. Everywhere, and all the time. So, it's very taxing. But it's very rewarding and very fulfilling.[11]

Given the expanded workload, home schooling virtually requires the full-time attentions of an adult household member. Sometimes families find creative ways to keep a parent home while still paying the bills. Cathy Ericksen's night shifts enabled her to be home with Sam during his waking hours. Tisha Jones, another single mother, found home-based employment in marketing. Kelsee Green lived with her mother, who helped extensively with her two granddaughters while Kelsee maintained an impressive career as an antitoxics activist. And on rare occasions, it is dad who stays home. Bill Pallone is the full-time parent for his two daughters, Carlen (age eight) and Ruth (age nine); his wife, a librarian, earns the household income. Surely there are other homeschool dads like Bill. "I want you to know that there is at least one father out there doing this job full time instead of being the bread winner," wrote one parent in a letter to the editor of *Practical Homeschooling*, a magazine for believers published by Mary Pride:

> I have been teaching my four adopted daughters for five years and thoroughly love the opportunity to invest in their lives.
>
> As a credentialed teacher, I am more qualified to instruct my children, and as an attorney, my wife is more qualified to support the family. So please do not direct all your articles to "Mom." Some of us dads are doing the job as well!

Another letter in the same issue came from a widowed mother who homeschools her three children on her own. "My secret?" she wrote. " In addition to the grace and mercy of God being extended daily, if you *choose* to educate your children at home, you can![12] Despite notable exceptions, though, I found throughout the movement that home schooling usually gets done by a more or less full-time mother who is financially dependent on her husband.

For most of the families I met, having a parent at home full-time has required some sacrifices. Eric Rayburn left a job in the ministry for a better-paying business position so that the family could afford to have Marci stay home. Heather Hughes talked about going without new furniture and other amenities so that the family could make it more or less on one income; Heather works part-time at an art store and also does sales work out of her home to pad the household's bottom line. Some people talked about giving up family vacations. One mother I met at a homeschool conference told me that her family rarely ate out, even when traveling far from home, as one way of making ends meet.

Some women make considerable career sacrifices to stay home. Lissa Foster, a mother of two, holds a Ph.D. in biology but left the field after finishing her degree to be at home with her children full-time. The family moved to Illinois when Lissa's husband, also a scientist, was given a postdoctoral fellowship at a prestigious university. Lissa's formal professional involvement now consists of teaching the occasional night class. Sitting in the Fosters' living room, a stone's throw from the university campus, Lissa explained her transition from graduate school to full-time motherhood: "I had been planning to get a postdoc here, but we couldn't find any infant day care for [my youngest], for one thing. And the day care for [my daughter] was just incredibly expensive. Even on a postdoc salary, with the cost of day care or child care here . . . it just didn't seem worth it to me to pay someone to watch my kids."

Staying at home was not what Lissa had planned on earlier in her career:

LISSA: For a long time we saw ourselves as just the typical, I can't remember what the acronym is for double-income-no-kids family.
MITCHELL: "DINKS"?
LISSA: Yeah. We were convinced we were that until I started getting closer to thirty. And I think it was like, around my twenty-ninth birthday, I became convinced that I had to become a mother before I was thirty. . . . I just suddenly had this urge to be a mom, and [my husband] went along with it. But even then, we discussed that we would always be in academia because that was all we had seen, not just through our families but through our friends. . . .
MITCHELL: Did you go right from college to graduate school?
LISSA: Yeah. Yeah. We had always assumed that that would be the road we would take, because that's what we were doing, and that's what we were choosing to train to do. Nobody in their right mind chooses to go into a Ph.D. program, finish it, and then stay home. It's just not done. I know I've really disappointed my professor in choosing this way.
MITCHELL: Oh, your mentor?
LISSA: Yeah. I know it really greatly upsets her because I'm not the first of her students to do that.

Lissa had hoped that her daughter, a kindergartner at the time of their move, would be able to get into a magnet school. The local district school was simply not an option:

We had been assuming that we would probably send her to [name of magnet school] or someplace like that. The private schools we couldn't really afford, and didn't really like. And the public school, we certainly weren't going to consider the one that we're in the district to, that's right across the street. . . . The cement, the playground, I don't think they even have a swing set, it's just cement.

The next stop was home schooling, in tandem with a support group that now meets regularly in the Fosters' neighborhood.

Lissa's account of her journey to full-time motherhood betrays some ambivalence. On the one hand, she claims to enjoy her current life. "I was just as happy to be at home," she concluded after talking about the limitations of the postdoc option. But she also talked hopefully about work possibilities, perhaps continuing to teach night classes at a community college. "If I can continue to teach night school, it gives me an out for what I've been trained to do, and a way of interacting in a more professional way." And there is a sober awareness of the path not taken:

> LISSA: And there are some days when I think about, I went through this whole program, I spent seven years for my Ph.D., and shouldn't I be doing more with it than I am? I guess it's that I got it that really counts, [I'm] trying to learn that having gotten it is what really counts. . . . If I do something it better be for my sake and not to make my mentor feel better about it, or to make my family happy. If I do it, it has to be because it's what I really want to do.
>
> MITCHELL: But sometimes, are you saying that you sort of go . . .
>
> LISSA: Yeah. Yeah . . . when [my son] gets real crabby or tired, or [my daughter] doesn't want to do this, she's just not in the mood to do her math on a particular day, and you just want to tear your hair out. . . . And that happens. But it would happen over different issues if they went to school.[13]

Like so many women who face the hard choices about how to balance work and family, Lissa's calculus includes many factors: her husband's career opportunities, her deep desire to be a mother, income constraints, and the range of opportunities for school and child care that are available to her household.[14]

Most of the women I interviewed, however, indicated a predisposition to full-time motherhood. As my time and familiarity with home schoolers grew, in fact, I came to suspect that their general commitment to home over work is part of what makes homeschooling mothers distinctive—at least compared with the women in my academic life, for whom the difficult divide between motherhood and career is a source of much theoretical and practical difficulty. Some like Lissa Foster ended up pursuing full-time motherhood despite their earlier plans, but for many others being a full-time mom is the realization of a long-held desire.

When Diana Coleman-Maxwell and I talked about her and her husband's childhood career hopes, she said, "He wanted [to be a doctor] since he was five years old, and I wanted to be an artist and a mom, freelancing at home . . . ever since I was in about seventh grade. So we're both real good at long-term plans."[15] Sally Norton spoke similarly: "I am a full-time housewife, a full-time mother, and I cherish that very much. I think that is incredibly valuable, partly because it's always how I thought as a child it would be."[16] Some of their husbands concur. "I remember in the early years that we absolutely didn't want anyone else raising our kids, it was going to be one of us," Gerald Turner said in a joint interview with his wife. Robert and Martha Edwards were in such unanimity about having Martha at home that the issue had not even come up for discussion. When I asked how they had "decided" to have Martha stay home-full time, the Edwardses replied:

> MARTHA: It was never a question, I don't think.
> ROBERT: That's how it's going to be. At least in my mind.
> MARTHA: I don't know that we ever really discussed it. I mean, it was just one of those things.
> ROBERT: If you don't disagree on it, you don't think of talking about it, you know [chuckles].
> MARTHA: It was just the way we were going.[17]

These parents are aware of other options. Diana Coleman-Maxwell has held many jobs throughout her adult life, from retail work to art and language instruction, as well as a range of volunteer activities; Sally Norton logged many years as an urban schoolteacher; Martha Edwards and Penny Turner both worked before they had children. Nevertheless, their accounts indicate that full-time motherhood has been the priority in their life plans.

These women also are aware that they are living in a world with changed rules about how women should put their lives together. They understand the broader culture's expectations that they be independent persons as well as wives and mothers. Diana Coleman-Maxwell said:

> The other thing that I find with home schooling, with all my life, it's been really weird because on one hand I kept my own name, on the other hand, I'm a stay-at-home mom. On one hand, [my husband] and I are extremely equal. You know, we don't consider [it] his income. It's ours, we have a family goal. And yet on the other hand, I build my life around his schedule. I am very much the little wife waiting at home.[18]

Diana talks about her biography as having multiple casts. It is partly traditionalist, but it also bears the imprint of liberal feminism. Other women seem to think of themselves as the heirs of these different influences, even if they are less enthusiastic about some of them. Peg Jesson, a mother of two, says that she and her husband "were very serious about me being home with our children." Still, she confesses that "I went through a very brief, ah, career hysteria when we'd been married for about a year. But I finally realized it was because I wasn't ready to have kids and I was afraid of getting ahead of myself." Peg recognizes her previous desire for a work life beyond her family, but she cheerily derides it as a kind of mental illness.

Whatever course women have taken to full-time domesticity, home schooling gives them the opportunity to transform home work into an extraordinarily elaborate project. To be a homeschooling mother means staying at home without "just" staying at home, a fact that is not lost on the women themselves. Consider how Peg Jesson talked about her encounter with John Holt's writings: "John Holt, ah, *How Children Learn* and *How Children Fail* are two books he's written which are very interesting. Another is the one that home schoolers read very often, *Teach Your Own*. It's a great book, it makes you feel like 'I can do this!' 'I'm a person!' You know, 'I'm not just a mom!'" These moms are not "just moms." They are teachers, administrators, domestic planning centers, hubs of taxing but fulfilling household enterprises. "I don't want to have my children grow up and remember me as the lady who always had the clean house," Peg explained. "I want them to remember me as the mom who spent lots and lots of time with them. And did wonderful things with them. And enabled them to do wonderful things. And went places and made projects and tried stuff, and had science experiments that didn't work [grinning]."[19] One of the things that home schooling offers, then, is a renovated domesticity—a full-time motherhood made richer by the tasks of teaching, and some of the status that goes along with those tasks.

Home schooling provides women with an expanded maternal role not just within the household but also far beyond it. Many mothers devote good portions of time and skill to maintaining a vibrant homeschool movement, from the grass roots on up. For, as we have already seen, home schooling is a collective project. Local support groups facilitate field trips, camping trips, curriculum and science fairs, teen socials, moms' nights off, and countless other events that ease and enrich the work of individual families while doing much to build community. In this local movement-building as in their homes, women tend to do the majority of the work.

One large Christian support group in suburban Chicago, for example, holds "enrichment days" for its membership nine times a year. On one sunny Friday the enrichment day theme was "ancient civilizations." The hundred children in attendance moved briskly through a four-hour schedule, participating in neatly planned activities that included mock Olympic games: a javelin throw with a plastic baseball bat, a shot put competition with water balloons. A portable sandbox was the site of an archaeological dig. In arts-and-crafts sessions miniature chariots were fashioned out of shoe boxes, laurel crowns from green construction paper. Bedsheets served double duty as costume togas. I counted four dads working that day and fifteen moms. Dads had taken to supervising the more physical events, recording the flight distance of bats and water balloons and explaining the rules of the wheelbarrow-style "chariot races." For the older children, one father served as referee in two games of half-court basketball. Girls played at one hoop, boys at another. One mother's comment indicated that the number of dads on hand that day was exceptional. "We're really glad that more fathers are helping with enrichment this year," she told me, her arm around a fat, official-looking notebook.[20]

This pattern is a common one. A HOUSE support group I attended often was maintained entirely by women. The group had a "chair" position, whose responsibilities included holding the key to the rented church basement where the meetings were held, calling meetings to order, and maintaining the roster of topics to be discussed at each meeting. Throughout the two years that I was most familiar with the group, the chair position was always occupied by a woman. So also were treasurer and newsletter editor, the only other formally designated administrative positions. The group had auxiliary activities—4-H Club, Science Club, and a *Kid's Creations* newsletter for children's artwork—all of which were coordinated by mothers.

If home schooling is a lot of work for any mother who does it, those who assume leadership positions in the homeschool movement have even more to do. I met many such women. Throughout the 1980s, Deirdre Brown homeschooled her own children while being one of the primary architects of the statewide HOUSE network. By the early 1990s, her older sons had reached adulthood, but Deirdre still homeschooled her youngest, Tate, while remaining a key player in HOUSE, a council member of the National Homeschool Association (NHA), and a part-time paid representative of Clonlara School. During the years of my research, Deirdre's phone lines (two) were so busy that she kept one number private and had an answering machine screen virtually all the calls on the other. Deirdre is an activist of national stature, but her commitment to home schooling is not as exceptional as her national credentials. Diana Coleman-Maxwell ably nurtured a small homeschool play group into a lively HOUSE chapter with almost eighty households over a five-year period. She somehow managed to be a key organizer in her local chapter, sit on the statewide

HOUSE council, work part-time for her local school district, and home-school her own two children.

As the homeschool population has grown, so, too, has the national market for curriculum packages, teaching aids, and household management primers of every description. Many women have risen to prominence as homeschool advocates and entrepreneurs. What began as a home-based effort for her own children became Rebecca Avery's The Weaver, the curriculum package used by the Rayburns and widely respected among believers. Patricia Montgomery, long active in the alternative school movement, is founder and director of Clonlara School, the correspondence program favored by many unschooling types.[21] Carol Ingram helped to devise the Advanced Training Institute (ATI) correspondence program used by Robert and Martha Edwards, Susan and Steve Jerome, and some five thousand other homeschool families.[22] Since then Ingram has had a varied career as an advocate and favored public speaker for homeschooling issues. No roster of home schooling's exemplary women would be complete without Mary Pride, the author and homeschool curriculum critic who is also publisher and editor of *Practical Homeschooling* magazine. The list of homeschool activists and businesswomen could be lengthened considerably.

Practical Obligations, Cosmic Explanations

Home schooling is largely a movement of women, but it is not nominally for women. What may seem like stating the obvious is deceptively important: the core incentive to home schooling is one's *children*, not motherhood. Women who already were inclined to stay home, and even some who were not, may find in home schooling a fruitful way of expanding their domestic work and enhancing their status. But at its heart home education grows out of a perceived obligation. The child's needs are in charge, not the mom's.

Consider that several of the women I met spoke about full-time motherhood as a virtual requirement of parenthood. As Lissa Foster discussed her decision to take a step back from her career in science, for example, she framed child care considerations in terms of what being a parent requires.

MITCHELL: What conversation do you have with yourself about that decision [leaving academia to stay home full-time with your children]?

LISSA: Even then, it was like the reason we chose the cooperative day care for [my daughter] is we both wanted to finish our degrees, but we both wanted to have time with her. We had made this decision to bring a life into the world; we both feel like we owe something to that. You don't just have a kid and throw it into other people's care. I'm not really supportive of that kind of idea. There's no reason to bring life into this world if you're not going to be there for it. So, you know, it sort of fits in with how we both think, and especially how I think, both of us, meaning my husband and me—for me to stay at home with them.

For Lissa a central responsibility of parenthood is raising one's own children. She implies that relying on other forms of care provision is reckless, like "throwing" the kids somewhere.[23] Others concur that firsthand care is a responsibility of parenthood. Peg Jesson talked passionately about putting off her other life plans in her children's interests:

It troubles me that a lot of women my age seem to have lost the perspective of delayed gratification. That you don't have to have everything you want now. Children need—it's like I can wait for what I want. I dream of going to seminary. It's a deep desire of my heart. I want to do that. But, I don't need to do that now. I can wait for what I want. But children can't wait for what they need. They need what they need now because they're little. And if they don't get me now, the attention I pay to them when they're eighteen isn't going to meet those needs that they have when they're three.[24]

Talking about her early days of motherhood, when staying home full-time cost her household considerable comfort, Sally Norton used a metaphor of investment to explain the incentive to stay home. As she sees it, sacrifices made for her children in the present will likely pay off as they mature:

For me to stay home with [my daughter] when she was first born, one chicken would last three main meals. We'd cook it once and eat it. I'd cook it again to get the meat off it and use those pieces in casseroles. I mean even the pieces we'd eat we'd save, in case there was any meat left. And then I'd boil the bones for soup and add dumplings. . . . We had no vacations. . . . I couldn't visit my mother-in-law, who was only in [the next state], because it was seven dollars with gas and tolls. I did not have that to go visit more than once a month. There was nothing, but we were investing in our child's future. That whatever we sacrificed now, whatever money it took now, from the time really almost before she was born, we would save later on. I have a happy, well-adjusted child. That doesn't mean it happens every time, but the percentages are in my favor.[25]

Although it is stated in different ways, the general message of these mothers' words is clear: staying home is best for the kids, valuable enough to trump other valuables like income, comfort, and career.

All homeschool mothers explain their decision to stay home in terms of their children's needs. But by themselves, such explanations can come up short. After all, many perfectly good mothers raise perfectly good children while going to work full-time. The broader culture offers a host of reasonable arguments about why it may even be better, in fact, for both mom and the kids if mothers are not full-time caregivers: less parental dependence and fuller socialization experiences for the children; financial autonomy and sturdier self-esteem for women. Making sense of the exceptional household commitment of home schooling often requires more elaborate accounting, and it is in the making of these larger accounts where the two sides of the homeschool movement diverge.

Somewhat paradoxically, some homeschool mothers make sense of their extraordinary commitment by rendering it invisible. They downplay the fact that home schooling has costs for women in terms of time, energy, and career opportunity. They overlook the asymmetry in workloads between mothers and fathers as if it were not there. Or sometimes they reach for an explanation in the realm of nature, accounting for their commitments in terms of a natural reproductive order. On the other hand, the believers do a lot to make full-time motherhood visible. They celebrate women's home labors by placing them within a divine plan for godly families.

Invisible Mother, Natural Mother

The appearance of much of the secular homeschool literature betrays a relative invisibility of grown-ups in general. Many homeschool publications give ample space to images of, and by, children. The covers of *Home Education Magazine* and *Growing Without Schooling* (*GWS*), the flagship publication of Holt Associates, typically center on children—sometimes with a grown-up or two, sometimes not. *GWS* also frequently includes editorials written by homeschooled young people ("young readers," as the magazine sometimes refers to them). Similarly, Clonlara School's newsletter, *The Learning Edge*, is thoroughly embellished by children's artwork from cover to cover. Letters from children and news of children's accomplishments fill the monthly issues.

But, of course, the accomplishments of homeschooled kids invariably require someone else's involvement, whether or not that someone else gets talked about much or gets her picture in the paper. Invariably, someone is keeping a watchful eye on children's progress, answering questions and asking new ones, making sure that young readers eat and sleep adequately or get to the doctor when necessary. In homeschool families that someone is very often a mother. Yet in the secular homeschool literature, mother can be hard to find. Sometimes she hides behind her children's artwork or disappears in long expositions of childhood potential. Not infrequently, she blurs into a plural "we" in collaborative discussions of home education.

Mother's invisibility is partly the result of a child-centered pedagogy. John Holt's written work repeatedly encourages parents to put faith in children before their own efforts. Holt's unschooling requires no particular teacher, no particular educational setting. "This book is about ways we can teach children, or rather, *allow them to learn*," Holt wrote in *Teach Your Own*, subtly making teaching a passive endeavor. Holt's rationale for the primacy of children's efforts over parental teaching is deceptively simple. "Children are not only extremely good at learning," he wrote in *Learning All the Time*, "they are much better at it than we are."[26] Holt taught parents to be wary of undue involvement in their children's learning every step of the way, encouraging both parents and children to follow their own life agendas. He concluded a chapter of *Learning All the Time* with a telling criticism of parental instruction:

> There's nothing wrong with offering [children] a suggestion, but there are several things you have to be careful about. First of all, both parents and children must know that it *is* a suggestion, which the child is free to refuse. If the child refuses to go along with it, . . . it is best to let the matter drop, and quickly. Don't coax, and don't keep on with the activity on the theory that if the child does it long enough he will eventually get to like it. Adults can learn to take "no" for an answer. . . . We have things of our own to do.[27]

Embedded in unschooling pedagogy, then, is a suspicion of authority distinctions between parents and children that tends to make parents disappear. By a rhetorical sleight of hand, teaching and teachers are pushed into obscurity. Children can teach themselves. Adults have things of their own to do. Mothers, fathers, and adults all blur together, their significance paled behind children's potential.

This hopeful obscurantism is common in secular homeschool literature.

Consider David and Micki Colfax's widely read *Homeschooling for Excellence*. The self-described California homesteaders came to public prominence in the mid-1980s when the national media celebrated their three eldest children's matriculation at Harvard. Leaving careers in academic sociology (David) and high school teaching (Micki), in the early 1970s the Colfaxes moved to a rural northern California homestead, where they began homeschooling their children. Understandably, the Colfaxes are often mentioned as exemplars of home schooling's potential.[28]

But where are Mom and Dad? Simply by their status as coauthors, the Colfaxes disappear into each other in the structure of their text. The authors use a plural pronoun throughout: "*We* decided to teach our children at home," "*We* tried to avoid any confrontation with state or local authorities," "*We* called ourselves the Rocky Mountain School."[29] Since husband and wife are home together, they have created work routines "with both of us sharing the teaching" while integrating home schooling into the "day-to-day life of building, clearing, planting, tending, and harvesting." Although the reader learns something about the couple's division of educational labor (David "has spent dozens of hours poring over math books," Micki "has done the same in pursuit of appropriate English and history materials") the Colfaxes give the impression that their contributions to their children's educations are at parity.[30]

Even so, the authors are reluctant to claim responsibility for home schooling's evident success. Parents need only provide certain raw materials for learning, they argue. Children will do the rest: "Most parents, we contend, are more than capable of providing their children with a better education than they could obtain elsewhere. All that is necessary are appropriate learning materials and opportunities, on the one hand, and a nurturing environment, on the other."[31] The Colfaxes admit that home schooling is a considerable drain on time and money, so much so that parents need to rethink household financial priorities and be wary of burnout. Yet they still speak of their pedagogical program in a Holtian language, claiming a commitment to their *children's* capabilities: "Some readers may conclude that despite our disclaimers, we do in fact have an educational philosophy. If so, it is only that children *will* learn, *will* aspire to excellence, if we recognize and respect their different interests and abilities and give them a chance to develop them."[32] Crediting success to their children rather than themselves, the Colfaxes depict a home education in which parent labors are secondary to children's potential.

This emphasis on children to the exclusion of parents has several important consequences. First, it tends to feminize the work in practice.

Rendering the homeschooling parent rhetorically invisible doesn't mean she isn't there. She *always* is—providing "the appropriate learning materials" and creating the "nurturing environment" her child needs. This parent is usually a mother, and she usually is homeschooling more or less on her own while her invisible partner earns the wages the household requires. Not talking about the specific roles of women and men in the project means that home schooling will more likely be women's work by default. As in conventional households, where not talking about the housework usually means that women do more of it, not talking about home-school divisions of labor means that more of the work goes to mom.[33]

But it is also true that in the homeschool world children are "where the action is," to quote the pregnant title of an essay by Erving Goffman. For home schoolers, children are what matter most. They unquestionably are the main business of the movement and, to hear parents tell it, the most exciting part of the work. This means that those who are closest to the children tend to enjoy not only the responsibility but also the status that comes with being close to the symbolic center of the cause.[34] Whether as mothers or movement organizers, women usually are closest to the kids, and they enjoy a palpable measure of social regard for being so. For example, I found that both work and attention were disproportionately given to women in the HOUSE support network. The chapter I knew best had a practice of asking people in attendance to introduce themselves at each meeting. This simple opportunity to claim an identity provided one gauge of how fathers see themselves in relation to mothers regarding home schooling. Men would often introduce themselves with deference to their wives in phrases like "I'm Don Walker. My wife, Mary, and I are homeschooling our two children, Ashley and Andrew. *Mary can tell you the rest*"; "I'm Bill Jones, *Sara's husband*." Often, fathers would defer entirely to their wives, passing the responsibility for introductions to them: "I'm Beth Wilson, this is my husband Tom, and we've been homeschooling our three children for four years now." Once a father was preparing to make his own introduction but was passed over in the circle by his wife. Just as the man was preparing to speak, his wife introduced herself, then her husband and children, while her mate remained silent.[35]

Throughout the activities of this statewide organization, women consistently were at the center of the action, men at the periphery. The HOUSE network organizes annual camping trips, events I attended on two occasions. Each campout liberally mixed work and play. Two business meetings and impromptu rap sessions constituted the working parts of each weekend; nature walks, horseback riding, fossil hunts, and campfires, the play. A handful of men participated in the first evening meetings during both weekends, but men were absent from or only peripheral participants at the other gatherings. During the afternoon meeting of 1992, the women spoke at length about the costs and rewards of the homeschooling life and about the ingrained tendency to instruct their children too much. At the afternoon meeting the second year, the group devoted its energies to discussing how the organization might formally respond to allegations of child abuse from neighbors, relatives, or the state, and how to deal with parents among their membership whose parenting practices they could not condone. As the women discussed issues arguably central to their cause, fathers devoted energies to caring for children, tending campsites, and engaging in more leisurely talk among themselves.

"You know, it's striking to me that the men are less involved in the meetings of the weekend than the women are," I confided to Cathy Ericksen during one conference weekend. Neither she nor I had much experience at camping, so we had pooled resources and set up camp together with her son, Sam. This gave us ample opportunity to talk, and at one point I chanced a conversation about men and women in HOUSE. "There are hardly any men, or no men at all, at the group meetings," I said, referring to the weekend's events.

"It doesn't surprise you, does it?" she replied quickly. "It's sort of always like that with home schoolers. You know, the men are usually working, they're at work all day, and the women are in charge of the kids."

"Yeah, but here, I mean the dads are here, they could be participating as well. I don't know, there are so many impressive, articulate women here, and the men just sort of stay on the sidelines."

"Yeah, but don't you think, I mean there are a lot of sharp women in home schooling, but a lot of the fathers just seem like more average guys."[36]

I responded equivocally, surprised by Cathy's bluntness. Nevertheless, her eagerness to compliment HOUSE women relative to its men is noteworthy, a sort of loaded recognition that fathers and mothers are not regarded equally.

Women tend to be at the center of the homeschool project even when their work as mothers is not explicitly talked about. Since kids are where the action is, and women are near them, they enjoy a good measure of status within the movement and likely within their households as well. But there is a downside to the relative invisibility of women as mothers, too. It puts women in an tight spot when they need to make sense of their commitments to outsiders or even to themselves. Why are you doing this?

skeptics and contrary inner voices sometimes want to know. This side of the movement only provides answers regarding the kids. In a culture that persistently reminds women to think about themselves as well as others, this paucity of self-centered reasons for home schooling can make it difficult for mothers to explain their child-centered commitment. Perhaps this is why many of these women make reference to nature, weaving a particular conception of natural living into their rationales for home education.

Moving closer to nature is common among some groups of home schoolers. Arda Ben Shalom, a HOUSE mom, said, "Another reason we're homeschooling, I guess, is because we're vegetarian." Arda didn't like the prospect of "dealing with my daughter in a public school situation and a lot of junk food and stuff."[37] Another HOUSE mom in Chicago, Sarah Michels, dreams of a life out of town: "I suppose someday I'd like to live in the country, and do some organic gardening. I've always hated being in the city because I get caught up in the pace. My ultimate dream is to move out somewhere west and have a lot of land [with] other people who would like to do organic farming."

"Everything I do is a little bit different," Sarah told me. "You know, I had my babies at home and nursed them extended periods of time. [I'm] trying to be really health conscious and vegetarian, trying to rid my home of those things that I read are bad for us." Comparing her own background with that of other women she knew, Sarah said: "People who homeschool are generally of a whole different mind-set. They are also people who are open to breast-feeding, many of them are also open to home birth. It all runs along the same line."[38]

Over time I found that that line often leads through La Leche League, a support and advocacy organization that encourages breast-feeding. Arda and Sarah had been active in La Leche, as had several other women I met through the HOUSE network. As another told me, "It's funny, one of our [homeschooling group's] early meetings, it was almost like everybody at this meeting was either a League member or a former League member, and it was like old home week."[39] Even a brief look at La Leche League literature indicates that its mission is a natural one. La Leche's ten-item "Philosophy" lists, first, that "mothering through breastfeeding is the most natural and effective way of understanding and satisfying the needs of the baby." As other scholars have pointed out, one of La Leche's central messages to women is that breast-feeding is more natural, and therefore better, than other forms of nurturance.[40]

92

Penny and Gerald Turner, also HOUSE parents, were especially articulate about their commitment to La Leche, breast-feeding, and home education. During our long interview we meandered back and forth between talk of La Leche and talk of home schooling. Penny appreciated La Leche because it provided her with like-minded support when she was a young mother. "I found a place for myself there. I felt like, wow. I found people that agree with the kinds of things that I'm reading about and that I'm feeling, so I liked it." Gerald is convinced that the breast-feeding advocated by La Leche is clearly the best option for his children: "The way I look at it, it's like, hey, when the choices are clear that one way is physically better, and definitely more in line with nature, and the only thing that's going against it is the materialistic yen of this country, the quick satisfaction—quick, quick, quick, stick something in his mouth and get him away from me, so that I can be free. Free for what?" Within seconds we were back to home schooling. Gerald continued: "And now finally it's school, it's the same thing. Yes there are a lot of nice advantages to a school, including major day care, OK? But we're not in family raising to have someone else be a day care sitter." Penny made the connection, too. "Many people that are La Leche League people go into home schooling. . . . It's kind of almost like a natural progression."[41]

But talking about home schooling as "natural" cuts both ways. On the one hand, it provides women with a sturdy rationale for their extraordinary commitment to children. It is difficult to argue with nature, and that rhetorical edge can be an asset when one is doing something unconventional. Appeals to home schooling as natural lend the project the quality of an imperative. Anything else is artificial, second-best. On the other hand, appeals to nature may tend to deepen women's obligation to the work while attenuating men's. If home schooling, like breast-feeding, is something that comes naturally to women, why should we expect someone else to share the load? Appeals to nature arguably help homeschool mothers explain their work in ways that are broadly sensible. But as feminist inquiry has shown time and again, that narrative satisfaction can come at the cost of thinking about divisions of household labor in more critical ways.[42]

Whether or not homeschooling mothers talk about nature, their universal reference to children's needs suggests that the movement's discourse about childhood exerts a powerful tug on behavior. Saying that one did it for one's children is among the most emotionally charged and culturally universal explanations one can give for action. This is why successful elaborations of children's needs can be enormously influential on how people think and what they do.[43] Once convinced that their children require home schooling, mothers may need little else to explain themselves. Still, there are other ways of imagining what homeschool motherhood is all about.

Godly Womanhood

Here is how Carol Ingram, keynote speaker for Illinois Christian Home Educators' 1993 state conference, opened a workshop titled "Schooling or Educating: Which Are You Doing?"[44] "[My husband] Bill and I just met about six and half years ago when at the ripe old age of thirty-eight I was convinced that I was going to be single forever, and God just . . . didn't have anybody out there for me to marry," she began.

> In fact, I decided I was just even going to quit thinking about it. And when I quit thinking about it, God moved . . . an Air Force officer . . . from Mississippi all the way up to the Great Lakes Naval Base. I mean, that's how creative the Lord is. And this Air Force officer . . . drove fifty miles, one way, to come to church on Sunday . . . where I was playing the piano for services. And our preacher decided that we ought to meet each other and kind of sat back there and did the matchmaking thing, [and] it didn't take long for God to reveal His will to us.

Thus this articulate, energetic woman described a major life change. Her account was notable not only because her personal history seemed to have little to do with the topic of her workshop but also because she so explicitly told that history in a divine vernacular. It was God who had brought her and her husband together, who had put them both in the same place at the same time, who had made his will—not Ingram's—apparent. "God had so arranged the circumstances of my life prior to meeting Bill that we knew we would never had children," she continued. "And as Bill and I talked during the days that we were engaged, Bill really felt that because of the preparation God had laid in my life for education that what we wanted to do is spend our lives strengthening those of you who have children to do the very best by them that you can possibly do. So that's our story and that's our perspective."[45]

A former Christian school principal, in recent years Ingram had become a full-time advocate of home education. When I heard her speak that Saturday in June, she had been introduced as the associate director of the Home School Legal Defense Association, working in its advocacy wing, the National Center for Home Education. At that time she was highest-ranking woman in this national organization, and one of the most visible proponents of home schooling among the believers. This, too, Ingram implied, was all part of God's plan.

Many believer women tell the story of their own journeys to home education in terms of God's will. Lola Wooster, a mother with two high school–aged daughters, explained her move from paid work to home schooling this way:

> LOLA: I was working part-time last year. And it was close to home. I was just a few blocks away. I was only a phone call away. It was at a bank and it would start at 1:00 and my husband was home at 4:00, and it was just a few days a week. And I thought it would work out. But it really didn't. It was too much pressure for me to try to keep the house going, keep school going, and trying to work. . . .
>
> MITCHELL: Was it a difficult decision to make?
>
> LOLA: It was. I didn't know whether we would be able to make it financially with me quitting. God was really dealing with me in an area where he was showing me that I was walking by sight and not by faith. I was looking at the numbers I saw on my paycheck and [my husband's] paycheck, and it was scary to quit. But I was physically stressed out enough that I just couldn't work.[46]

Jerry and Jennifer Kullom similarly implied a relationship between their faith and their household decisions. They both had been working full-time when their second child arrived. As Jennifer explained:

> We just sat down one day and decided that we didn't want strangers raising our children, you know, even family, it still wasn't their mother and father. So it's not the same. And then, we became Christians somewhere in the middle of that, too, so we were also under the conviction that it really wasn't what God wanted. . . . We'd been under the conviction that [my working] was wrong, and the practical aspects just all pointed that I ought to be at home.[47]

Like many working parents, Lola Wooster and the Kulloms had a hard time meeting all the demands of home and children. In both cases the solution involved having Mom stay home. Notably, though, they talked about their decision with reference to God's will. Lola described her frustrations with work as a lesson in faith; Jennifer told me that having two full-time working parents "wasn't what God wanted." If many of the women I met in secular groups made reference to nature when explaining why they homeschooled, many women I met through Christian organizations alluded instead to divine intentions.

As my files of homeschool materials grew, I began to discern a parallel difference in how the work of home schooling was represented visually. Images in venues like *GWS*, *Home Education Magazine*, and Clonlara's *Learning Edge* tend to highlight children and put grown-ups at the periphery. But believers' publications often focus on parents as well, especially mothers. In the countless photographs, sketches, and computer graphics that embellish the believers' literature, home education is depicted as a project of children and their mothers. In an advertisement for A Beka Video home school, a woman at work in the kitchen looks on while her son gets a televisual lesson at the dining table. An ad for a "household organizer" calendar product depicts mother and child pointing happily at the device affixed to a refrigerator door. A flyer promoting "The Little House Primer," a study guide for the books of Laura Ingalls Wilder, promises that the product has been "mother and child tested and approved." Christian Liberty Academy assured *Chicago Tribune* readers that "*Mothers* with limited formal education are producing children of exceptional ability and achievement."[48] If on the other side of the movement mothers are marginal or invisible, among the believers they are often at center stage. Sometimes they even get star treatment. *The Teaching Home* magazine carries full-color photographs of homeschool families on its front covers. Featured families regularly contribute a "Cover Story" about themselves that runs as editorial in the issue. Together the cover photos and the features, which are written by parents, lend "everyday" home work celebrity importance.

Relative to other home schoolers, believer advocates write a lot more about mothers and fathers as well. A favored biblical reference in writings about believer women is in the New Testament book of Titus, an epistle written by Paul:

> But as for you, teach what befits sound doctrine. Bid the older men to be temperate, serious, sensible, sound in faith, in love, and in steadfastness. Bid the older women likewise to be reverent in behavior, not to be slanderers or slaves to drink; they are to teach what is good, and so train the young women to love their husbands and children, to be sensible, chaste, domestic, kind, and submissive to their husbands, that the word of God may not be discredited.[49]

Sometimes simple reference to these verses is used as shorthand to describe a certain kind of womanly sensibility, as in an advertisement for a curriculum resale business called The Titus Women's Potpourri. The full-page ad featured a graphic of an open Bible, its pages marked with the reference "Titus 2:3–5."[50] The Christian Homeschool Fellowship Web site features a message board called "Titus 2," on which women exchange advice on such matters as meal planning, housekeeping, and spousal communication.[51] For a presentation targeted to women at one of Gregg Harris's homeschool workshops, speaker Cheryl Lindsey offered the title "Titus Two Living in a Feminist Age."[52] On other occasions the verses serve as a catalyst for longer exegeses on Christian womanhood, as in Mary Pride's *The Way Home*. Originally published in 1985, by 1990 the book had reached its eleventh printing.[53]

In her introduction to *The Way Home*, Pride presents the book as an exposition of Titus 2: "Each section of this book is dedicated to one of the womanly roles listed in Titus 2:3–5: loving your husband, loving your children, homeworking, being kind and subject to your husband, and what happens if we do (or don't do) all this."[54] The book's eighteen chapters are divided into six sections, each of which begins with a phrase from the passage of Titus. With headings such as "Back to Wifeliness," "Back to Babies," "Back to Mothering," and "Back to Homeworking," each section is an excursus upon a different component of godly womanhood. The book is a call for Christian women to abandon the false promises of women's liberation and return to their homes. The subtitle on the book's pink-and-white cover promises a journey "beyond feminism, back to reality."

Just as other homeschool authors construct ominous schools to build their conceptions of childhood, Pride constructs an ominous feminism to build an archetype of godly womanhood. Rendering modern feminism's stock rhetoric of liberation and oppression a two-edged sword, she speaks of feminism as itself an oppressor. "Today's women are victims of the second biggest con game in history," she begins. "The first," she adds parenthetically, "was when the serpent persuaded Eve she needed to upgrade her lifestyle." Pride goes on to list a wide array of woes wrought by feminism, which include no-fault divorce laws, growing rates of female alcoholism, and the decline of the male family wage, "all in the name of Liberation."

Women have pushed through the "liberated" divorce laws which allow husbands to collect alimony from wives and allow adulterers and perverts to retain custody. *Women* are the ones working feverishly to remove children from their parents' care and place them in state institutions. . . . All over America, in your town and mine, right now women are working to abolish the traditional family, to legitimize infanticide, homosexuality, and adultery. They have succeeded in making abortion legal; now they are struggling for the right to murder one's child once he or she is born—or better yet, to let the State decide which children shall or shall not live. This total rejection of women's unique biological role is also called Liberation.[55]

To combat the trouble, Pride offers a womanhood of full-time mothering. This kind of womanhood has its own blessings:

> Don't you enjoy holding a sweet, warm little baby and watching him nurse contentedly at your breast? Don't you treasure that first little smile as your baby drinks you in, the most important person in his world? Isn't it satisfying to make a yucchy little bottom all clean and sweet . . . ? . . . Loving our children means just *enjoying* them and not fretting about the time it takes to serve them. . . . The mother who likes her children will find that they are a blessing.[56]

Like godly motherhood, godly wifehood is typified by the same rewards, since for Pride a necessary purpose of Christian marriage is to produce children. "Children are the essential fruit of marriage, not a mere accidental side-effect," Pride writes in a chapter called "Beyond the Me Marriage."

> Husband and wife unite in God's plan not for themselves alone, but for the sake of the fruit they will bear as well. Woman's role then begins to emerge as something distinct from man's. Neither man nor woman sees marriage as an end in itself . . . but as a medium for the great responsibility of subduing the earth, in which each party has a role assigned by God.[57]

Within this image of the sexes, women have little choice but to follow the path God has laid for them. "*You and I don't have a choice between slavery and uncontrolled freedom. We have a choice between slavery to self-indulgent sin or slavery to God.*"[58]

A prominent player in the homeschool movement, Pride weaves advocacy of home schooling into her discussions of broader moral themes in chapters with titles such as "Who Owns Our Kids?" and "The Times, They Are A-Changing." For her, home education is part of God's directive that women be "homeworkers"—guardians of children, nurturers of husbands, and, ultimately, powerful agents of social change. "Homeworking will not usher in the Millennium, but it will change society," she promises. "And if homeworkers don't reconstruct society, the feminists will."[59] Godly womanhood and the home work for which it is designed are framed as components of a broader social and moral project for godly women.

Believers also have a good bit to say about dads. Also available for the believer bookshelf is *The Homeschooling Father*, by Michael Farris. Former Moral Majority activist, legal counsel for Concerned Women for America, and founder of the Home School Legal Defense Association, Farris is probably the best-known advocate of Christian home schooling in the nation. His book on fathers lays out a model of believer fatherhood built around the theme of benevolent leadership. Farris writes: "All Christian fathers need to exercise real spiritual leadership in their families. In home schooling families, the need for spiritual leadership is particularly acute. Home schooling fathers who fail to provide reliable spiritual leadership are asking their wives and children to fight a Spiritual Revolutionary War without power or weapons."[60] Farris is careful to describe men as agents of authority, not sources of it. Ultimate authority lies with God. "Fathers do not have the job of directly supplying the spiritual power their families need," Farris writes. "That is God's job. But a father has the responsibility to see to it that God's power is flowing freely to each and every member of his family. A father is to serve as the family 'pastor,' providing spiritual leadership for his home."[61]

This leadership has both cosmic and practical components. On the one hand, the Christian father is responsible for the spiritual lives of his children. In a list of twelve spiritual goals of Christian parenting, Farris includes, first, "My child will be sure of his or her salvation" and, second, "My child will love and understand God's word."[62] Leadership also includes the practical discipline of children. "When you are away at work," Farris writes to fathers, "your wife has the responsibility of disciplining your children." But "when Dad is home, he needs to bear the primary responsibility of administering discipline in the family." As the ultimate authority in the believer household, the Christian father is the ultimate rule enforcer: "By having Dad clearly in charge of discipline, there is greater stability than where there appears to be two people in equal authority. The Bible says that no man can serve two masters. The principle is true for your children. They need the assurance that comes from having Dad clearly in charge when he is at home."[63]

Yet for all his authority, the homeschooling father is encouraged to be a benevolent partner. In a chapter titled "Helping Your Helpmeet," Farris addresses the ways that husbands ought to encourage and facilitate the labors of their wives: "The plain truth is that moms do the vast majority of the work in home schooling. As dads, we are asking our wives to take care of housework, cooking, laundry, childcare, *and* teaching our children. That is a *lot* of work." By way of assistance, Farris offers "(1) reliance on the Holy Spirit" and "(2) a dad who helps."[64] One of the best ways dad can assist is to give his wife respite from her daily labors. "A regular mental break, even if it is just for thirty or forty minutes, is a great source of comfort to home schooling moms." In addition, Farris encourages men to schedule other special times for the couple to be together alone: "Take your wife out to dinner at least twice a month—even if it is only for fast food. There's nothing that says you have to eat fast and leave."[65] Dad also can help by lending an ear to his wife's troubles:

> Your wife needs to know that she is not home schooling alone. She needs to know that you view this as a team effort and that you are willing to help her shoulder the tremendous responsibility. . . . Find out how she is doing with the levels of responsibility. Determine where she needs the most help. Discuss ways your help would be the most meaningful to her.[66]

Leadership and nurturance are thus dual components of the same male leadership role.[67]

Texts like these by Pride and Farris are distinctive only in their degree of elaboration and in the celebrity of their authors. Farris's arguments about homeschool fathers, for example, have many echoes. "One of the most notable features of the home education movement is that it is pretty much a women's movement—at least down in the trenches," writes Phil Lancaster in an article for believer fathers called "It's *Your* Home School." "In the day to day battle of planning and teaching, scheduling and organizing . . . it is the mother who bears the brunt of the work, at least in the vast majority of homeschooling homes. . . . So if homeschooling is going to be an option at all, it is going to have to be the responsibility of our wives, right?" The question is asked rhetorically, and it is answered unequivocally, in boldface: "Wrong! you are responsible."[68] Beverly Somogie, cover mother for a 1994 issue of *The Teaching Home*, noted that her husband, Gary, "is the 'principal' of our school. . . . He oversees all of us, making sure that I haven't lost my mind and that the children do their lessons."[69] And the believers' general faith that gender roles are divinely complementary is ubiquitous. Borrowing directly from the biblical book of Genesis, a phonics workbook I purchased at a Christian curriculum fair asks junior readers to fill in some loaded blanks: "God made a w_man to live with Adam. God made a woman to hel_ Adam."[70]

Believers sometimes explained their home work to me by alluding to such ideas. When I asked Marci Rayburn to talk about her decision to leave a teaching career and be home with her children, she explained eloquently:

> I think it would have to do with who God made me to be, and, I was just terribly uncomfortable with someone else caring for my child, and it was just a very strong leading from God that I needed to stay home. And once I *was* home, I was really at peace. And I felt that this was where God wanted me to

be, at this season in my life. And I felt, too, that he had gifted both of us to educate [our daughter], and so I had more of a desire I guess to be at home, because I would be doing that and it would be even more fulfilling than just being a mom. That it would be using my talents and my abilities.[71]

Still other clues indicate the believers' concern about putting divine will for men and women into practice. Several parents said that daily devotions were the Dad's job. The Kulloms specifically talked about dad's "administrative role" in homeschool households. ATI, the curriculum program chosen by the Edwardses and the Jeromes, essentially requires that fathers be involved in the homeschool program. A spokesperson for the ATI curriculum, a young man who had himself been homeschooled, told me during an interview:

ATI really is for the whole family. Educating the whole family. So there's quite a vital ministry to fathers in the program. You know so often in homeschooling households there's a problem of improper balance between the mother and father, between the husband and the wife. I mean, and this is understandable since so often the woman is doing most or all of the work of home schooling, all the planning and the record keeping. And it's easy for the father to say, "Oh that's her job," and he ends up losing his proper position of authority, of leadership in that family. And the Bible is clear that it is the father's job to see to the education of his children. He may *delegate* that responsibility, or part of that responsibility, to his wife, but the education of the children is *his* responsibility. And that can take different forms. Like, in my family, my mother is the one who does a lot, most of the planning and the work with the children, and she will bring her plans to my father, and he'll basically say, "Yes, of course, yes, that's good, go ahead," but the point is that it is his authority to delegate. How it's delegated may be different in different families, but that order of authority is very important.[72]

That ATI is serious about the involvement of homeschooling fathers is indicated by its strict policy about divorce. ATI's 1994 application literature specifically warned applicant families, in italics, that "future divorce brings disenrollment."[73]

But despite some poignant affinities between the words of ideologues like Pride and Farris and what many believers say and do, I did not find the kind of strident scripting of motherhood and fatherhood outlined in books like *The Way Home* and *The Homeschooling Father*. True enough, several believer women talked about God's will in their decisions to stay home. Peg Jesson offered a mild chastisement of working mothers when she told me that "a lot of women my age seem to have lost the perspective of delayed gratification," implying that women who pursue careers while having children are selfish. Sally Norton spoke derisively of day care (in Sunday school, she said, "You can always tell the daycare kids. . . . They are either more boisterous, more demanding, or they are the super quiet in the corner, shy, or the terribly miserable kid").[74] Nevertheless, I found that there was considerable distance between how the advocates talk about men and women and how the believers' rank and file talk about themselves. Not contradiction, but distance—partial employment of language (God's will) or practice (men leading devotions or playing administrative roles)—rather than wholesale embrace or dismissal of what the advocates have to say.

A common finding of research among conservative Protestants in other settings is that theory and practice rarely match cleanly on issues of gender. In theory, for example, conservative Protestants often preach wifely and womanly submission. In practice, wives may have a lot of say in household and congregational decision making. In theory, mothers are supposed to stay home full-time with their children. In practice, mothers who work are not heavily sanctioned.[75] The same is true among homeschooling believers. True enough, compared with other home schoolers, the believers make more room for male leadership in their organizations. When HOUSE convened its statewide conferences, women tended to be the ones who sat on the council and conducted most of the organizational business. But Illinois Christian Home Educators is overseen by a board of directors composed primarily of husband-and-wife teams. At the ICHE annual conference in 1993, a man opened the proceedings and welcomed the audience. When officers were introduced, they were men. Wives were recognized subsequently, then rose to accept applause. The Home School Legal Defense Association (HSLDA), Michael Farris's concern in northern Virginia, employs many women, some in positions of considerable authority; still, during my visits in 1993 and 1999, I learned that all of its staff attorneys were men.

But it is also true that women are often the lead spokespeople for Christian home schooling in their households. They are the local experts, who know the details of the project and typically have the day-to-day responsibility for it. In homeschool work beyond the household, believer women often are the primary engines of local and regional support groups. And more than a few, Mary Pride and Carol Ingram among them, have made formidable careers as homeschool leaders while preaching submission to husbands and the Heavenly Father.

In the end, I concluded that what is most remarkable about the believers' talk about gender and family is not the degree of fit between talk and practice, but rather the sheer amount of talk. Any feminist worth his salt would concur that putting home and work together remains a difficult task especially for women. Stagnant wages for large sectors of the middle and working classes mean that many households require two incomes to maintain what they regard as an acceptable lifestyle. Women's wages are far from being at parity with men's. The majority of women with children in this country now work, but their spouses remain reluctant to take up a fair share of housework and childcare. The United States has no national child care policy. Day care options for millions of households are either slim, absent, or unaffordable. Women face contradictory pressures to be both independent persons and committed mothers.

At the same time, the standard for what counts as good mothering has risen considerably. Here again, homeschool families are exceptional only in degree: mothering is a much more elaborate enterprise generally than it was even a few generations ago. As Sharon Hays points out, "Child rearing ideologies vary widely, both historically and cross-culturally. . . . The idea that correct child rearing requires . . . copius amounts of physical, mental, and emotional energy on the part of the individual mother is a relatively recent historical phenomenon."[76] If anything, the hard choices faced by working mothers have been exacerbated by the culture's more elaborate expectations of contemporary mothers.

In the face of the formidable obstacles women face in assembling coherent and feasible life plans, the believers' elaborate talk about gender and parenting represents an admirable effort to imagine a more ideal work-family system. And while it is expressed in a language far removed from the verbosities of social science, their imagination betrays considerable sociological sophistication. The believers often say it is very important that mothers stay home. But the talk does not end with celebrations of maternity and admonitions that home and work do not mix. Also on the table are detailed examinations of fathers' roles, both as committed breadwinners and as nurturant helpmeets to their wives. Home work gets redefined to include considerably more than cleaning floors and packing lunches. Women are admonished to be committed full-time to their children, but their submission to God's plan is also explicitly recognized and celebrated from pulpits and on the pages of glossy magazines. A wide array of career-like opportunities remain open for believer women as organizers, administrators, advocates, and entrepreneurs even while they are full-time mothers. The sheer elaborateness of the believers' talk about mothers and fathers indicates that they are aware of the complicated linkages between motherhood and the broader institutional organization of gender, work, and social status. They understand, in other words, that a lot needs changing if women are going to stay home full-time. And even if reality rarely conforms neatly to their plans, at least there *are* plans—utopian perhaps, but something to work toward, something tangible to talk about.

Of course, this utopia comes at a price. For all people but especially for women, the believers' vision scripts many central features of biography. A woman is strongly encouraged to marry, to have children, and to be primarily a homeworker. Her domestic industry will be encouraged and assisted by her husband, but it also will be formally subordinate to his judgments. If a woman wants something other than the divine plan, her desires will be regarded as heretical at best and, at worst, blasphemous. Men are similarly obliged to marry, have children, and assume a family role that is largely predefined. If this is what heaven looks like, not everyone will want to go there.

Homeschooling believers have a lot to say about Christian families, but their characteristically traditionalist talk should not be mistaken for the entirety of conservative Protestant discourse on domestic issues. It is important to remember that in the conservative Protestant world there are multiple positions in the conversation about gender and family. Despite the critical press given to more traditionalist voices, students of the debate have noted that it includes a range of positions from traditionalist to feminist.[77] That the believers' homeschool literature tends toward the conservative side suggests that many of the movement's most successful entrepreneurs—Pride, Farris, Bill Gothard of ATI, Welch and Short of *The Teaching Home*, Gregg Harris, and others—have come largely from American Protestantism's far right wing. Their collective accomplishment has been to create a Christian home education that is intellectually coherent but also decidedly hostile to some basic tenets of liberal feminism. There are other, equally vital, points of view. Many Christian women, after all, have made deep investments in their own careers. Many have a more gender-neutral conception of God's will. It is not surprising, then, that not all committed Christian home schoolers are interested in the version of home schooling promulgated by the believers' most visible advocates.

When I asked Lissa Foster to talk about the religious composition of her HOUSE chapter, she said:

> I'd say the majority of the people are Christian faith, but they just aren't Christian home schoolers, they're home schoolers who happen to also be

Christian. That does seem to be a difference between being a Christian home schooler or home schooling [and Christian]. . . . There are a few people in [our] group, I know we have a few Muslim families. . . . I know at least two Chinese people, an Indian couple.

Lissa appreciates the ecumenism. "I don't want [my children] to ever grow up thinking that one way is right and one way is wrong. I really like the diversity of our group," she says. Lissa calls herself a Christian, but "we're just not really, like fundamental or literalist Christians. We're Christians but not in that way." Lissa's version of her faith is unproblematic in HOUSE, which explicitly welcomes families regardless of their religious background.

But the Fosters were planning a move to a different state, one well-known among home schoolers nationally for its large and strong Christian support network. Lissa spoke cautiously about finding a homeschool community after the move:

MITCHELL: Was I correct in hearing you indicate some apprehension about the support group options [in your new home]?

LISSA: A little bit, since the [name of Christian] group is such a strong group, and I'm a little bit concerned about whether we would be able to fit in with their group or not. I mean even if we are Christian, and we do sometimes do Bible studies and do devotions every night with the kids. . . . We've run into some of the people being against women working outside the house, which I definitely do. I didn't this year, but I have in the past taught night school at the community college. I'd like to continue doing that, and I know that that causes a problem with some of the more fundamentalist Christian groups. Also the issue of evolution. We are both biologists; it's something we both teach. . . . We have no problem with the idea of creation through evolution, but we're not seven-day Creationists, which I know it can really be an issue for some people, too.

Like many of its peers in other states, the Christian organization in Lissa's new home has a statement of faith that includes basic tenets of conservative Protestant theology. Lissa did not sound certain about the details, but she worried that her stance on evolution might be problematic:

So we're a little bit concerned about that because I can't join a group in good conscience knowing that this is what they believe, and this is the only thing they believe, to lie to them and say, well I'm going to join you because it's convenient for me. . . . I don't want to lie to them. And I know that the parent group of [the state organization] leans more to that way, . . . so we do have a little bit of apprehension about that.

Despite what she had heard about the organizational landscape, Lissa remained optimistic. "But there are other groups that are forming [there] for people who are more like we are," she added hopefully.[78]

As is true with their teaching styles, home schoolers' diversity of faiths is only roughly reflected in their organizations. By the mid-1990s, in cities across the country, mothers and fathers typically were obliged to choose between explicitly Christian groups and explicitly nonsectarian ones. And where conservative believers set the terms of what "Christian" meant, mothers like Lissa who read their Bibles differently found themselves looking elsewhere for people to talk to, people who thought their way.

Authority and Diversity

A SINGLE CARVED SIGN named the site of Clonlara School. Located on a side street in Ann Arbor, Michigan, its four modest buildings were all painted dark green and tucked beneath shade trees. Bits and pieces of childhood were evident on the grounds: climbing equipment, a tire swing, and a playhouse. To reach the office I walked through a little garden where narrow walks outlined beds of flowers. At the center of the garden was a monument, a wood pole bearing the message "May peace prevail on earth" in several different languages.

Although the school was serving four thousand children a year, when I visited in 1994, Clonlara's main office occupied less than four thousand square feet in an old house whose layout still bore traces of its previous use. I discerned a parlor, a day porch, and a dining room from the contours of walls covered with snapshots of smiling children and countless works of children's art. Staff members, mostly women, sat at desks in the crowded front rooms. I would meet many of them soon: Rachel, who at the time of my arrival was trying to nurse her child, type, and talk on the phone simultaneously; Greta, mother of two and active in a group called Informed Home Birth; Beth, who had previously worked for a housing advocacy organization; and Marlin, who first learned of Clonlara through the local food cooperative.

Over the course of my visit, I would be impressed that the school had a palpable coherence to it. The work histories and political orientations of the staff, the loose conceptions of who was boss, and the open classrooms in Clonlara's day school all seemed part of a broader pattern that I could discern but could not easily label. None of the candidate terms—*counterculture, progressive, alternative*—fit most neatly. This uncertainty contrasted sharply with my experiences among the believers, who often labeled their organizational culture for me. The believers call their organizations "Christian," "godly," or "evangelical," as in Christian school, godly home, and evangelical church. Primers about how to live in these organizations can be purchased in religious bookstores, and the ideals that animate them can be heard from pulpits. On the other side of home education there are fewer such luxuries, but nevertheless breast-feeding at work, "peace on earth," and the food co-op all seemed to go together somehow, components of a shared sensibility that many home schoolers said they felt but few could name. Thankfully, one of the Clonlara staff members lent me some excellent candidate terms.

Kyron had been working as a receptionist in the school's offices, sending her children to Clonlara's small day school. During my visit the office staff held an afternoon party for her. Soon Kyron would be leaving because she and her partner were moving to a small acreage out of town. "I'm not a city person, I'm a country person," Kyron explained. "I like being home, like tending children, like the home-based work. Being self-sufficient, that's the kind of life I want." Kyron planned to keep her children at home after the move. "Oh, yes, I want to homeschool. But I don't think of it as a separate kind of a thing. It's more like my whole way of doing things." As we continued to talk, I learned that Kyron's sister, a born-again Christian, was also a homeschooling mom. She seemed to mention her sister as much for contrast as comparison:

> It's interesting my sister homeschools, too, but she does it differently. She's a born-again Christian, and she says she's homeschooling because she's a Christian. She uses a curriculum, she uses KONOS [a religious program]. And it's funny because in many ways we think similarly about what we're doing, but she does it in a Christian way, that's the way she talks about it, talks about why she's doing it. And I do it in a, I don't know, I talk about it in a different way even though we're doing the same thing. She's talked to me about her beliefs, but that's just not how it is for me. Earth-based and heaven-based, is how I think about it. We're doing kind of the same thing, but hers is heaven-based and mine's earth-based.

"Do the two of you get along?" I asked.

> Oh, yeah, we get along pretty well. We've sort of agreed to disagree on some things. We don't see each other too often, she's still up in [another town], and I've been down here, so we're not together much. And she has her circle of friends there, people from the church, Christian home schoolers. And that's fine for her, seems to work real well for her. That's sort of like her family now, her church, and her homeschooling friends. . . . And I have mine, too. It's interesting we are from the same family, grew up together, but that's not how our lives are put together now.[1]

The distinction between the two ways of doing things was difficult for Kyron to spell out directly, more amenable to metaphor than to straightforward elaboration. Like Kyron and her sister, sometimes home schoolers who think contrarily get along pretty well. They might move largely in different circles or, when they do encounter each other, somehow agree to disagree. But very often the difference between earth-based and heaven-based has pulled home schoolers in such separate directions, or perhaps made them such different people, that diplomacy is difficult, and cooperation even more so.

We can make a more detailed, if less poetic, sense of the distinction between earth-based and heaven-based by borrowing from the tool kit of cognitive science. Cognitive psychologists and cultural sociologists often use the term *schemata* to describe templates of understanding that people use to make sense of the world. Schemata are "knowledge structures that represent objects or events and provide default assumptions about their characteristics, relationships and entailments under conditions of incomplete information."[2] Like the image on the box of a jigsaw puzzle, a schema helps us to assemble small bits of knowledge into a coherent whole. Think of lived experience as an ever-accumulating pile of puzzle pieces: while the flow of life sends us a cacophony of stimuli, schemata enable us to order the information into comprehensible patterns. They allow us to get a sense of a big picture, even when some of the pieces are not in place.

Of course, life is a lot less tidy than a parlor game. With human sense making there is never one right solution, no one best way of making sense of a situation. Not infrequently people find themselves disagreeing about how to assemble the big picture. Different biographies and cultural traditions imbue people with disparate and sometimes competing ideas about how to put the details together. Such differences can make it hard for players to cooperate, and may even lead to factions in the party. In the course of my work, I learned that at the core of the difference between earth-based and heaven-based home schoolers are incompatible ideas about the nature of persons and of legitimate authority. This means that home schoolers tend to have different guiding images—different schemata—for how to assemble themselves into collectivities. The difference has not been without its consequences: a dynamic, talkative, and diverse movement on the one hand; miscommunication and division on the other.[3]

Some home schoolers assume that persons are essentially good. They believe that, if so allowed, people will tend to make good decisions that are in their own best interests. They believe also that individuals are rightfully autonomous. People may work under certain leaders or under the constraints of certain rules, but they do so of their own choosing. Believers think differently. First, and in keeping with central tenets of Protestant theology, they assume that people are both good and sinful. This sin nature, as believers often call it, means that people can make the wrong decisions if left to choose on their own. Second, believers are more willing to grant that under the right conditions, some people can appropriately direct the affairs of others. Parents can direct children, for example, and godly leaders their flocks.

Such different ways of thinking about people and their rightful relations have significant organizational repercussions. They have led home schooling's movement builders to make different decisions how to fit people together into collectivities and how to allocate labor and authority. As these contrary sensibilities have been built into the organizational structure of the homeschool world, they have affected patterns of cooperation between homeschool groups and subtly channeled patterns of recruitment to the cause.

The story I tell in this chapter and the next is about what happened through the 1990s as home schoolers found themselves disagreeing about just what their movement should look like and how it ought to function. I recount some pivotal years in the history of home schooling, a history that offers larger lessons for social movement scholars. First, it reminds us that people really do attempt to turn their ideals into organizational reality. When building their organizations, activists try to give practical expression to their visions of how the world ought to be, and often they succeed. Second, homeschool history shows that people can become committed to certain ways of doing things even when those ways are not efficient. Partly because they come to represent some philosophical or political ideal, organizational forms can be intrinsically meaningful, so much so that they are hard to set aside even when they do not serve practical ends very well. Finally, this history demonstrates that differences of opinion about apparently mundane matters can sum to formidable organizational trouble. Disagreements over little things—like what to call a group, or how to coordinate a phone tree or write a purpose statement—often signal larger differences in organizational sensibility that ultimately can inhibit or prevent cooperation.

IMAGES OF ORGANIZATION

As I have described, different home schoolers have contrary ways of thinking about children and their parents. John Holt argued that children are inherently sensible individuals, poorly served by teaching methods that encroach on their ability to make their own choices. He claimed that the best path of learning is one that children pursue of their own volition. Of course, children are free to cooperate with one another and with chosen authorities, and we have seen already that unschooled children often do so. They entertain each other at support group meetings, join science and 4-H clubs, and enroll in classes at the local community college. Significantly, though, the explanations for these activities are framed in terms of children's choices. And because children are individuals, with distinctive preferences and proclivities, their behavior is difficult to predict.

In time I learned that this conception of persons informs how its adherents think about home schoolers as a group. Over a coffee shop breakfast with Deirdre Brown, I offered that her wing of home education was typified by a kind of anarchic ideal. Inclusives conceive of people as autonomous individuals, I said, who rightly choose their own direction. To illustrate what I was saying, I took several packets of sugar from the table between us. I defined each one as a person and laid them out randomly.

"Yes," she said, "but what happens is that people come together, because they have common interests, so it looks more like this." Deirdre took the packets and arranged them in a circle. She did not disagree that people make their own choices, but she amended my image to show how choice-making individuals could come together to form an organization. To depict how constituents did this, she used the image of a circle, in which people come to the collective as equals.[4]

Afterward I took stock of a feature of meetings that I had long taken for granted: the physical organization of bodies. At HOUSE support group sessions and statewide camping trips, a circle was the default arrangement of persons. Before support group meetings began, attendees would often devote considerable energy to rearranging the furniture to form a circle. At the state level, council meetings and group discussions invariably were carried out in circles.

Other clues indicated just how seriously home schoolers like Deirdre take the notion of individual autonomy. At one HOUSE state council meeting, for example, a group of regional representatives joked that their group was hardly a group at all. "We're not an 'organization.' We're a loose coalition of individuals."[5] The comment met with chuckles, as if to indicate that such was true in theory if not entirely in fact. On another occasion, a local HOUSE chapter decided it wanted a way to share expertise; members of the support group were bearers of multiple skills, they reasoned, and they wanted a way to connect interested parties with talented ones. But what to call it? Perhaps because I was a graduate student (or perhaps simply because I was on hand), a couple of the mothers asked me. One of them said, "I don't want to use the word 'teach,' you know. It's not for people to 'teach' people." The women were having trouble finding words that fit their intent. I suggested a metaphor—a skills bank. "Skills

111

bank. Yeah. You put something in, and you take something out." The term stuck. Teaching metaphors, which might imply hierarchy, were spurned. But a metaphor that highlighted the collective amassing of resources and individual volition (*you* put something in) was acceptable.[6]

Believers tend to think about things differently. As I indicated earlier, they share the belief that children are unique individuals, but they combine this faith with an ardent concern for child discipline and protection. In believers' households this concern takes the form of admonitions that children need guidance to keep them from untoward people and beliefs. For believers, keeping children out of school is as much about keeping them from ungodly influences as it is about meeting their individual needs. In the home, believers are admonished to train their children in Christian living even while they are allowed to mature as unique persons.

This difference in pedagogy implies a starkly different relationship between individuals and authority. While other home schoolers defend the central importance of letting children make their own choices, the believers contend that children's autonomy must exist within a framework of parental control. This model of authority extends beyond the relationship between children and their parents. As described in the previous chapter, believers also have a model of an ideal family structure that scripts distinctive roles for mothers and fathers, women and men. On the other side of the movement, theorizing about family formation is notable for its absence.

Beyond the family, too, the believers conceive of a divine order in which God, the ultimate and transcendent authority, delegates earthly leadership to particular men and women. The believers' is a Protestant divine, in which no single earthly person or organization has ultimate authority. Rather, there may be many human instruments of God's interests, multiple authorities, which leaves room for considerable discretion for people to choose their earthly leaders. And like the rest of us, godly leaders are fallible, prone to sin, potentially errant or irresponsible vessels of divine will. Nevertheless, the believers' organizational schema is clearly hierarchical. Some people have more authority than others, and multiple individual interests may legitimately be subsumed under collective ones.

This hierarchical conception of authority is often invoked implicitly. As we have found already, it is built into the way believers talk about how children should be treated, how wives ought to behave with their husbands, and how husbands should be sensitive to divine will. But sometimes the schema is made quite explicit. I found that I didn't need sugar packets to discern it, because very often the picture was drawn for me. A sequel to

The Way Home, Mary Pride's *All the Way Home* includes a chapter on household organization. Employing a tongue-in-cheek style, Pride asks her readers:

> Who is in charge of this outfit, anyway? According to the Bible it works like this. God, Company Owner. Tarzan, Chief Executive Officer (CEO). Jane, Plant Manager. Boy, Trainee. Not hard to understand. We can also pretty easily see what is wrong when Tarzan and Jane start battling over who should be boss. Alligators hang out below to eat whoever falls out of the tree.

To illustrate her point, Pride provides her readers with a telling labor tree. Titled "The Biblical Chain of Command," the image looks like this:

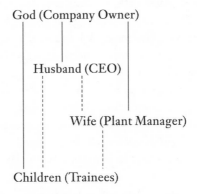

The accompanying legend indicates that the solid lines represent "direct authority," dotted lines "delegated authority."

A similar hierarchy is sketched by Gregg Harris in his instructional videotape "Child Training, God's Way." In a discussion about child socialization, Harris argues that young children tend to use their older siblings as role models for their own maturity. To illustrate why his claim is true, Harris provides a picture:

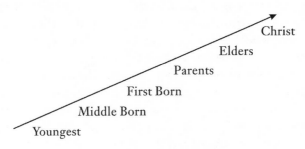

"Everyone is reaching for higher levels of maturity . . . but who is raising whom?" the graphic's caption reads.[8] The assumption is that parents are more mature than children and thus rightfully direct them. So, too, are church elders more "mature" than parents, and Christ the most mature of all.

As with the home schoolers in the HOUSE group, the believers lend other more subtle cues regarding how they think about human relations. HOUSE meetings of all sorts consistently met in circles, but I was more likely to find traditional speaker-audience configurations at believer gatherings. For the support group meeting where I met Pamela Eckard, Sally Norton, the Kulloms, and the Witkowskis, chairs in a church basement were arranged in neat rows, with a center aisle and furniture in the front for speakers (I was allowed to speak facing the group, in front, when I made a request for interviews). The sessions I attended at the statewide conferences of Illinois Christian Home Educators were held in auditoriums where speakers were at podiums. When I attended two of Gregg Harris's Christian Life Workshops, Harris stood both before and above his audience, on stages in a gymnasium and a church. At the "ancient civilizations" enrichment day held by a large suburban support group, one portion of the day was devoted to a formal instruction session, held in a church sanctuary. At this session the moms stood at the front, facing the children who were seated in pews.[9]

There were other clues. Once when I called a Christian mother to arrange an interview, I received a call back from her husband. He was concerned that I had taken the liberty to arrange a meeting with his wife, in private, without his consent. I could only apologize. Clearly, my assumption that a woman could schedule her own interview was not shared by the man on the other end of the line.

Sensibilities, images, schemata. Whatever we call them, they exist in our heads: actual behavior is a lot less tidy, and home schoolers' behavior is no exception. As mentioned earlier, there are some important features of home schooling's organizational landscape that the schemata fail to see. The self-motivated, self-teaching child of unschooling, for example, requires more or less full-time attention from another person. The heavy parental obligation of unschooling remains whether or not people acknowledge it. And the infrastructure of home schooling as a social movement is largely maintained by women—many of them entrepreneurial, many of them with hefty reserves of reputational clout—even while much believer discourse preaches a message of female domesticity and submission. The point is not that the models are always true to reality, but rather that the models are the primary referents people use to make sense of reality. These images of organization are consequential because people employ them when building organizations-in-the-flesh, and when they elicit participation in their cause. The images also serve as standards by which certain configurations of labor, authority, and scarce resources can be called honorable, problematic, or immoral.

Because they have different conceptions of what an ideal organization *should* be, home schoolers have built two quite distinct movement infrastructures. Committed to ideals of individual freedom and ideological diversity, the inclusives have created an organizational system that is built around individual decision making and that amply accommodates difference. Committed to an ideal of godliness, the believers have created a system that is built around leaders and that discourages dissent.

HEAVEN-BASED

Wendy Doyle greeted me warmly at the door to her office at Christian Life Workshops (CLW), the ministry of the popular home education advocate Gregg Harris. The tidy facility was located on the same property as the Harris home, and it housed a range of related industries: Noble Publishing Associates, which purveys homeschool curriculum enhancements and household organizers; *New Attitude*, a magazine for homeschooled youth founded by Harris's son, Joshua; and CLW, which appeared to be the flagship concern. Its product was seminars staged by the elder Harris to recruit and embolden Christian home schoolers.[10] An announcement for a 1994 conference in the Chicago area promised two days of lectures by "some of the most experienced and visionary voices in the national home-school community today"—among them Gregg Harris, Joshua Harris, and Doug Phillips, then director of the Congressional Action Committee (CAP), the lobbying arm of the Home School Legal Defense Association (HSLDA).[11] The event was to be held in a large Protestant church in the Chicago suburbs. The cost of registration and tuition for the conference was forty-five dollars per couple, and attendees could save money by registering early or signing up in groups of five or more. Support group leaders who came with ten or more group families, "Christian Foreign Missionaries (active but on furlough)," church pastors, and single parents were admitted free of charge.

115

Sitting in her office, Wendy handed me a one-page list of job descriptions for the six employees who directed the workshops from Harris's backyard. As the director's assistant and national events coordinator, Wendy had the job of scheduling Harris's seminars around the country. When I met, her she had been at CLW for two and a half years, and she described her work with the confidence that comes from experience. "I'm the events coordinator for the workshops, I do all of Gregg's scheduling, and I work with the local teams to arrange the workshops and seminars. Here's my calendar," she added with a grin, motioning toward a laminated wall poster that covered half of an office wall.[12]

I asked Wendy about the relationship between CLW headquarters staff and the local "teams." "Well, say you want to do a workshop in your area," she began. "You'd call and say, we'd really like to have a workshop, what can we do? I'd take the call, and we would schedule a workshop in your area. We like to work six months in advance, you really need six months to do all of the planning and organizing. And we'd find a time."

"So you rely on local people for organizing the conferences?" I asked.

"Yes, that's right. Whenever we go for a workshop, we work with a team of eight people in coordinating the event. . . . They each have specific jobs. It's actually quite a bit of work. It can be really good, challenging work if you're the sort of person who likes to be organized and efficient, and we provide a plan for the work, too."

As she spoke, Wendy retrieved a fat binder from the corner of her desk. It was a planning manual for the local workshops and conferences, and she referred to it as she continued to explain. "There's a publicity captain, one for registration, . . . the facilities captain . . ."

Inside the manual was a pull-out flowchart, with rows listing discrete jobs for eight local workers: the local coordinator, prayer captain, publicity captain, facilities captain, registration captain, bookstore captain, exhibit hall captain, refreshments captain. Columns blocked out periods of time on the approach to the conference date: 20 weeks, 16 weeks, 12 weeks, 8 weeks, 4 weeks, 2 weeks, 1 week, and 1 day prior. With 64 cells, the resulting table divided up the labor into clearly articulated, bounded tasks. At 16 weeks prior to conference date, for example, the prayer captain was expected to "Pray for the Event. Recruit volunteers to pray. Call or visit team members." At 4 weeks prior, the exhibit hall captain was to "Make initial map of Exhibit Hall" and, at 1 week prior, "Create a final map of the Exhibit Hall Area." Also at 1 week prior, it was the job of the refreshments captain to "Verify volunteers, refreshment donors & equipment." Few details were left to chance.[13]

I remarked to Wendy that this level of organization was quite impressive.

"Yes, it really is organized. And it really has to be that way because there's so much to do. Some people get kind of f. . ." Wendy seemed hesitant to use the vernacular.

"Freaked out?" I offered.

"Yes, freaked out about it because it seems like there's so much work, and some people get upset at the manual, that everything's so set up, but it really needs to be."

"And a lot of this organization was in place when you came on the job?"

"Yes. Most of it." Placing her hand on the manual, she said, "This represents years of work really, Gregg pulling this together."

Over the course of our conversation, it became clear that the success of Harris's endeavor relied on the prayerful, practical support of scores of volunteer associates across the country—eight conference captains at each conference site, the teams of assistants that each captain enlisted, and host families who housed and fed Harris and ferried him to his appointments.

From one perspective, the organizational sophistication of CLW resided in its central offices. Here, after all, was the control center for CLW's national operations. Here is where the binder was housed, alongside the very person who pulled it all together, Harris himself. Here in the office was where we might first try to assess how "organized" the project was. To make this assessment we might look, for example, at the degree of coordination between local groups and the CLW office, or at the extent to which the process of holding a seminar was similar from city to city, or at how financial records were kept, or at how easy CLW's workers were to replace.[14]

But if we kept our focus on the Oregon offices, we would miss two important components of the social system that made Harris's ministry possible. We would miss, first, the universe of established organizations on which CLW depended. CLW often held its seminars in buildings of local religious concerns. Christian Liberty Academy was the site for the first Harris workshop I attended; a subsequent workshop in the Chicago area was held in a local church. A promotional flyer for an "Advanced Home Schooling Workshop" (for "the special needs of experienced home schooling families") in London, Ontario, listed the venue as a local church.[15] These organizations supported Harris's ministry with more than their physical plants. As sociologists such as Aldon Morris and Christian Smith have explained, religious organizations carry a distinctive moral weight in the society. Churches especially lend the projects they house a civic respectability that they otherwise might not have.[16] Harris's use of religious organizations was thus good for his ministry in both practical and symbolic ways.

There is yet another significant component of CLW's organizational system, one that resides in the heads of the local volunteers who enabled Harris's show to go on. CLW relied on people who are comfortable with being directed. The coordination of labor for the workshops was clearly top-town. The planning manual explicitly scripted the jobs of a host of volunteers at each workshop site and placed those volunteers into hierarchical relations. The manual invoked a sports vernacular to designate authorities ("publicity captain," "facilities captain") and designated discrete tasks for each of them. According to Wendy, each captain worked under the general supervision of the local coordinator, who in turn was answerable to the CLW offices. The success of the workshops depended not only on the generation of volunteer labor but also on CLW's ability to coordinate that labor. An explicit, hierarchical organization of volunteers enabled CLW to replicate its workshops again and again across the country. The volunteers and the venues changed, but the orchestration of actors remained predictably, efficiently the same.

This kind of organizational model can only work in a social universe in which people are willing to work in hierarchical relationships with one another. Harris's concern had the luxury of doing business in a world in which deference to authority is commonplace. The believers are generally comfortable with the notion of hierarchical social relationships, having rehearsed them in their pedagogies and to some extent in their families as well. This willingness to accept hierarchical arrangements is easy to take for granted, perhaps—until it is not forthcoming. That "some people get upset at the manual, that everything's so set up," as Wendy said, indicates that not everyone is willing to play along. Still, the evident success of the system suggests that Harris and his colleagues had figured the plan quite well; by the early 1990s, CLW claimed that over seventy thousand parents had attended its workshops.[17]

Years ago, Gregg Harris had Wendy's job. In the early 1980s, Harris moved from the Midwest to work as a conference coordinator for Raymond and Dorothy Moore, then headquartered in Washougal, Washington. Business differences forced Harris and the Moores to go their separate ways, but Harris remained in the Pacific Northwest, near Portland, Oregon, nurturing his own concern in tandem with other blossoming leaders in the Christian homeschool movement. In the early 1980s, Christian Life Workshops engaged the services of Peggy Allen, who was employed by the

Moores as an office worker but also provided office services on a freelance basis out of her home. As Peggy recalls, "My first clients were *The Teaching Home*, Gregg Harris with Christian Life Workshops, and the Home School Legal Defense Association. Those were my three customers, and of course at that time they were quite small, they were just starting out."[18] Allen's early clients grew to be organizational giants in Christian home education, and their practical relations with one another endured.

The headquarters of *The Teaching Home* (*TTH*) magazine are a short drive away from CLW headquarters. Since its first issue in 1980, *TTH* has matured into a nationally distributed glossy. By 1994, its four-color covers were appearing bimonthly in the mailboxes of over thirty-seven thousand subscribers.[19] Like other homeschooling magazines, *TTH* has extensive columns for letters from readers, as well as features pertaining to the mechanics of home schooling. But two things make *TTH* distinctive from other homeschooling periodicals: its centrality in a national movement communication network and its decidedly "Christian" editorial policies.

Through much of the 1990s, the magazine had "newsletter editors" in forty-one states. These editors were associated with state-level home school organizations and were responsible for regional editorial pages that appeared in the center of each *TTH* issue.[20] Subscribers in Illinois, for example, received an "Illinois Update" stapled into their subscriptions. In the March/April 1994 issue, Illinois readers learned about the upcoming Illinois Christian Home Educators (ICHE) convention and could take note of a "Legislative Day" in Springfield hosted by their state's Christian Home Educators Coalition (CHEC).[21] Additionally, *TTH* regularly listed addresses and phone numbers for homeschool organizations in all fifty states.[22]

In the same issue, *TTH*'s "Convention News" column trailed over six pages. It included announcements for state conventions and curriculum fairs in thirty-nine states (eight were listed for Texas alone). The spring itinerary of Gregg Harris's Christian Life Workshops tour was listed, along with CLW's toll-free information number. CLW also ran two advertisements in the March/April issue. Two-thirds of page 36 were devoted to ads for Harris's workshops and his CLW "Home School Favorites" publications.

Legal and political matters related to home education receive extensive coverage in *TTH*. Much of this editorial content is supplied, however, by another homeschool organization—HSLDA. Each issue of the magazine features a "Legal News" section compiled by HSLDA. For March/April 1994 this section included updates on homeschool-related legal issues in eleven states and Puerto Rico. At the end of the column, *TTH* ran this editor's note: "Home School Legal Defense Association offers prepaid legal defense and has served the home-school community for 10 years in an outstanding and reputable manner. We highly recommend membership." As he regularly does, Farris also had contributed an editorial to the issue. Titled "Homier Than Thou," it was a plainspoken admonition for home schoolers to not be braggarts with one another: about the number of children they had, for example, or about whether they baked their own bread.

Stapled into the middle of the issue was an HSLDA membership application.

Striking to even a casual reader of *TTH* is how expressly "Christian" it is. The editorial voice of the magazine is clearly religious. "We hope that this magazine will benefit your family and bring glory to our wonderful Lord," offered the publishers at the end of a brief column welcoming new readers in March/April 1994. Features are peppered with Bible verses. A two-column feature titled "Teaching from a Biblical World View," for example, includes references to seven different Bible passages. A sidebar lists "Christian Men of Science," among them Isaac Newton and Louis Pasteur. A feature on early childhood education includes a section titled "Practical Ideas for Teaching Children to Memorize Scripture."

The publishers are clear about the religious nature of their product. A purpose statement, printed in every issue of the magazine, explains:

> The purpose of *The Teaching Home* magazine is to provide information, inspiration, and support to home-school families and organizations.
>
> *The Teaching Home* publishers, Pat and Sue Welch, have purposed that the organization and all of its activities and publications will be consistently and forthrightly Christian to the honor and glory of the Lord God.

Directly below its purpose statement, *TTH* presents readers with a text titled "We Believe," which articulates a fundamentalist theology:

> The Bible is the inspired and infallible Word of God and constitutes His completed and final revelation to man. The Bible, in its original autograph, is without error in whole and in part, including theological concepts as well as geographical and historical details.
>
> God has existed from all eternity in three persons: God the Father, God the Son, and God the Holy Spirit. . . .
>
> All men are in violation of God's righteous requirements and His holy character both by nature and act, and are therefore under His wrath and just condemnation. . . .

Salvation is offered as a gift, free to the sinner . . . in the sacrificial death of Jesus Christ alone.

"God's Plan of Salvation" is also printed in each issue, instructing readers in Protestant Christian conversion.

Given the religious tone of virtually every page, one might wonder why *TTH* editors choose also to include summaries of basic tenets of their religion in every issue of the magazine. Saving souls would seem not to be the express purpose of a publication called *The Teaching Home*, and in any case given the nature of the magazine, the theological statements would seem to be preaching to the choir. Why, then, do the publishers place the mechanics of their faith in the foreground?

The Teaching Home does its work in a movement characterized by wide variation in religious preference, pedagogy, and worldview. In the midst of such ecumenism, *TTH*'s explicit statements of religious faith have an important symbolic function. Unbelievers who continue to flip the pages can consider themselves forewarned. The religious statements also have symbolic functions among the believers who are the magazine's primary audience. First, they make clear to believers just what *TTH* means by "Christian." *TTH* is not only not a secular periodical; it is also not a Catholic or a Mormon or even a liberal Protestant periodical. Its "Christian" is a conservative Protestant faith. *TTH*'s theological statements render the magazine exclusive of other Christianities by definition.

Still, we might wonder why *TTH* would need to make its theology so explicit, especially for readers who likely are already familiar with this usage of the term *Christian*. A second answer is that an ideologically diverse movement creates considerable uncertainties among activists and constituents about who thinks like they do and who does not. Cooperation is greatly enhanced if people share assumptions about who one another is and how they are to work together—a sociological insight as applicable to corporate boardrooms as it is to social movements.[23] But how am I to know who thinks like I do? Like bumper stickers with the ancient, telltale fish logos still popular among conservative Protestants, *TTH*'s statements of faith tell believers that they and the magazine inhabit the same cultural world.

Once we think of *TTH*'s belief statements as symbolic in this way, the appearance of the word *Christian* throughout the magazine, and, indeed, throughout the movement, takes on a new relevance. Perhaps it matters, for example, that it so often appears in the names of believers' state-level organizations. Sharing the page with the statement of faith in March/April

1994 is a list of *TTH*'s affiliated forty-one newsletter editors, along with the names of the statewide organizations of which they are members. Twenty-eight of these forty-one organizations have the word *Christian* in their names: Illinois Christian Home Educators, Christian Homeschoolers of Hawaii, Utah Christian Homeschool Association, and so on. Perhaps it also matters that Illinois Christian Home Educators, the statewide umbrella organization the Jeromes helped to found and in which they and the Edwardses are still involved, has a statement of faith that looks very much like that of *The Teaching Home*.

The symbolic nature of statements of faith likely has further import in *TTH* given the magazine's advertising policy. *TTH* promises readers in every issue that it "is very selective in accepting advertisements." Each issue contains a "Resource Directory" that indexes the advertisements by page. At the top of the directory, the editors offer that "we can recommend advertised products and services for your consideration."

With *The Teaching Home*, Pat and Sue Welch have created a coherent representation of believer home education. Happy homeschool families adorn each cover. News from a wide range of homeschool organizations fills the magazine's pages with pertinent current events nationwide. Perhaps most important, organizations that a home schooler might not otherwise see as connected become practically linked: a legal services firm provides homeschool news to the magazine, which in turn encourages its readers to use the services of that firm; Christian Life Workshops advertised in *TTH*, and in turn the magazine gave CLW explicit endorsement as an approved advertiser. Finally, calling the entire publication "Christian" lends a particular cast to all of the magazine's various contributors—they are, by editorial extension, defined as "Christian," too.

Like all representations, *The Teaching Home*'s vision of Christian home education occludes some important features of the empirical world. Religious home schoolers and homeschool organizations of nonfundamentalist or non-Christian faiths are not part of this picture, nor are those believers who desire a more ecumenical movement. But in another sense this exclusion is itself an organizational accomplishment. *The Teaching Home*'s editorial policies help to link a movement world of decidedly shared cultural sensibility. When you read this, or buy that, or take this party's advice, the magazine implies to its readers, you have a sense of the kind of people with whom you are dealing.

Peggy Allen's third client, the HSLDA, in subsequent years became the largest and perhaps most visible homeschool organization in the country. The legal services firm that began as a shoestring operation in 1983 claimed over thirty-seven thousand dues-paying members ten years later, some 90 percent of whom were, by HSLDA's own accounts, evangelical or fundamentalist Christians.[24] Along with its rapid growth came a move east, toward Washington, D.C., and growing clout in the homeschool world. When I first visited HSLDA's comfortable Virginia offices, the organization was well on its way to becoming the nerve center of a national movement infrastructure.

HSLDA provides its member families with full legal counsel if they ever are approached by school or social services authorities, or brought to court as a result of their homeschool activities. In the early 1990s, the standard annual fee for HSLDA membership, per family, was $100. Families active in some local and regional support groups may purchase membership at a slightly reduced rate. HSLDA thus enjoys the endorsement of many grass-roots organizations. Members of many Christian support groups in Illinois, for example, receive group discounts for HSLDA membership.

HSLDA is more than a legal services firm, however. Part of its accomplishment has been to efficiently link the furthest reaches of the believers' grass roots with a central hub. Since 1990, creating and maintaining this network has been the job of a service arm of HSLDA, the National Center for Home Education (NCHE). Housed in the main offices of its parent organization and funded by a portion of HSLDA's dues revenue, NCHE's founding mission was "to serve state [homeschool] leaders by providing information and federal legislation of concern to home schoolers."[25]

During the year of my first visit, homeschool advocate Carol Ingram was serving as NCHE's associate director. I had heard Ingram in her appearance as keynote speaker at ICHE's 1993 state convention; I soon was impressed that her vivacity and enthusiasm were just as strong in her office as they had been onstage before that audience of hundreds. As we talked through most of an afternoon and again the following morning, Ingram sketched the features of an impressive organizational system.

We began by looking at literature from NCHE's 1993 National Christian Home Educators Leadership Conference. Held that November in Williamsburg, Virginia, the event had drawn 287 attendees from forty-two states, Puerto Rico, and Canada. Flipping through the attractively bound conference program, I asked Ingram for whom the conference had been designed.

"Well, this particular conference is unique in that we limit the membership to people who are officers or board members of statewide organizations. Or national organizations, or the kind of people that would be your

123

speakers on the national homeschool circuit."[26] Williamsburg was targeted to those advocates in leadership positions at the statewide level and beyond. "So we do limit [the national conferences] for the simple reason that we don't want it to get so big that we lose the ability to really interact discussion-wise at that level." The 1993 conference was the sixth of its kind. "We move it around the country so that every five or six years [leaders] have a reasonable chance of having it at least somewhat nearby."

The back pages of the conference program listed the names of all registered attendees and the organizations they represented. Some people had traveled from as far away as Maine, Oregon, or New Mexico to attend. Steve and Susan Jerome from ICHE were listed as registrants. Over fifty state and regional advocacy organizations were represented, many of them titled with the catchy acronyms that name so many sites on the homeschool map: CHEF (Christian Home Education Fellowship of Alabama), FEAST (Family Educators Alliance of South Texas), and MATCH (Missouri Association of Teaching Christian Homes).

I was curious about NCHE's rationale for limiting attendance at Williamsburg to a certain, high level of leadership. "What needs are you trying to address at that level that are distinctive?" I asked.

"Well . . . in a way they're not distinctive in that [the needs] will be different from other levels but they're . . . the same needs on a different level. And so what happens at this conference is that it is like a support group for the state leaders. You know, just sort of like your pastors' conferences are . . ."

"A retreat . . ."

"Yeah. We're not like that. We're in home schooling, so this is, you know, not a retreat. This is a move forward." She chuckled at the half joke. "Just teasing you with that." Ingram smiled at me, then continued. "We're trying to broaden their horizons. We're trying to help home schoolers, we do a lot of things because of the nature of what we do here at the national center. We are very legislatively oriented, somewhat lobbying oriented, and so we bring to the state leaders something they can't get anywhere else unless they do it on their own."

"And what is that?" I asked.

"And that is information about what's [happening] on the national scene legislatively that can have an impact on a family's ability to keep homeschooling. And the issues are not always going to be specifically homeschooling bills. . . . You have things that impact on family rights [for instance] that curtail parents' ability to make choices." She went on to give some examples of current proposed legislation that NCHE was combating: stricter federal enforcement standards for child immunization, and congressional passage of the United Nations Convention on the Rights of the Child.

The bulk of the sessions in Williamsburg were devoted to more practical concerns of maintaining efficient movement organization. There were sessions titled "Good Accounting Principles for Home School Leaders," "Using Computers to Simplify Everything Your Organization Does," and "Managing Your Organization: A Look at the Vital Role of Board Members."[27] Such sessions offered advice on how to tackle the more mundane aspects of mobilization. The one devoted to computer use, for example, included discussions of how leaders could use computers to do accounting, maintain newsletter mailing lists, and exploit the Internet to disseminate information.

A Saturday morning general session titled "Capital Alert" was devoted to a presentation regarding Congressional Action Program (CAP), HSLDA's lobbying arm that had been inaugurated in January 1993.[28] Led by HSLDA president Michael Farris and CAP director Doug Phillips, the session outlined HSLDA's efforts to build a political advocacy network with constituents in every congressional district in the nation. Conference literature described CAP as "a grassroots defense of the home school family." Working in tandem with state-level homeschool organizations, NCHE/CAP staffers were building a fax and telephone network that would link the Virginia offices with volunteers across the country. If NCHE/CAP determined that pending legislation deserved the support or opposition of home schoolers, it could use the CAP network to generate phone calls and letters to Capitol Hill.[29]

What the Williamsburg conference offered, then, was an opportunity for NCHE to nurture a national social movement apparatus. Workshops on computer literacy, sound accounting principles, and grassroots activism might help make organizations more efficient. Simply bringing people together from across the country facilitated conversations that might otherwise be impossible. And by providing information to prominent local and regional activists, NCHE could count on disseminating conference news back down to the grass roots.

NCHE's annual conferences are predicated on a deceptively simple assumption: there is a hierarchy of homeschool leaders. This notion, so basic that it may be taken largely for granted, is a vital part of the architecture of NCHE's efforts. The cover of the Williamsburg program announced that the event was a "Leadership Conference." Ingram made clear that the conference was not for everyone, and not just for every "leader"—only those

125

at a certain "encompassing level," as she described it. The entire event was predicated on the idea that organizationally, the homeschool world is organized as a pyramid.

Ingram emphasized that NCHE was not dictatorial in its relationship with the believers' rank and file. "It's not a top-down thing, where we're saying, 'okay home schoolers . . . this is what you need to do.' It's not that at all. It's an advocacy kind of thing where we provide the information. We believe you're capable thinkers. You decide what you want to do." Still, I wondered how it might be possible for NCHE to avoid speaking without some measure of authority. After all, if NCHE called its annual events "leadership" conferences, was it not, then, a leader of leaders?

From talk of Williamsburg, we moved on to a discussion of NCHE's other year-round advocacy efforts. Ingram explained, "Now we also provide to the state leaders . . . a monthly mailing, that whole series of red notebooks out there on the bookcase are the mailings we've done since our inception." She pointed out her office door to the adjacent hallway and a shelf full of three-ring binders. "And that will be anywhere from eighty to two hundred pages of material about ten to twelve times a year, where we will capture articles and issues—many times we'll give them articles on both sides of an issue because we're dealing with a level of leadership [where they] can hone through it."

I asked Ingram who received NCHE's mailings. "Well basically there's a whole network of statewide organizations. So whenever we hear of a new state organization that we don't already know about, we will write to them and let them know who we are and what we do. And if they're interested in our services, they basically ask for them and get them."

I asked who received the information and how recipients were chosen.

"The way we keep our mailing list working is, once a year we ask them for a response survey. If they don't return the response, they're cleared out of the mailing list. Because you just have to keep it current. And we're probably dealing with about 220 leaders. . . . [The mailings] cost us about $150 per person per year. And so it is a costly venture."

"So the contact organizations don't pay a fee for that?" I asked.

"No, not at all. It's purely a service thing. Which is why it gets kind of interesting," Ingram continued. "I've been watching on the Internet lately, there have been some people that are really offended by the fact that we refuse to send the mailing to them."

"Oh really?"

"And it's one of those uncomfortable things where, you know you just can't send it to everyone that asks. And so you've got to know what their level of statewide influence is. And yet sometimes home schoolers can be a very rights-conscious group and can be very unhappy, [saying,] 'what do you mean you're restricting the information?'"

"So what happened?" I asked.

"Well, the lady who called in was from Illinois. She wanted the mailing, and I explained to her that it costs us and therefore we restrict it to two people per state-level organization. I said, are you in leadership of a state-level organization that is currently not receiving [the mailings]?"

"So she called for the information . . ."

"Right. And I just wasn't able to give it to her. She was of the mind-set that nobody should have the right to restrict information. And I guess that she put her complaint on the Internet, and several others picked it up and, you know, it's not the kind of thing we're going to discuss on the Internet. It's not worth the time."

I asked Ingram which organizations in Illinois did receive the NCHE mailings: ICHE, APACHE (a regional Christian support group down-state), Christian Home Educators Coalition (CHEC, a state-level political organization), Christian Liberty Academy, and Bill Gothard's Institute for Basic Life Principles. All Illinois recipients, then, were what *The Teaching Home* would call Christian organizations.

"And I mean it's definitely not a Christian/non-Christian thing," Ingram continued. "Clonlara's on our mailing list, Holt Associates is on our mailing list, and for quite a while, NHA [National Homeschool Association] was on our mailing list, . . . now several of them through the years have fallen out of our mailing list just because they didn't return our questionnaire, and so I mean that's the nature of the game."

Still, Ingram was clear that NCHE is primarily a Christian organization, even while it understood that not all homeschool organizations were. "And there is a little bit of controversy," she said, "in some circles of home education between organizations that are quote unquote 'exclusively Christian,' and organizations that are Christian but serve everyone, and organizations that are non-Christian. And there seems to be a tremendous tension generated by those who are in the organizations who are non-Christian, not understanding why the Christians are, you know, not being like Jesus and loving them all."

Somehow, our talk had careened into a broader discussion about big differences among home schoolers.

"I think a lot of what causes that [is] . . . it's a very interesting error in thinking," she said.

And that is we tend to assume that there's this group over here called Christian, and there's this group over here called nonsectarian or non-Christian,

127

or whatever you want to call it, "secular." And in the middle there is some big entity called "neutral." And the secular people constantly appeal that "All right we're willing to be neutral." . . . And the fact is there are not three groups. You know, scripturally speaking, "He who doesn't build with me scatters abroad." We are either saved or we're lost. We're either in a Christian world reference or we're in a non-Christian world reference, we're not in a neutral world reference.

Ingram's words helped me make sense of how NCHE could include some non-Christian groups on its mailing lists despite the fact that it primarily serves believers. Like its parent HSLDA, NCHE is not for Christians exclusively, but it nevertheless promulgates an exclusively Christian cause. Nonbelievers might have access to NCHE services, at least to some degree, but only at the discretion of its standing authorities.

At the heart of the believers' organizational schema is a general acceptance of hierarchy. When it organized its local programs, Christian Life Workshops relied on the assumption that hierarchies are legitimate. NCHE assumes that believer home education is put together hierarchically when it selects attendees for its annual "leadership" conferences and when it makes choices about which local parties will receive its mailings. And by calling some movement personnel "leaders" and treating them specially, NCHE actively nurtures a hierarchical organizational system that distributes resources (like information, and network contacts, and prestige) unequally.

But just how is one to know who thinks in terms of leaders and captains, and who does not? This is really a part of larger questions: Who thinks like I do? With whom can I get along? One way of addressing these generic uncertainties is to use common markers of shared sentiment as proxies for more general similarity. The editorial policies of *The Teaching Home* suggest that markers of conservative Protestant Christianity help create the boundaries of believer home education. Carol Ingram, and the lady from Illinois, indicate that HSLDA/NCHE does its work at a blurry patch of the divide.

EARTH-BASED

"Cold water. Use cold water for oatmeal." I had been scrubbing cereal bowls, somewhat unsuccessfully, under a hot stream. Noticing my trouble, the woman on rinse duty had offered the advice. "It's something about the starch in the oatmeal, I think. It comes off better with cold."[30] For what-ever reason, the cold water worked better. While we finished the breakfast dishes, my partner in the dish room talked about her support group back home, her homeschooling activism there, and her interest in the NHA. It was easy to talk with her, that chilly October morning in 1992, the second day of a weekend conference of the NHA. Even after months of research, my interactions with the believers had remained rather formal, but the individualists granted me admission to the flow of their most mundane movement business. During that 1992 weekend they asked me for rides to the airport and for help sweeping floors and washing dishes, and they al-lowed me to sit in on all administrative meetings. The relative inclusion I was offered among these home schoolers was, perhaps, partly because I looked more like them. Deirdre Brown later joked that I was an honorary member of the NHA Council on account of my Birkenstock sandals; I was told that the council required them. But subsequently I realized that this willingness to include me was also a consequence of looser rules about who is one of "us."

I was not the only one doing chores that weekend. Except for a hired cook, all the work of the conference that fall was accomplished by volun-teer labor. As attendees arrived, they were asked to sign up for a series of tasks—cleaning bathrooms, sweeping cabins, helping in the kitchen, and doing dishes. This voluntarism was not without its troubles. Several times during the weekend, the two women informally in charge of these matters chided the group for leaving some jobs undone. A graduate student eager to blend in and a few of the heartier volunteers took up some of the slack.

As among the believers, this wing of home education is maintained largely through volunteer labor. But the organization of voluntarism is different in groups like the NHA. While believer voluntarism is supported by an assumption that hierarchy is legitimate, home schoolers like Deirdre Brown work under the assumption that individual persons have primary discretion about whether and how to participate. This makes for sluggish organizations in practice.

The NHA was founded in 1988 by a group of home schoolers active in the National Coalition of Alternative Community Schools (NCACS), an advocacy organization peopled by progressive educators from around the country and long supported by John Holt. Many home schoolers amenable to Holt's unschooling philosophy had found support for their cause in NCACS through the early 1980s, when home education was still new, still beyond the media spotlight, and still clearly linked to the progressive school movements of the previous decade. The NHA emerged from its parent organization during the same period that home schooling was enjoying rapid growth nationally.

While informal membership estimates for the organization ran as high as 500 in the early 1990s, the NHA's 1992 balance sheet indicated that the organization had fewer than 150 members paying the fifteen-dollar annual dues.[31] NHA's 1992 national conference, held at a YMCA campground near Cincinnati, Ohio, drew 173 participants (80 adults) from sixteen states.[32] The 1993 conference, held at the same site, counted 96 participants (41 adults).[33] At both events, most attendees were from the midwestern, northeastern, and midsouthern regions of the United States.

Although considerably smaller and poorer than the believers' NCHE, the NHA and its conferences similarly link prominent advocates from around the country. Among those at the NHA's 1992 conference were many whom NCHE staffers might have called leaders: Larry Kaseman, executive director of the Wisconsin Parents Association (WPA), a nonsectarian advocacy organization that serves as a legislative watchdog for home schooling in that state; Patricia Montgomery, director of Clonlara School; Maggie Sadoway, a homeschool mother who is very active in Massachusetts homeschool politics; and Deirdre Brown of Illinois HOUSE. Yet only one of these advocates, Patricia Montgomery, was registered for the NCHE conference in Williamsburg the following spring.

From its parent NCACS, the NHA inherited a progressive organizational structure. NHA bylaws outline a highly democratic organization. Each dues-paying member has a vote in decision-making events, and major organizational decisions are made by majority votes of the entire membership. Additionally, the NHA membership regularly elects delegates to its administrative council, whose decision making is governed not by majority vote but by consensus. According to the NHA's consensus rules, all council members must agree on a course of action before the council proceeds.[34]

Yet even the formal depiction of organizational structure provided in the bylaws understates the level of democracy present in the NHA. During the 1992 conference there was considerable discussion about just what constituted an NHA member. If a homeschool family paid NHA dues every year, did that mean that the family had only one vote in organizational business? Some members were more specifically concerned with whether children of members had voting rights independent of their dues-paying parents. While no changes to the bylaws were made as a result of these discussions, it was informally decided that each member of a dues-paying family—children included—could vote independently. Further, since votes among the membership were conducted by a show of hands and without any formal procedure for certifying membership, in process the NHA's business was conducted by those present regardless of their membership status.

The effectiveness of a participatory democracy, however, depends on who agrees to participate and how participants enact their participation. For one thing, people have to show up. During the NHA conferences in 1992 and 1993, none of the scheduled sessions I attended started on time. People would assemble in meeting halls and chat during the minutes surrounding the scheduled time for an event; ten to fifteen minutes into the scheduled session, someone would begin proceedings with a "we really ought to get started." Often, the problem was that no one person had been designated as responsible for directing a particular session, so that business generally commenced by mutual agreement of those present. "That's okay, we're on homeschool time!" one woman said after a scheduled session began particularly late. Less than perfect timeliness is almost a given for any event involving multiple parties, of course. But "homeschool time" clearly meant something different among these home schoolers than among the believers. At ICHE state conventions in Illinois, for example, speakers and discussion leaders often bemoaned schedule delays and frequently encouraged participants to mind their watches. At the NHA conference, lapses in punctuality were joked about.

Uncertainty about who might show up and when, though, sometimes had more significant consequences. Each national conference of the NHA is also a meeting time for the NHA Council, the administrative body charged with conducting the organization's business. NHA bylaws stipulate that formal council decisions can only be made when a two-thirds quorum of council members is present. In 1992 and 1993 the council consisted of nine members, so a quorum required six in attendance. But at the 1993 meetings only five council members were on hand. The council secretary had resigned abruptly for "personal reasons" unspecified to me; another council member from the East Coast was adopting a new child that weekend; a new member from a western state was unable to attend because of family troubles and obligations at work; and a fourth had failed to show up for the meetings two years in a row.

On the agenda were issues that many present agreed were crucial to the operation of the organization: decisions about how to go about securing 501(c)(3) nonprofit status; reformatting the NHA newsletter, the *Circle of Correspondence*; pursuing paid help for an overworked, volunteer office coordinator; and planning the 1994 meeting. But what could the council do without a quorum? Debating this question took up a considerable amount of time. One member asked if reducing the council to eight members would do the trick, since the bylaws allowed for flexibility in the number of council seats. He took a moment to calculate whether five of eight was equivalent to two-thirds. Would .625 of the council be close enough to a quorum? This figure didn't sit well with everyone at the table. "You can't have a fraction of a person," one member quipped. Another option was to elect a new council member, but doing so would be a logistical challenge. An election would require a vote of the entire membership, and typically the council held a call for nominations and published candidate bios in its newsletter beforehand. There was agreement that abridging those conventions would be politically unwise, and that carrying them out at the conference would unduly tax an already tight schedule of meetings. But no one was comfortable making consensus decisions on the council without a quorum, since doing so would violate the bylaws. After much discussion it was decided that the council would finish out its meetings that weekend in conference ("we'll discuss the issues," as one member said) but delay making significant formal decisions until its next meeting.

Nonattendance is a generic administrative problem, of course, but most organizations have mechanisms for punishing it. Informally, offenders may be chided for failing to live up to their duty or curtly encouraged not to let it happen again. Sometimes formal sanctions are used to discipline the offender, as when, for example, dismissal or demotion is made the price of absenteeism. But the NHA has few formal or informal tools with which to punish its no-shows. Informally it is a "volunteer" organization that has only a few carrots. Formally, NHA bylaws stipulate that council members may be suspended "for cause" by a two-thirds council vote and removed by a majority vote of the general membership; however, this option was not used even for chronic absentees—likely, I suspect, because invoking such mechanisms would have been too politically drastic relative to the infraction. The formal mechanisms weren't supple enough, but that was hardly the only problem.

I never heard the word *leader* used to describe anyone in the NHA, not even members of the council. The kinds of leaders that NCHE takes for granted have little place in the organizational schema that informs the composition of the NHA. This theoretical equality is not without its troubles. Because its members assume that their organization is composed of choice-making individuals, few demands can be made on individual members who make choices that gum up the NHA's work. Instead, the NHA has to rely on people to actively *choose* to participate: to show up for meetings, volunteer to wash dishes, and carry through on standing commitments.

On the first morning of the 1993 NHA conference, thirty grown-ups and their children learned a new game. Part consciousness-raising exercise, part "Simon Says," the game began with an announcement from a workshop facilitator: "We are a diverse group of people. This exercise provides a place for the awareness that, in spite of our diversity, we can come together for common goals. This awareness is simply that—no attempts are or should be made in labeling any individual. And so I invite you to STAND UP IF. . ." The facilitator, the same woman who had shared dish duty with me the previous year, continued by reading a long menu of potential identities. Members of the audience were told to stand up if

> you are now living in southwest Ohio . . . northwest Ohio . . . [if] you are originally from the eastern U.S. . . . from the Midwest U.S. . . . from a different country . . . [if] you are a single parent, a parent with a partner, a stepparent, a grandparent, [if] you are living in a committed relationship . . . if you are a young person, [if] your heritage is Latino/Latina, African-American, . . . European, Asian . . . [if] the church, synagogue, temple, or other religious service is an important part of your life . . . [if] you grow a garden . . . recycle, [or] have written a poem, painted a picture, or created any work of art in the last year . . . [if] you wish you were or are glad you are homeschooled.[35]

By the end of the exercise everyone in the room was standing. Chuckles at the novelty of the game peppered the audience, as did comments, spoken through smiles, that this—diversity—was what the NHA was all about.

The "Diversity Acknowledgment Exercise," as the NHA conference literature called it, opened a workshop titled "Forming and Working with Inclusive Statewide Networks and Organizations." Among the topics discussed at the 1993 workshop were "working with a wide variety of people" and "keeping the goal of inclusiveness clearly in mind." Along with its commitments to democracy and voluntarism, the NHA has an explicit commitment to social and ideological diversity. Its literature for prospective members promises that "NHA is committed to emphasizing the diversity of homeschoolers while encouraging the acceptance of homeschooling as an individualized approach to education."[36] But living up to this commitment has proven difficult for the NHA even at the most basic level of organizational process.

Consider the following situation, discussed at length by the NHA Council during the 1992 conference. One council member, a Jewish woman from the West Coast, had been unable to attend the event because it had been scheduled between two Jewish holidays. Disgruntled, she wrote an open letter to the NHA membership that was subsequently published in the organization's quarterly publication, the *Circle of Correspondence*. "Dear Friends," the letter began:

> When I volunteered to serve on the Council of the NHA, I knew there would be conflicts between the various meetings and activities of the organization and the running of a traditional Jewish household. Simply traveling and keeping kosher is an experience in itself! This year, one of these expected conflicts did, indeed, arise. The annual Conference was scheduled between two holidays, and there was no way I could attend. . . . I have been assured by the Conference Committee that they will carefully look at their calendars before selecting the next Conference dates, and that conflicts such as those we have seen in the past will not occur again. Yes, there is an entire month on the Jewish calendar that should be avoided, and yes, the number of families that observe these days is small. Yet if we ask ourselves "who does it *hurt* to avoid these days?" and then "who will be excluded if we ignore these days?" we can perhaps get a better perspective on the issue.[37]

Many council members at the 1992 meetings were aware of their colleague's dissatisfaction with the dates, and one long council session was devoted to scheduling the next conference to accommodate her wishes in 1993.

But the task was difficult. Earlier in the weekend, council members had decided to hold the conference at the same site the following year. Since the campground was booked through the month of August, a summer date was out of the question. September weekends were a possibility, but Rosh Hashanah fell squarely in the middle of the month, and Sukkot, the Jewish harvest festival, fell on September 30. The autumnal equinox, which one council member celebrated as a pagan holiday, fell on another candidate weekend. Another complication was that the campground facilities were designed for three-season use and were poorly heated. A running joke throughout the weekend had been the challenge of open-air cabins on crisp nights and chilly showers on frosty mornings. Any date later in the autumn would be out of the question.

Despite the fact that the dates overlapped with Columbus Day, the Council decided after much debate to hold the next conference from October 7 to 11, 1993. "We'd really like to accommodate everyone, but any date we choose is going to be a problem for some people," one council member said.

"Right," said another. "If we try to accommodate everybody, then we'll never have a conference."

However, the disgruntled member in absentia was perturbed for another reason also: the council's decision to hold the meeting in the same place two years running. Her letter also included the following:

> The [Cincinnati] site sounded great. . . . But what's this I hear about next year's Conference at the same site? What happened to moving this event around the country?
>
> According to memory, both the Conference and the Council Meetings were to be held in various locations. More families could become involved in this way. As for Council Meetings, surely these must rotate around the country. To do otherwise will create unnecessary hardships for our Council members and their families. My greater fear is that our volunteers will be limited to those with large pocketbooks. Now, the concept of "regional" conferences has been brought up. This is something that I can fully support!

"At any rate, the best of luck to those of you who have volunteered to plan and organize these regional events!" the letter continued. Part of the problem, though, was that no one had volunteered to host the general meeting elsewhere. While several council members expressed eagerness to hold the 1993 conference at a different site, no one had offered to do the local footwork necessary to coordinate the event in their hometown. These details, however, seemed of lesser importance to the disgruntled council member than the moral risks that came with scheduling over religious holidays and staging the 1993 event in the same spot: "Being a national organization that includes 'everyone' is never easy, and demands a high degree of sensitivity. Let us work on nurturing that sensitivity for all of the small communities that make up our greater homeschool community at the national level," the letter concluded.

Sufficiently honoring the diversity of its membership proved difficult on a practical level, then. The NHA did not want to exclude this Jewish member, but it was hard to find a date that was simultaneously workable within other constraints. Nor did the council wish to exclude its members on the East and West Coasts or those with small pocketbooks (part of the reason the conference was held at a campground, in fact, was to keep costs to families low). But the only way the NHA could conduct a conference was to have someone *volunteer* to do the organizing. Largely because only one party had come forth to do so, the NHA returned to the same site in 1993.

The NHA's commitments to participatory democracy, to voluntarism, and to diversity are sincere ones. The organization seeks to conduct its business in ways that honor the freedom of individuals to make their own choices and to honor the outside ideological commitments of its constituents. But seeking to enact those ideals has some practical costs. The NHA's spurning of most formal leadership roles, its hesitancy to discipline its members, and its efforts to make sure that "everyone" is included make it difficult to conduct even the most mundane aspects of organizational business: getting scheduled, getting started, getting a quorum, and cleaning up after everything else is done.

As with the believers' designation of things Christian, these other home schoolers have signposts that succinctly summarize broad differences in philosophy and organizational sensibility. Through the 1990s, explicit statements about nondiscrimination became common ways of marking subtler cultural territory. During my field research, for example, Illinois HOUSE revised its purpose statement to read as follows: "The purpose of this network is to support families in exercising their right to homeschool regardless of age, color, creed, ethnic background, family composition, financial condition, gender, learning disabilities, race, religion or lack thereof, sexual preference, or special educational needs."[38] During these same years, many unschoolers became fond of saying that their organizations were "inclusive," in contrast with many believer organizations, which they regarded as "exclusive" on the basis of religion. In practice, however, this inclusiveness does not include everyone. Over time I learned that those under the inclusive umbrella represent a distinct segment of the homeschool world: those who are comfortable participating in organizations that actively seek diversity, and those who are uncomfortable in expressly Christian organizations.

This marker of diversity is paradoxical, then. Those who are inclusive share a fundamental ideological similarity. By acceding to the ideal of inclusiveness, they also accede to a goal that excludes many believers. One might participate in either an inclusive movement or a Christian one, but as home education matured through the 1990s it became increasingly difficult to participate in both.

FROM SENSIBILITY TO SOCIAL STRUCTURE

When Kyron at Clonlara School talked about heaven-based and earth-based home schoolers, she alluded to a broad difference in how people think about themselves and their work. At the heart of the distinction are contrary ways of thinking about collective life. While the believers betray a general acceptance of hierarchy, unschoolers are more skeptical of vertical social arrangements in general and are relatively more concerned than the believers with protecting individual autonomy. The difference shows up when home schoolers talk in hypothetical, abstract terms, as when Deirdre arranged the sugar packets, and when Mary Pride and Gregg Harris sketched out ideal family and spiritual relationships. It also shows up in the day-to-day choreography of movement work: in deceptively mundane decisions about how to arrange the chairs at a meeting, or in what words to use when describing new projects (remember the "skills bank"). The difference between earth-based and heaven-based also shows up when home schoolers make practical decisions about how to turn their ideals into durable organizations.

Organizing requires making decisions. What will our organization look like, on paper and in process? What will be its purpose? Who will it include, and whose needs will it best serve? As these decisions get made, broad sensibilities about how the world is or ought to be assume a concreteness that is consequential both within the new organization and beyond it. Inside, decisions come to be made partly on the basis of the rules. At organizational borders, the rules are used by outsiders to appraise an organization's purpose and to predict whether membership or cooperation will be possible. What an organization looks like on the outside can thus have significant consequences for how distinct parties coalesce (or not) into working coalitions.

When the National Homeschool Association drafted its bylaws in the late 1980s, the founders worked hard to create a set of organizational rules that would put its democratic and egalitarian sensibilities into practice. The bylaws made membership open to literally anyone, gave voting rights to all members, and created a council with a rotating membership governed by consensus and strict quorum rules. Once the bylaws were in place, they had consequences independent of the ideals that inspired them. The lack of a quorum at the 1993 meetings caused considerable trouble for the council, which discussed the problem at length. But the council members did not talk in broad philosophical terms about why they had a quorum rule. Instead, they talked about how the rule might be met or gotten around (was .625 close enough to two-thirds?), and in the end agreed to simply talk rather than make formal decisions. Once in place, it was the rule of quorum that mattered, not the democratic sensibility behind it.

Quite literally, organizational decisions make the world. When the National Center for Home Education holds annual "leadership" conferences, it presumes that the homeschool universe is composed of leaders and followers. But the conferences also help create the leaders that NCHE presumes exist already. What better way to make grassroots leaders than to have a powerful national organization anoint them with hotel reservations and registration badges, supply them with useful cues for making their support groups run efficiently, introduce them to movement elites from around the country, and supply them with political and legislative information perhaps unattainable to them in any other way? By designating a category called leadership, and distributing resources on the basis of that designation, NCHE helps manufacture the personnel that it claims merely to serve.

At organizational borders, practical decisions about who an organization says it is shape patterns of interorganizational cooperation. Illinois Christian Home Educators has a name and a statement of faith, both of which tell outsiders that ICHE is up to a certain kind of business. Only those support groups that accede to ICHE's statement of faith can participate in the network and enjoy the information flows that go along with it (remember, for example, that ICHE sends personnel to NCHE conferences and is a recipient of NCHE mailings). Among home schoolers, what you say you are matters. It is no accident that *The Teaching Home* relied on ICHE, not HOUSE, for its regional newsletter information in the 1990s; that over half of the organizations supplying newsletter copy to *TTH* in 1994 had the word *Christian* in their names; that most of the curriculum advertisements in *TTH* are purchased by religious suppliers; and that Gregg Harris's Christian Life Workshops schedule was listed in the magazine's "Convention News" column. By the same token, not saying "Christian" can lead to crossed signals, as in the confusion Carol Ingram described when the lady from Illinois requested, and was denied, information from the nominally nonreligious NCHE.

What organizations say they are also affects patterns of movement recruitment. Illinois Christian Home Educators maintains a phone line for fielding homeschooling inquiries. Callers are offered an information packet that represents a decidedly Christian home education. Included in the fat mailing are homeschool testimonials by Christian parents, a list of curriculum suppliers heavily weighted toward the religious market (The Weaver, A Beka, Christian Liberty Academy, and KONOS are listed, but not Clonlara School), a sample copy of *The Teaching Home*, a ten-dollar credit coupon for a *TTH* subscription, and a membership application to the Home School Legal Defense Association.[39] A single phone call to ICHE thus links the inquirer to a web of services linked by their "Christian-ness." By contrast, people who knock on HOUSE's door are offered admission to a different homeschool world. A visit to the HOUSE Web site provides guests with links to a rainbow of homeschooling organizations that includes the Islamic Homeschool Association of North America, Jewish Home Educators Network, the National Association of Catholic Home Educators, and Latter-day Saint Home Educators' Association, as well as ICHE, the Moore Foundation, and the Christian Home Educators Association.[40]

We can think of decisions about how to organize, then, as the construction work through which sensibility gets turned into social structure. Decisions about how to organize embed our ideals in practical arrangements of persons and resources, and into rules about how to do things, that are more concrete and less flexible than the thinking that informed their design. Since the very purpose of formal organization is to render particular ideas and social relationships more durable, the very act of organizing precludes other alternatives. Perhaps the support group networks in Illinois would have been less polarized, for example, if HOUSE had not long ago forbidden Christian groups from organizing under the HOUSE name. Perhaps some Christian organizations would have written less restrictive statements of faith, had their authors known that women like Lissa Foster ("We're Christians but not in that way") might look elsewhere for support because of how those statements are worded. As it happened in Illinois and beyond, "inclusive" and "Christian" have become embodied in essentially incompatible membership, participation, and authority rules. In the process, the contrary cultural tendencies in the homeschool world have become more fixed.

Thinking about organization-building as the intermediate work that turns sensibility into social structure helps us more fully appreciate the labors of prominent activists. These men and women have done more than work hard. They also have *thought* hard: about how to talk about their work, how to transform philosophy into practice, and how to build a homeschool movement that will outlive the commitments of particular individuals. Of course, they have not done all the thinking on their own. All of them have borrowed heavily from the organizational traditions that are most meaningful to them and with which they are most familiar: Deirdre Brown and her colleagues in the NHA from the progressivist organizational forms of the 1960s and 1970s; the Edwardses, the Jeromes, and other believers from the organizational cornucopia of conservative Protestantism. Nevertheless, at its birth contemporary home education was something new under the sun—a new technology, we might say, with distinctive personnel requirements, legal and normative impediments, and ideological rationales. Thus, the task of giving this innovation sturdy organizational form has required a good measure of inventiveness. Perhaps this is one reason why homeschool advocates are so often intellectuals, and why I ended up having such heady discussions with Robert and Martha Edwards, the Jeromes, and Deirdre Brown.[41]

Of course, builders must make their plans in a manner that is sensible to those whom they wish to have inhabit their cause. Constructing a homeschool movement has required considerable organizational innovation, but it is innovation constrained by what potential home schoolers will find honorable or acceptable. As with art and food, people have distinctive organizational tastes. Not all palates can be pleased simultaneously. It is hard to imagine, for example, that HOUSE parents would be very pleased with rules that prohibited them from breast-feeding in public, or that asked them to find baby-sitters for their small children in order to attend a convention. Such rules are routine, however, at the annual conferences of Illinois Christian Home Educators. Likewise, given that even the word *leader* is taboo among them, we might expect some NHA members to become suspicious if their council members were to attend NCHE leadership conferences. And as I described in Chapter Two, parents make choices about support groups to match their own lifestyles and pedagogical preferences with those of the group. Such variation in taste means that movement builders need to be sensitive to the proclivities of those they wish to serve. The same organizational forms will appeal more and less to different parties.[42]

Now that the organizational architecture of home education is largely in place, not everyone has to think as hard, or even necessarily share the organizational sensibilities that informed the movement's design. Home schooling is easier today than it was twenty years ago. One can now simply join organizations that others worked years to build. And the designs of those organizations now have consequences, whether or not all their current inhabitants approve of every detail. This is an important way in which the movement elites who design organizations have influence far beyond their numbers. HOUSE is run by consensus, for example, even though in the course of my fieldwork more than a few members complained to me about the inherent inefficiency of consensus rules.

Decisions about how to organize can be fateful over the long term, too. Organizations that are built with a tiered system of authority and responsibility, like NCHE, are better equipped to make hard decisions and complete complicated tasks (like national conferences) routinely. And when an organization explicitly names and trains "leaders," it has a built-in means of reproducing itself across generations of activists. But the NHA has no clear mechanism for reproducing its core; instead, it must wait for activists to volunteer for higher commitment and then train them on an ad hoc basis. At the same time, the NHA's radically democratic decision-making procedures are not infrequently an impediment to getting the work done. Whether the architecture of the NHA is strong enough to outlive the commitments of its core members is an open question.[43]

Like the NHA, HOUSE is governed by consensus, and administrative business is carried out by a "coordinating council" made up of regional representatives. Each HOUSE chapter is formally obliged to appoint a representative to this body, but at the September 1993 council meeting I attended, only seven of the state's nine active groups had sent representatives. According to HOUSE bylaws, these absences do not impede group decision making, so the meeting proceeded. Other people were present as well: all the council delegates were women, but some had come to the meetings with their husbands. Deirdre Brown also was present and was appointed to facilitate the meeting.

Over an hour of the meeting was taken up by a long round of introductions. As I listened to people take their turns, I found that the fault line between inclusives and believers seemed to be showing up everywhere.[44]

"I'm Liz Walton, from Summerville. And I am the group, basically, from Summerville. I am it. We've got a lot of Christian home schoolers in the area, and they're very organized, they've got a lot going on. And for a while in our HOUSE group we had people who were Christians, who had that orientation, and they've just sort of gone into those groups. So we don't really have a group down there now, but I just sort of keep going. We have it there as a resource for people."

"I'm Mia Jenkins, from the infamous Winterton HOUSE group. There is currently no group, no HOUSE group in Winterton."

"Infamous?" someone asked aloud.

Deirdre Brown answered, apparently knowledgeable of the situation there. "Yes, the group disaffiliated because some people thought it was anti-Christian."

Mia Jenkins added, "I don't know about that, but the group just sort of stopped happening."

Deirdre continued. "There were some people in that group who wanted it to be more of a Christian group, and because of HOUSE's inclusion policy, because they didn't want to do things that were specifically Christian . . ." She paused, thoughtful, then continued, "I mean the HOUSE people, the non-Christians were fine with having Christians in the group, but the problem was there were a lot of people in the Winterton group who wanted to do Christian things, wanted it to be more of a Christian group, and so they disaffiliated and started their own group."

Jenkins revised Deirdre's account. "Actually, it didn't quite happen [that way], but when I got these bylaws I could tell it was just going to be like a time bomb. I mean once these people saw the stuff about, you know, 'sexual preference and religion, or lack thereof,' I knew that was just going to be the end of it. They wouldn't have gone for it."

Deirdre seemed to accept the revised story. "Yes. I mean it's okay, they wanted to do their own thing, and that's all right, but they couldn't do their own particular thing and call it a HOUSE group, so they ceased to be HOUSE. And so there are a lot of home schoolers in Winterton, but there's no HOUSE group there."

The introductions continued: women from several other towns talked a bit about their groups. Then a woman from Mayland spoke:

"There currently is no HOUSE group in Mayland. There was a group of home schoolers [there], but it's now run as a Christian group, so there is no HOUSE group per se. But we still keep going. I keep going with it and [knowing] that others will, you know, come in time."

Those signposts—*Christian, inclusive, secular, diverse*—were coming to mark an increasingly consequential divide. Very soon, as home schoolers ascended to a new level of national visibility, that division would prove fateful.

Politics

In 1993, the following classified ads appeared in an issue of *Home Education Magazine*:

HOUSE FOR LEASE on organic wilderness. . . . We homeschool our children (6½ and 4) and would like to share farm activities/chores with another homeschooling family. You can even further develop one of the following cottage industries: market garden edible landscape nursery permaculture; goat dairy cheese; natural colored wool-fiber artist; timber thinning-milling; guest cottages. Please send SASE to . . .

Enlightened, intelligent, alternative-minded young woman needed. Midwife and homeschooling mother of four daughters, ages 3½–11, and their father, are searching for the right person to join our family to assist in child care, housekeeping, and educating. . . . Nice home on quiet river in the woods. Primarily vegetarian health foods diet. . . . Write soon and tell us all about you. . . .

National Homeschool Association advocates individual choice and freedom in education, serves those families who homeschool, and informs the general public about home education. Write for a free copy of the NHA newsletter. . . .[1]

Home Education Magazine (*HEM*) does for many unschooling types what *The Teaching Home* does for believers. Like *TTH* a bimonthly with a national circulation, *HEM* provides a public forum for the exchange of homeschooling information and lends a public face to the inclusive side of the movement. A large letters section in every issue enables readers from across the country to swap wisdom, and a "News Watch" column summarizes articles in the popular press to keep readers up-to-date on what the rest of the world is writing about home education.

Another *HEM* column, "Taking Charge," serves as a sort of ongoing instruction manual in homeschooling activism. In it, Wisconsin advocates Larry and Susan Kaseman analyze the changing face of homeschool politics and provide advice about how their readers should seek to ensure their homeschool freedoms. One column published in the winter of 1993, for example, was titled "A Manageable Approach to Political Action for

Homeschooling."[2] Trailing over five pages, the column suggested that home schoolers make personal visits to their state legislators and attend local school board meetings as ways of maintaining the legitimacy of home schooling in the public eye. If each home schooler were to devote "perhaps 15 hours" to activism, the Kasemans pleaded, "we would be that much closer to . . . convincing people that homeschooling is one acceptable alternative among many as a way of raising children."

As part of their manageable approach to political action, the Kasemans' column encouraged readers to participate in "statewide inclusive grass-roots homeschooling organizations." Just what they meant by *inclusive* was described in some detail.

> Such organizations believe that each family must make its own decisions about curriculum, approach to education, personal beliefs, lifestyle, etc. . . . Such organizations are usually careful not to take direction from people and/or organizations outside the state . . . [since] such outsiders may use and direct state organizations for outsiders' own goals and in ways that are not in the best interest of the members and the homeschooling community.

To help readers find their way to inclusive groups, the Kasemans added that "a list of such organizations may be found in this magazine."

Sure enough, *HEM* had devoted two pages near the back of the issue to names and addresses of homeschool organizations across the country. The listing featured entries for organizations in thirty-nine states. Readers could be assured of the inclusive character of the organizations by reading the editorial note printed at the top of the listings:

> One of the most frequent requests we receive is from parents searching for "a good local support group." Most people indicate that they are seeking a group which welcomes all homeschoolers, regardless of religious, philosophical, or educational preferences. Unfortunately, in recent years some groups have required adherence to a religious statement of faith as a prerequisite for membership or for holding office within the group. . . . The groups listed below welcome a broad spectrum of homeschooling families. We will not list exclusivist or closed groups.

As with the directory published in *The Teaching Home*, *HEM*'s listings represented only a select portion of organizations serving home schoolers at the grass roots. What differed were the selection criteria.[3]

By the early 1990s, home schoolers were divided into two quite different movement worlds. They read different publications, attended different support groups, and heeded different kinds of advice about how to act politically. Ultimately, the difference meant that a relatively small and homogeneous group of people would orchestrate public opinion on the movement and shape the political climate for home education.

A LINE IN THE SAND

The May–June 1991 issue of *HEM* included a special section titled "Homeschooling Freedoms at Risk." The feature carried two polemical articles, one written by *HEM* editors Mark and Helen Hegener, the other by "Taking Charge" columnist Larry Kaseman. Also included were several letters from home schoolers around the country, two strident essays, and excerpts from homeschool bulletin boards on the Internet.[4] The Hegeners thought the feature so significant that they made reprints of it available at cost to home schoolers across the country. I first saw the feature at a HOUSE meeting, where Deirdre Brown presented copies of it to the group for free.

The articles warned that some Christian leaders were inaccurately, and unjustly, attempting to speak for the homeschool movement as a whole. "A view of homeschooling has been actively promoted which advances the notion that there is only one way to homeschool, and which ties that one way to an extremely narrow range of social and political support," the Hegeners wrote. "A sense of community has been lost and our homeschooling freedoms are being threatened."

The Hegeners outlined a scenario in which a handful of Christian leaders were assuming definitional control of the entire movement: "The problem is a small group of individuals, their organizations, and their associates, whose actions have resulted in dividing the homeschool community, breaking down networks of support and communication, and artificially imposing an exclusive hierarchical order." The Hegeners named names: Michael Farris, president of the Home School Legal Defense Association; *The Teaching Home* publisher, Sue Welch; Gregg Harris of Christian Life Workshops; and homeschool researcher Brian Ray were listed as core activists dedicated to building a distinctively Christian home education. Others were indicted, too. HSLDA attorney Chris Klicka, advocate Sharon Grimes, Mary Pride, and "dozens of local and state leaders" were among those who "directly and indirectly provide support for the centralization of power and control" in the homeschool movement. The authors saved their most potent venom for Michael Farris. They alleged that he had "repeatedly tried to position himself as the preeminent spokesperson for the homeschool community," even while the legal acumen of Farris and his organization was, as far as the Hegeners were concerned, suspect. The tonic to such illegitimate authority was to raise a multitude of individual voices. "To maintain our freedoms," they wrote, "each and every one of us has to be able to define our own positions, assume our own responsibilities, and make our own decisions based on personal beliefs. We can accept no less." The Hegeners also were suspicious of Farris's organization, HSLDA: "Legalistic arguments and professional hat tricks will not gain us any greater degree of homeschooling freedom. We need to rely instead on the kind of good old fashioned wisdom and sound judgment that we can gain from our own experience."

The Hegeners bulwarked their accusations by surrounding the article with other voices. Linda Winkelreid-Dobson likened the Christian homeschool "experts" in question to "bitter pills"—expensive, hard to swallow, and not very effective besides.

> Think about it. You're a new homeschooler and you hear of a workshop within traveling distance. You gladly dig into your pocket and plop down money to hear what the "expert" has to say. He says you must spend thousands of dollars for a proper home education. You believe him. And he just happens to have thousands of dollars worth of material to sell you.

Essay by essay and letter by letter, the special issue of *HEM* offered a bald critique of the other side of the movement. The believers were after authority and control, while the inclusives wanted democracy. The believers were interested in making money and centralizing power, the inclusives in grassroots empowerment. HSLDA pursued legal protection for the movement as jacket-and-tie attorneys and often fumbled; other people went to court as just plain folks and usually won. Distributed nationally through the magazine's subscription base, and through the more informal networks that carried offprints and gossip, "Homeschooling Freedoms at Risk" prodded home schoolers within earshot of *HEM* to question the believers' intentions.

The *HEM* feature framed the believers' exclusivism as a newly potent threat to the cohesiveness of the homeschool movement. The efforts of a small Christian elite to control the movement undermined what the Hegeners called "the homeschooling community," an inclusive, if perhaps imaginary, coalition of everyone who homeschooled. Larry Kaseman reiterated the idea of a unified homeschool movement in his article for the *HEM* feature when he wrote: "In order to maximize our strength, we must work for unity (but not uniformity) among homeschoolers. To be the most effective we can be in protecting our freedoms, we must focus on the one thing that homeschoolers agree about: the freedom of a parent to choose an education for his child consistent with his principles and beliefs." But while home schoolers might have agreed on some core rationales for their cause, the differences between them were many and subtle. Merely reminding home schoolers that they agreed on some things would prove to be insufficient glue for people who often thought of themselves as essentially different from one another, and engaged in essentially different projects.

Even as early as 1991, homeschoolers had gone a long way toward building their variant ways of thinking into the structure of the homeschool world. Many local support groups were by then expressly "Christian" or nonsectarian; regional associations like ICHE and HOUSE already were organized differently and had different kinds of people at their helms. And believer advocates like Farris, Welch, and Harris already had been working in tandem with one another for years. Over those years they had developed a vision for what a decidedly Christian home education ought to look like, and they had created an organizational apparatus for making that vision a reality (in other words, the Hegeners' accusation that believer leaders were acting corporately was correct; whether that corporatism was godly or profane depended on who one asked). Of course, the inclusives had built an organizational system, too, but it was a considerably smaller, less centralized, and less well coordinated operation.

Once this organizational system had been built, it had profound effects on the amounts and kinds of cooperation that were subsequently possible within the cause. The Kasemans were correct: believers and inclusives did agree on certain issues of individual freedom and parental rights. But by 1991 two things mattered at least as much. First, by the time the *HEM* feature was published, home schoolers were living in an organizational edifice that tended to divide them in two. You heard different news, met different kinds of people, and had access to different services depending on where you lived in that edifice. Your perception of the movement as a whole was shaped largely by the people you knew and by the organizations that met your immediate needs. Those who disagreed with your basic vision of things were easy to disregard, or demonize, because you didn't know or rely on them in any consequential way. Homeschool history demonstrates how a movement's organizational system can separate people, information, and resource flows in ways that exacerbate ideological differences.

147

Second, the construction of an organizational system means that other kinds of self-interest become embedded in a cause. By 1991 it wasn't just about philosophy anymore. At stake were questions about who would get to speak for home schoolers nationally, who would get the glory for the movement's precocious growth, who would be able to make a decent income by selling homeschool products and information, and whose vision of home schooling would make history. This is why the Hegeners and their colleagues were so angry. The homeschool house had largely been built, and the inclusives were finding themselves relegated to a minor wing.

The Great Divide

One evening in the winter of 1992, Cheryl Marcus invited me to her home to introduce me to her great passion, the Internet. Cheryl had been active in computer chat groups for some time; still an utter Internet novice myself, I was eager to learn from her what "on-line" really felt like. In the party room that night were Ruth Hawes, a mother in Tennessee; Gayle Smart, a home schooler in Chicago; Cheryl; and myself. In the middle of our conversation the topic meandered to "stereotypes" about home educators. The exchange was peppered with *gs*—cyber grins.

⟨Ruth⟩ I do wonder if the stereotype of homeschoolers doesn't make some homeschoolers wary of becoming involved with groups?
⟨Gayle⟩ What stereotype, Ruth?
⟨Ruth⟩ Cover of the Teaching Home stereotypes.
⟨Gayle⟩ Major shudder!!!!!
⟨Ruth⟩ And yes I do know quite a few folks who closely fit the stereotype.
⟨Cheryl⟩ Oh, you mean like me ⟨g⟩. Excuse me while I get my apron and take my home-baked cookies out of the oven.
[. . .]
⟨Ruth⟩ Actually I think there are two stereotypes. The other one is the cover of the Rolling Stone (in the old days) type.
⟨Cheryl⟩ Gayle which cover would you prefer ⟨g⟩?
⟨Ruth⟩ I really must get THAT approved cookie recipe from you someday. ⟨G⟩
⟨Ruth⟩ Which cover? Well, I sure wish I had a home as clean and neat as those on TH . . .[5]

When they spoke of the "cover of the Teaching Home," Ruth, Gayle, and Cheryl were referring to the families featured on each cover of the believers' flagship magazine. Typically pictured in orderly living rooms or well-tended yards, these families invariably address the camera with smiling faces. The stereotypes invoked on the Internet that night indicated how their users understood some of the differences between home schoolers. The believers bake cookies, keep spotless houses, and get approval for much of what they do. The inclusives are freer spirits and social renegades with one foot in the counterculture.

The believers also understand that their ways of life are often different from those of many inclusives. One evening I told the Edwardses that I had become particularly interested in the different ways home schoolers go about organizing themselves. I said it seemed to me that the Christians tended to run different kinds of households and organizations than the secular groups did.

"Oh yes, so different. So different," Martha responded. She continued by talking about when she and Robert first investigated home schooling by attending early HOUSE meetings. "I remember from our days in the HOUSE group, you know, this idea of children as good and virtuous in themselves, and what children needed was the space, and the freedom to develop on their own, so that they would flower on their own if only the parent would let them. . . . And that's just so unlike how we think about it."

Robert speculated that the non-Christians' support groups might be run differently, too. "I imagine there are differences between the Christian and the secular groups, too. You [Mitchell] would know more about this probably, because of your work with HOUSE and you've been to Holt Associates [Holt's organization in Cambridge], but I would guess that the secular groups are really mostly women's groups. By that I don't mean 'feminist,' but kind of run by women."

I concurred. "Yes, I think that's right. In fact, I write about those groups, that wing of the movement, as being a women's movement in the sense you just described. Not a feminist movement, but run mostly by the work of women."

"That's interesting," Martha added, "because we really do draw on the men in our families. That's really been happening more lately, that the men are getting much more involved in home education."

We went on for a while like this, exchanging insights about how the Christians and the "non-Christians" get their household and movement work done. At one point I forwarded a question I had long been wrestling with myself: "I'm wondering if you can help me think something through. I've been interested in how home schooling really grows from different traditions, with different philosophies, and I'm wondering if it makes sense to think about there being one home education, one movement, or really two movements." From the brief pause that followed, I got the indication that the Edwardses weren't sure how to respond. Perhaps they hadn't thought about home schoolers in this way. But they seemed to think it was an issue at least worth considering.

Martha replied by referring to apparently essential differences between home schoolers.

> Well, I see what you're saying, and you're right that there are people who are homeschooling who think so very differently about it. I mean we see home education really as a part of something else, it's a part of a whole commitment to something, to our lives as Christians. And that's what gives us the strength to continue home schooling despite all of the challenges. It's the Lord who gives us the strength to do it. And I think that those people who are doing it who are not Christians must be special kinds of people, there must be something inside of them that gives them the motivation to do this—if they don't have the faith that we have that gives us *our* strength.

The difference between the two camps may be partly philosophical and partly organizational, but at least for Martha it also has to do with a deeper distinction: between those who take their strength from the Lord and those who seem to take it from themselves.

There was another question I wanted to ask the Edwardses, but I was unsure how to go about it. I had many indications that inclusives were critical of believers. Did parallel criticisms run in the other direction?

Martha responded, "Well the thing is we just don't hear about them very often, don't see them very often. You know we're active in our groups and relationships, and we don't really have much contact with them. I mean, I know those groups are out there, . . . but to be honest we just don't hear about them much."

Robert added, "And you know I think as the movement has grown, it's our understanding that by and large most of the people who are home-schooling are Christians. And these other groups are there and they've been there from the beginning, but they're really the minority, so it would sort of make sense that we would hear less about them." What survey data were available at the time indicated that Robert was correct: Christians were the majority of home educators in America. Perhaps part of the reason the inclusives were resentful was because, at least numerically, they were a marginal portion of the cause.[6]

The dimensions of difference between home schoolers were many, then, and they ran deep. People had known this for years, of course, and had long understood that there were limits on what issues might bring home schoolers of every stripe together. Some success at unifying home educators across philosophical and organizational divides had been achieved in the past—in Illinois most notably through the Ad Hoc Committee for Illinois Home Education Legal and Legislative Matters, a watchdog group that, from the beginning, had been made up of a plurality of home schoolers.[7] As time went on, however, being active in the home-school movement increasingly required either-or decisions—or having them made for you.

A chance conversation at the 1993 NHA conference helped me understand the nature of such choices.[8] A contra dance was held on the first evening of the weekend, but, weary from my five-hour drive, I had left the party early. The path from the dance to the main campground was un-lighted. As I walked the path, two dots of light whirled ahead of me in the distance. Giggles and voices indicated that the bearers of the beams were children.

"Don't shoot!" I said, holding up my hands in mock surrender.

"Give us your money!" a woman's voice said.

"Take everything I've got!" I replied. By now we were close enough that our faces could be seen in each other's beams.

It was Nichole Thompson, a mother I recognized from a HOUSE camping trip the previous month. Although she had been instrumental in organizing that event, I had never spoken with her at length. She lived far downstate from my home in Chicago, and when I had met her earlier, I had thought her reluctant to talk with me. That evening, though, we warmed to each other. She inquired about my work: whether I had chosen a title yet and what the focus of my project was.

"Well, I've found I'm very interested in the differences between the different kinds of home schoolers, the . . ." What words to use? "The exclusives and the inclusives," I settled on the local vernacular. "It seems to me that the differences go real far."

"Have you had any luck being able to talk to them?" she asked.

"Well, I started learning about home schooling with the Christian groups. Then I found HOUSE. But I've had good luck with the Christian groups, too."

She popped back, "They've gotten a lot more radical in the past few years. That's the way it seems to me at least."

"How do you mean?"

"Well, there's a lot more issues they're pulling into it. Like in my group, I'm part of a Christian group in [my city], and when I started years ago there were, there was a Muslim family, and a couple of pagan families, and a Jewish family. Now we're the only non-Christian family in the group. It's a good group, we get a lot out of it. But in recent years they've added a lot more things to the agenda. It's not just about home schooling. . . . I remember I went to one of those Gregg Harris seminars, and halfway through the first meeting they were handing out little pairs of feet." She was referring to lapel pins worn by many pro-life activists. The pins depict two tiny footprints, ostensibly those of an unborn child. "I was so angry, I wrote to him [Harris], and I said I don't see what this has to do with home schooling, and I want my money back. And they sent my money back."

"Oh, he did . . ."

"Yeah. I mean, we're Taoists, and so I don't have any problem with Christianity really. I don't mind singing 'This Little Light of Mine;' I don't mind Bible verses. I figure it's part of the world, and so the more my children know, the more they're exposed to, the better off they'll be. Because they'll learn to understand differences and tolerate differences."

"Sure, sure," I concurred. Nichole continued by talking again about the Christian group, called Chateau, that she was a part of back home.

"They [Chateau] do have a statement of faith. But the way it's worked out, the group started a long time ago, about fifteen years ago, and at that time it was Christian but they were originally interested in supporting home schooling, so they wrote into their bylaws that anyone could join. Although they do also stipulate that a person cannot hold office in the group unless they are a Christian, so it's the one group I'm a part of that I feel I can legitimately not make that kind of contribution to."

As we made our way down the hill, Nichole continued talking, this time about a different Christian support group in her hometown. "But there's another group in town, CANDO, they have a statement of faith and they really enforce it. The first meeting I went to I read the bylaws and [one] bylaw . . . said you had to be a Christian. They were going through the bylaws in the meeting, it said you had to sign the statement or believe the statement to be a member, and down under another of the bylaws it said that the bylaw about being a Christian could never be changed."

"Uh-huh."

"And so I said, I asked if this was true, if you had to be a Christian, and the women smiled and said 'yes,' and so I left. I said, 'I guess this group isn't for me.' And apparently I left three of the women in tears. But I just thought, well it's not me. You're the ones who said it. That there's nothing I can do about that."

152

There is a third homeschool organization in Nichole's hometown, a HOUSE-affiliated group, in which she also participates. "I go to the one group, Chateau, and I have HOUSE too."

"You said you stay with the one group, Chateau, because it's a good group for you. Can you tell me what you mean by that? I mean I think I know, but could you say a little more?" Saying this, I felt like the world's most wooden ethnographer. Nichole obliged me nevertheless.

"Well, it's a big group. And they're very active, so some things are just easier. Like my tapes. They're from the educational TV station in town, and Chateau has access to it. I can get the videotapes through Chateau. With Chateau I can buy the tapes for sixteen dollars, but with HOUSE the same tape is twenty-seven dollars. And with [the local performing arts center] tickets, I can get those through Chateau. We've been trying to get the ticket option with HOUSE, but with Chateau we can get them early and I just am not as sure with HOUSE."

Nichole recounted what happened when she brought up the issue of arts center tickets to HOUSE. "I said to the group, don't you think we should have a contract with the arts center, some sort of guarantee, have a contract that says we promise to buy tickets? But it's been a problem because there are some people in the group who don't want to have any policy, they don't want to have any policy at all, so it's been hard."

"Any policy?" I queried, not quite understanding.

"Well, yeah, they don't want to have any structure, *any* structure at all," she emphasized, "nothing formal. There are two people in the group who feel that way. Well now one of them, the most vocal one, is gone now, so maybe it will be less of a problem. But this one person was against any structure, anything formal at all. I mean, he didn't even want to have topics for the meetings, you know, where you decide what you're going to talk about beforehand. He didn't even want *that* much structure. He wanted it to be totally free-form, and it's hard to do things when it's done that way. I mean with consensus, and that everything has to be agreed upon."

The three support groups in Nichole's town have different participation rules. This both constrains her choices and forces her to make some. CANDO's Christian statement of faith means that Nichole cannot in good conscience be a member of that group. Chateau welcomes her even though she is not a Christian, but participating in that group means that Nichole must accept the fact that there are more things on the agenda of the organization than she might prefer. She is welcome to participate in HOUSE, but that group is small, has fewer benefits for her, and apparently is stymied by organizational limitations. Ultimately, then, Nichole is obliged to fit her identity and her desires into an organizational landscape not entirely of her own making.

Other home schoolers face similar dilemmas. In 1989, Laura Witkowski and her husband, Allen, talked with me at length about the relationship between their Christian faith and their decision to homeschool their four children. Dedicated Christians and also academics, they had moved to the Chicago area when Allen accepted a job at a local college. Four years later, when I bumped into Laura at an ICHE state conference, she confided that she had come to feel "kind of out of place" in the Christian support group she attended, and she was not sure where she might go to feel more at home. She said that she missed the relative ecumenism of a support group they had left behind in a large southern university town, and she hadn't found a group near her new home that felt the same.[9]

People bumped into the division in the homeschool world beyond their support groups as well. One evening in the fall of 1993, I gave Cheryl Marcus a ride to the HOUSE meeting that we both attended regularly. On the way I told her that I was planning a trip to visit HSLDA's headquarters in Virginia. "That should be interesting," she said with a clear note of sarcasm. I asked what she meant.[10]

"I feel like I'm becoming infamous with HSLDA, and I've never even met these people."

"What are you talking about?"

"I'd heard that HSLDA does this series of communications about breaking legal news. You know, stuff that's happening right now, and they send out fax alerts to people, to group leaders and newsletter editors, to get the information out, and they send out information about legal issues. And I thought it would be good to send that information out over the computer networks. So I called and asked about receiving it." Cheryl told me she had spoken with Carol Ingram at NCHE. "I told her what I was doing and why I wanted the information. I told her it would be a good way to, you know, get the information out. And she basically gave me the runaround."

"The runaround?" I asked.

"We talked about it, and she said she would have to get back to me, and then she called me back and said that she wouldn't be able to give me the information."

"Why not?"

"Well, I asked her why not, and first she said, 'It's very expensive to send the information out, and so they only send it to statewide networks.' And I said, 'HOUSE is a statewide network.' 'Well, it would have to be to a named officer,' she said. And I told her that I *was* a named officer. And then she said it was still a problem because HSLDA wouldn't be able to 'control' how the information was used."

"I see . . ."

"And that really made me mad. Those two words, 'information' and 'control.' I mean as far as I'm concerned the information should be free, it should be available to everyone. And you know she said something about wanting to make sure that there wouldn't end up being misinformation, legal misinformation. And I mean, I don't know, that's just the way it is. You share information, and you really can't determine, you're not responsible for if it gets interpreted properly. But the information should be free. And I thought, you know, how do they 'control' the information with the people they *do* send the information to?"

A few minutes later Cheryl summarized her consternation: "It just seems to me that one of the best things home schooling has had going for it is its unity. Maybe I just want to go back to the good old days, but it's just that I think home schooling is what unites us—our common interests as home schoolers. We went a long way with that. And now I think that groups like HSLDA are just shooting home schooling in the foot, trying to divide us up."

Just who was doing the divvying was difficult to determine, however. For Cheryl the cause of the disunity was the believers' exclusiveness. But hadn't the *HEM* articles been one of the first public efforts to name names, to lay blame? Wasn't it also the case that the inclusives' ideal of diversity encouraged people to go their own way? Weren't home schoolers like Robert and Martha perfectly free to leave HOUSE groups and organize their own support groups however they chose? Taking a few steps back from any one opinion made me skeptical about laying blame for the divisions. They were not just among individuals. They were cultural divides. And some of them had been given consequential organizational expression.

Reputations were dividing up, too. At the January 1993 meeting of a HOUSE support group, a couple who attended regularly brought news of troubles with their county's school district. The mother related the story: "Our school district office is sending out a form for home schoolers to fill out, they say they want to make sure that children are receiving the right instruction. . . . We heard that there's one family in the county that they've brought in, that they're taking to court. And so we're certainly keeping an eye on that."[11]

Others in the room said that they also had heard this rumor.

The woman continued, "And we've learned that if there's legal trouble, there's an organization called . . ." She searched in her notes for the piece of paper on which she had written a name. She continued, reading, ". . . the Home School Legal Defense Association."

I could almost hear hisses in the room. The responses came so quickly, from so many different people, that I found it impossible to connect comments to specific people in my field notes.

"You don't need help from them. Home schooling is perfectly legal in Illinois."

"School districts will say you need to do this and that, but that's because they don't know the law."

"HSLDA is a business. They're selling services. But you don't need them. They're *lawyers*, they're a group of lawyers who have decided to work on home schooling, and so they're selling their services to people. They try to push their services even when you don't need them."

"They're expensive. They charge a hundred dollars a year, and you don't need them."

The mother responded, "Well, actually, if you're a member of a group it's eighty-five dollars. It's only eighty-five dollars." Apparently she had heard of HSLDA's discounts for members of certain support groups.

"But you don't need their services," another detractor responded. "And there are other things about HSLDA that people should know. . . . They give you misinformation. They tell you that you have to register with the school district and they make you have a curriculum."

"They're *lawyers*, and lawyers need laws to do their work, so they're pro-regulation."

Lawyers. The dirty-word inflection of the term was in use that evening: lawyers trying to drum up business, motivated only by money, and, perhaps most damning, giving out faulty advice. Among the members of this HOUSE group, at least, the legitimacy of HSLDA was close to nil.

Others would continue to be impressed with HSLDA. In the years between my first two interviews with them, Robert and Martha Edwards had moved into leadership positions at the state level. In 1993, I had seen Robert address an audience of two thousand people at ICHE's annual state convention. There he had welcomed the assembled as a named officer on ICHE's state board. As per ICHE policy, Robert and his wife had been invited by ICHE's standing board members to join this highest tier of leadership among the believers in Illinois.

By virtue of Robert and Martha's ICHE Board membership, ICHE had paid their way to some of the national leadership conferences sponsored

annually by HSLDA/NCHE. Although they had missed the 1993 conference in Williamsburg, Robert and Martha had attended the 1992 and 1994
events, and were quite enthusiastic about NCHE's efforts. As Robert described it, "At the national conference, the leadership conference every
year, we'll get information about what's happening in Washington, things
that are occurring at the national level that we ought to be informed of.
The people at the National Center, really see it as their job to keep us
informed about what's going on at that level."

"So information comes down to you through the conferences . . ." I
queried.

"Through the conferences, and they'll send things to the state organizations, too."

Martha interjected, "It seems like we're always getting information from
somewhere, about news really from around the country. It's pretty remarkable to me that God has raised up people to fill those needs, to keep us
informed of things." She got up to find some examples of recent mailings
they had received.

I said to Robert, "Yes, it just seems to me that the movement is really
well organized." By "the movement" I meant the believers' cause, the one
that Robert and Martha had helped to build.

"Yes, I think that's true. With the phone trees in each state we can really
reach a large number of people very quickly. That's part of the reason they
send this information to leaders, so we can get the word out."[12] The phone
trees Robert referred to were the grassroots telephone networks actively
encouraged and supported by HSLDA/NCHE. Under the system,
HSLDA/NCHE was able to distribute political and lobbying information
to designated regional leaders across the nation. Regional leaders were
charged with disseminating the information to the grassroots. The system
made it possible for HSLDA/NCHE to coordinate the lobbying efforts of
thousands of home schoolers across the country with considerable
efficiency.

On Capitol Hill

In the winter of 1994, the U.S. House of Representatives considered passage of H.R. 6, a $12.7 billion reappropriation of the Elementary and Sec-
ondary Education Act (ESEA). The act had been consistently re-funded
since its inception as part of Lyndon Johnson's War on Poverty program;
the 1994 appropriation included funds for teacher training, school facili-

ties enhancement, art education projects, and a parental literacy program among its many provisions. The Clinton administration hoped that H.R. 6 would make history by distributing federal education dollars to schools largely on the basis of local poverty levels. That hope died, despite the bill's eventual passage, when many representatives realized the administration's allocation formula would sap money from their home districts. But the course of the legislation proved to be a significant milestone in the history of the homeschool movement. Controversy over a single amendment to the bill deepened the wedge between home schoolers and demonstrated to Congress the believers' ability for effective political mobilization.

In early February, California Democrat George Miller counted a minor victory when his amendment to H.R. 6 was approved by a House Education and Labor subcommittee. Miller's amendment stipulated that states would be required to demonstrate that all their teachers were formally certified in their assigned subject areas to receive funds under some H.R. 6 provisions. Written in a single sentence under Section 2124 (e) of H.R. 6, the original Miller amendment read:

> ASSURANCE.—Each State applying for funds under this title shall provide the Secretary with the assurance that after July 1, 1998, it will require each local educational agency within the State to certify that each full time teacher in schools under the jurisdiction of the agency is certified to teach in the subject area to which he or she is assigned.

The full committee also approved the amendment with little dissent on February 8, though members also approved a clarifying amendment by Richard Armey, the Texas Republican, that states could use "alternative" certification procedures.

Such was the status of the amendment until the following week, when a home schooler in New Jersey called Armey's office to ask if Miller's amendment might require homeschooling parents to be formally certified. In response to the inquiry, an Armey aide called HSLDA to inquire about the potential impact of the amendment for home schoolers.[13]

A prominent Republican congressman long active in party politics, Armey had endorsed the bid of Michael Farris, HSLDA's president, for the Virginia lieutenant governorship the previous year. Farris had lost the seat in the general election but had made national headlines when his supporters swarmed the state's 1993 GOP convention earlier that year to nominate him. The Farris nomination campaign had made the state convention one of the largest in U.S. history. Farris was a highly visible figure in GOP politics by the middle of the decade, largely through the grass-roots efforts of Christian home schoolers. It was little surprise, then, that when Armey's office had a question about home education, it turned to Farris's office, despite the fact that other national homeschool organizations would have been available to field the call. The National Homeschool Association, Holt Associates, and Clonlara School were visible movement players that also had the expertise to inform Armey's staffers. But their greater service to the inclusives rather than the believers arguably put them further afield from Armey's political frame of reference.[14]

The call to HSLDA proved more consequential than Armey might have imagined. The day it was received, Farris met with his legal staff to determine the potential impact of the amendment on home schoolers. HSLDA concluded that Miller's teacher certification assurance might enable some states and school districts to require that homeschool parents be formally certified. Their reasoning was based on the definitions of "elementary school" and "secondary school" in H.R. 6:

The term "elementary school" means a nonprofit day or residential school that provides elementary education, as determined under State law.

The term "secondary school" means a nonprofit day or residential school that provides secondary education, as determined under State law, except that it does not include any education beyond grade 12.

The problem, HSLDA attorneys concluded, was that many states claimed at least some jurisdiction over private school and homeschool programs. Since home schools were both "nonprofit" and "residential," this reasoning went, some state and district officials might be technically empowered to require teacher certification for home schools.

Later that day HSLDA learned that an effort by Armey to exclude home schoolers from the terms of H.R. 6 had failed in committee. Armey had offered an amendment to exclude both home schools and private schools from federal oversight via H.R. 6 provisions. The proposal failed because some committee members suspected that it might inhibit private schools that wanted them from receiving federal funds. Hearing this, Farris called Miller's offices to inquire if the wording of Miller's assurance might be changed to explicitly exclude home schoolers. Farris was told that the congressman believed the change unnecessary, since the legislation had not been intended to regulate home schools in the first place. It was then that HSLDA activated what proved to be a remarkable lobbying machine.

On February 15, 1994, HSLDA sent an "urgent alert" through its fax network. The message framed the Miller amendment as a fundamental threat to homeschool freedoms. Posted from "Michael P. Farris, Esq.," the fax alert warned readers that H.R. 6 "contains a provision which may be interpreted to require all home school parents to be certified teachers . . . an effective ban on home education for more than 99% of home schoolers." To a constituency long skeptical of state education authorities, the alert was like a match to kindling. The inflammatory tone of the fax hurried the spark along: "We are in a crisis mode. . . . Call, fax, or send an overnight letter to your Congressman immediately."[15] The rationale for immediate action was the congressional calendar: "H.R. 6 will come before the House of Representatives for a vote on February 24," the fax warned. By the evening of February 16, letters with a similar message had been sent also to all of HSLDA's thirty-eight thousand members. Branching beyond its own mailing lists, HSLDA began courting the support of neighboring organizations. In a matter of days the giant Illinois-based correspondence school Christian Liberty Academy and *The Teaching Home* magazine were disseminating the news over their mailing lists as well.

In addition to the fax and mail blitz, HSLDA lobbyists also assembled sixty homeschool volunteers in the Washington area to make personal visits to the office of every representative on the Hill. Volunteers were briefed about H.R. 6, especially its teacher certification amendment, and instructed to provide each representative's office with HSLDA's position statements on the issue. According to HSLDA reports, all 435 congressmen's offices had been visited by midafternoon, February 17th.

As it happened, the council of the inclusives' National Homeschool Association had scheduled its regular winter meeting, held in Chicago that year, on February 19 and 20. Attendees had begun to assemble at a volunteered home on the evening of the eighteenth. As they arrived, they began swapping stories about the commotion caused by HSLDA's messages. Few had heard the news directly—HSLDA membership was anything but encouraged on the NHA council—but they had gotten word of the issue from other home schoolers in their local areas. Attendees from Illinois, Ohio, Wisconsin, and Montana told me that their phones had been ringing off the hook, with callers frightened and confused: Was HSLDA correct in its claims? Were homeschool freedoms on the auction block? What was the best thing to do? Over that weekend and through the harrying week that followed, inclusive advocates across the country struggled to come to terms with HSLDA's warning. For better or worse, HSLDA had created a national movement issue, and the inclusives were being forced to address it.[16]

Several seasoned players were convinced that the Miller amendment was not nearly the threat that HSLDA was making it out to be. In a letter dated February 20, Clonlara School director Patricia Montgomery sent her word on the issue to Clonlara's enrolled families.[17] "When . . . I had a chance to examine HR 6, I realized that the potential for impact upon home schools . . . was not serious enough to sound a wide-ranging alarm. Cause for concern? Yes. Cause for panic? No." Montgomery told readers that, according to Congressman Miller's office, H.R. 6's definitions of "school" had been changed to include the word *nonprofit* to exclude *for-profit* schools from garnering federal funds. Montgomery also reminded readers that "nonprofit" meant something quite specific in legal terms, notably a designated 501(c)(3) status for which only formal organizations (not individual homeschool parents) were eligible. She pointed out that the Miller amendment would pertain only to schools applying for funds under some ESEA provisions, and, she argued, "It's hard to imagine home school parents applying for funding under the ESEA *even if they were eligible.*" Finally, Montgomery noted that before the Miller provision could become law, it would have to pass not only in the House but also in the Senate, where debate of H.R. 6 had not even been scheduled.

Others thought similarly to Montgomery. Pat Farenga and Susannah Sheffer, administrators at Holt Associates and publishers/editors of *Growing Without Schooling*, wrote in a public notice on the issue that "even leaving aside the question of varying interpretations of H.R. 6, nothing so sweeping would have happened on 2/24," the date the House was scheduled to vote on the bill. Farenga and Sheffer pointed out that the bill would still need to come before the Senate, and that "furthermore, the changes that the crucial section of the bill refers to are not supposed to take effect until 1998, so . . . there was never any question of homeschooling being outlawed immediately."[18] The Kasemans' Wisconsin Parents Association (WPA) agreed that the Miller amendment was hardly catastrophic. "Several factors greatly reduce the threat from the Miller amendment," the WPA announcement read. The rationale for calm on the issue spread over two pages.[19]

Perhaps Montgomery summarized this position on the Miller amendment most clearly: Cause for concern? Yes. Cause for panic? No. More troubling to many inclusives than the threat of the amendment, in fact, was the political harm being done to home schoolers by HSLDA's lobbying strategy. The amendment in question was but one sentence of a piece of legislation that, when ratified, contained over five hundred pages of text. Yet HSLDA's initial fax alert urged readers to tell their congressmen that

161

they "oppose H.R. 6"—the entire omnibus funding bill rather than a single amendment to it. Home schoolers were being encouraged to send calls and letters to the legislators with arguably extraneous demands, and many in-clusives were upset that HSLDA's instructions were tarnishing home schoolers' image on Capitol Hill. "It's making us look like we're a bunch of idiots," one council member lamented over the NHA meeting weekend in Chicago.

Whatever Representative may have thought of home schoolers, there was no question that they were getting *a lot* of calls from them. By Febru-ary 16—a mere two days after HSLDA had sent out its fax alert and before the NHA Council had even met on the issue—a few Capitol Hill phone lines were already jammed. Some members of Congress reported receiving hundreds of thousands of calls each. Representative Armey had trouble getting through to his own office.[20] But HSLDA had only begun. By the end of the week it had already made contact with major players in the religious media to carry their message nationally. CBN had visited HSLDA headquarters to tape the story for *The 700 Club*, and James Dob-son's prominent *Focus on the Family* radio program had scheduled a discus-sion of the issue to air over its thirteen hundred syndicate stations. On Monday, February 21, Rush Limbaugh discussed H.R. 6 and the home schoolers' lobbying blitz, spreading the news to an even wider constitu-ency. "God knows how many phone calls I've got because Rush Limbaugh had given my phone number out," Democrat William Ford later told the press.[21]

In the week that followed its initial fax alert, HSLDA honed its strategy. By Friday, February 18, Representative Armey had became the official sponsor of a "Home School/Private School Freedom Amendment" to H.R. 6. Written as a collaboration between Armey's office and HSLDA, the amendment stipulated: "Nothing in this Act shall be construed to per-mit, allow, encourage or authorize any federal control over any aspect of any private, religious, or home school." Farris wrote in a letter to House members that H.R. 6 was the "equivalent of a nuclear attack upon the home schooling community."[22] HSLDA promised that this amendment would defuse the bomb.

Other home schoolers disagreed. During its meeting in Chicago on February 19 and 20, the NHA Council had begun to assemble what it called an "ad hoc coalition of homeschooling organizations" to counter HSLDA's claims about H.R. 6. The coalition ultimately included fourteen groups, among them Clonlara, Holt Associates, the Islamic Homeschool Group of North America, Jewish Home Educators' Network, Latter-day

Saint Home Educators, *The Drinking Gourd* (a "multicultural" homeschool magazine), and the Moore Foundation.

Coalition organizers—notably, several members of the NHA council—worried that HSLDA's "Home School/Private School Freedom Amendment" would do home schoolers more harm than good. Larry and Susan Kaseman feared that by expressly including mention of "home school[s]" in federal legislation, perhaps for the first time, home educators might pave the way for further federal regulation. "Such regulations are written by bureaucrats to further define and clarify laws so they can be more easily implemented, administered, and enforced," the Kasemans wrote later of the issue. "They have the force of law, so federal regulations concerning homeschooling could be as serious as a federal homeschooling law."[23] Other council members feared that the HSLDA amendment might prevent needy private schools from receiving federal funds if they wanted them. Their conclusion was that the Miller amendment needed revision, but not in the manner that HSLDA proposed.

By the end of the weekend the coalition organizers had devised their own way to address the problem. Working in tandem with Michigan Democrats William Ford and Dale Kildee, they drafted a "clarifying amendment" that changed the wording of Miller's teacher certification assurance. The proposal inserted the word *public* before "school" in Miller's sentence and added a phrase that explicitly excluded private and home schools from the teacher certification provision.

Satisfied that this strategy would eliminate any risk of the legislation to home schoolers, the NHA coalition advocates contacted HSLDA, inviting them to support the proposal as well. But by the weekend of February 20 HSLDA was already riding the crest of its own wave. HSLDA declined the coalition's invitation and continued to press for its own legislation.

The coalition proceeded with its efforts. Early the following week, volunteers from the Washington area, working on behalf of the NHA coalition, hand-delivered letters to every Representative on the Hill. The opening message of the letter read: *"There is no one group who can speak for all homeschoolers.* However, the following homeschooling organizations, . . . each of whom provides a forum for the exchange of ideas among homeschoolers, have endorsed the *clarifying* amendment to H.R. 6, Section 2124 (e)."[24] Now there were two homeschool amendments, and political support for them was beginning to take on a partisan dimension: Democratic sponsors offered one solution, Republican Dick Armey another.

And still the calls kept coming. Capitol Hill switchboards were jammed on several occasions the week of February 22, garnering national media coverage. HSLDA continued to sound its alarm to amenable listeners. On Wednesday the twenty-third, for example, Farris appeared on two radio programs: the *Beverly LaHaye Show*, nationally syndicated and carried by many religious stations, and Pat Buchanan's show, broadcast live from Arlington, Virginia. By the end of the day, HSLDA had created a veritable spectacle of its lobbying campaign.

Most likely because of the partisan overtones the issue had engendered, Armey remained committed to the HSLDA amendment despite the efforts of Democratic congressmen to resolve the dilemma another way. By the time the issue came to debate on the House floor that week, the Democrats had opted to scrap the Miller amendment altogether while adding language that indicated the bill did not affect home schoolers in any way. The coalition's clarifying amendment and the legislation it had sought to fix were off the table. The Democrats also urged the Rules Committee to make the homeschool issue be the first item of debate on the House floor the next day. "The goal is to spare every member of Congress another weekend of phone calls," explained Congressman Kildee.[25]

But Dick Armey wasn't finished. "The phones don't stop ringing until I pass an amendment on the floor," he told the press. "Half of the members have committed to people that they were going to vote for my amendment."[26]

On Thursday, February 24, both amendments came to floor vote. The Democrats' amendment came up first, and it passed, 424 to 1. George Miller, the author of the original certification amendment, was the only dissenter. The Armey amendment passed later that afternoon by a vote of 374 to 53. Not one Republican voted against it. After spending almost five hours of floor time debating the certification provision and the amendments, the House adjourned for the weekend.

While Armey (and HSLDA) insisted on the necessity of the second amendment, even some of his party colleagues were skeptical that the additional legislation additionally benefited anyone. "It was more show than substance, because I believe we had already taken care of it with the Ford amendment," William Goodling of Pennsylvania told the *Congressional Quarterly*.[27]

But the show had been remarkable. Literally overnight, HSLDA had turned a single amendment into a political spectacle and a minor media sensation. Sending its fax alerts to homeschooling leaders across the country, HSLDA was able swiftly to ignite a chain reaction among constituents eager to write and call their congressmen. Several times over the subsequent days, phone lines and switchboards on the Hill jammed with the deluge of calls. HSLDA's good connections with the conservative and religious media turned this sizable ripple into a wave when well-known personalities such as James Dobson, Beverly LaHaye, Rush Limbaugh, and Pat Buchanan carried HSLDA's message to even broader constituencies. So potent was HSLDA's siren call that even its detractors couldn't ignore it; the fax alert induced them to devise a legislative "solution" to what many of them believed was only a marginal problem to begin with.

In the end there was little doubt that HSLDA had both created the controversy and earned primary credit for its resolution. Although it cannot be known for certain what the fate of the Miller amendment would have been had HSLDA not become involved when and how it did, the available evidence suggests that the legislation became a "homeschool" issue only after HSLDA defined it as such. Once HSLDA had publicized the Miller amendment among home schoolers, the initial response of the inclusives was a reserved caution. Cause for concern? Yes. Cause for panic? No. That many inclusives were more upset with HSLDA's politics than with H.R. 6 policy indicates how fundamentally HSLDA had defined the issue even among its detractors.

And of course, the believers got public credit for it all. When the *Congressional Quarterly* carried a two-page story on the phone blitz in its February 26 issue, it devoted ten column inches to a discussion of HSLDA. The article made no mention of the inclusives' ad hoc coalition, or of the split between home schoolers who supported the Armey amendment and those who did not. Similarly, coverage of the final House vote on the amendments carried by the Associated Press made no separate mention of the coalition efforts.[28] When the *New York Times* carried the AP story the morning after the vote, the paper used boldface to describe the events as "a bow to the religious right."[29]

Culture and Mobilization

Just how was HSLDA able to pull off this feat? Previous scholars of social movements provide some helpful answers, pointing to the importance of money and other material resources in gaining the ear of standing authorities and showing how important practical, mundane relationships are in distributing news of a cause and eliciting support for it. But the standing answers go only so far in explaining the homeschool case; they fail to reach the cultural bedrock on which this movement's resources and social networks have been built.[30] Homeschool politics enable us to better discern this deeper stratum of cultural organization.

A resource mobilization approach would likely emphasize the role a well-funded organization played in enabling believers to take control of the H.R. 6 controversy. Consider the wealth of HSLDA, the believers' mobilization control center. If even 80 percent of HSLDA's approximately thirty-eight thousand member families in 1993 paid the minimum $85 annual membership fees, the organization would have had an annual gross income of over $2.5 million from those membership fees alone. This conservative estimate goes far in explaining how HSLDA was able to keep a sizable professional staff, administer its fax network and mailing lists, and maintain regular phone and travel contact with its national constituency in the months and years before H.R. 6.[31] When news of the Miller amendment reached HSLDA, it was equipped with the material resources it needed to get the word out: fax, photocopying, and word processing equipment, and a budget sufficient to put thousands of dollars toward postage and phone time. Additionally, HSLDA was able to enlist a host of volunteers across the country, people already practically linked to the organization by virtue of membership, to help disseminate the news.

By contrast, the National Homeschool Association had paltry resources with which to spread its version of the story. The NHA had an annual budget that was counted in the thousands—not tens of thousands, and certainly not millions—of dollars. It had no full-time staff, operated out of a volunteered home, and continually depended on in-kind contributions even to hold its semiannual council meetings. A situation as big as H.R. 6 became greatly strained the resources of the NHA. The council had to rely on private household phone lines to do much of its communication during those crucial days in February, and it was forced to use consumer copy shops to produce many of its mailings even in the heat of the controversy. In short, the NHA's coalition effort was a shoestring operation. Like HSLDA, the NHA relied on volunteers across the country, but it enlisted volunteers without the benefit of a firmly established, formally organized fax and phone network that could be activated on command. Clearly, the believers' more formidable resources do much to explain how they were able to create and then steer the H.R. 6 issue so determinedly.

But to say that HSLDA had many resources while the NHA had only a few do not tell us much about how this disparity came to pass. For that we need a cultural explanation. HSLDA generates income by offering a service—legal counsel—that is valuable only if people believe that they need it. Some home schoolers are suspicious of HSLDA precisely because of the financial dimensions of HSLDA's advocacy. "They want to sell their damn insurance," one embittered advocate on the NHA side of things told me once in reference to HSLDA. "They need to keep people scared of the law so that they will run out and buy this insurance to protect themselves."[32] The believers disagree. In the wake of H.R. 6, several believers in Illinois said that the lobbying effort had only solidified their support for HSLDA. For many believers the organization had "saved" home schoolers from a serious threat—or, as some would later explain to me, God had saved home schoolers through the vehicle of HSLDA. HSLDA's resource mobilization, then, is dependent on the reputation of the organization before its clients. Pivotal to HSLDA's relative wealth has been its ability to embody the prestige of the legal system and to market that prestige to a constituency with cultivated apprehensions about the intrusions of the state into their lives. In this sense HSLDA represents cultural entrepreneurship at its zenith: the manipulation of established systems of meaning for novel, and perhaps self-interested, purposes.

Previous scholarship also encourages us to consider the social networks in which the H.R. 6 controversy bloomed. Certainly the believers had a well-funded headquarters and volunteers around the country to support it. Just as important, though, was the coordination of those resources in a hierarchical system. Through its fax tree, HSLDA was able to disseminate word on the crisis that its grassroots leaders found definitive. Everyone got the same news and the same instructions on who to write, what to write, and when. The believers' pyramidal network structure enabled HSLDA to orchestrate a national constituency of volunteers. Arguably it was this orchestration that made the lobbying blitz so impressive. By contrast, the inclusives relied on more informal relationships between organizations and constituents. To be sure, the inclusives also had a movement network, one sturdy enough for them to build their ad hoc coalition in a matter of days, but they did not match the speed of the believers in getting their word out. Nor, it seems, did they match the numbers of persons HSLDA was able to reach with its single, definitive voice.[33]

But an emphasis on network structure cannot by itself explain what made the believers' organizational system so effective. First, it cannot explain what made the news that traveled through the network so compelling. When HSLDA put out its fax alert in Michael Farris's name, it sent news of a crisis to those who were predisposed to honor the legitimacy of the messenger. HSLDA had for some time been positioning itself at the top of the believers' organizational pyramid, but it had done more than just sit there. Through its sibling organization, NCHE, HSLDA had sponsored special conferences specifically for grassroots leaders. HSLDA had long supplied legal news to the believers through its editorial contributions to *The Teaching Home*. Consistently true to its membership agreements, HSLDA had frequently fielded calls from skeptical school officials, put out fires with social service agencies, and taken more than a few homeschool cases to court. Regular mailings to the membership consistently reminded people of HSLDA's legislative and judicial successes. Through years of effort, Farris and his team were well positioned reputationally as well as ecologically. Because his organization had laid such a solid reputational foundation in the eyes of many believers, Farris could do more than suggest that home schoolers go into action. He could, rather, tell them that it was "imperative that all home schoolers call their Congressman/woman immediately." To a constituency that had paid good money for HSLDA's legal expertise and seen Farris come through on his promises, this call to arms had the weight of legitimacy behind it. HSLDA relied not only on network connections, then, but also on its constituents' beliefs about the integrity of Farris and his organization.

By contrast, the NHA had a thinner reputational legacy on which to build its call to action. The NHA had regularly sponsored annual conferences and printed a quarterly newsletter, but it had sought to do very little other than link a national constituency. Its purpose statement included no services comparable to the legal advice or news editorial provided by HSLDA. It was ever reluctant to speak authoritatively for all home schoolers. It was decidedly not in the business of nurturing leaders. Consequently, when H.R. 6 hit, the NHA had fewer reputational resources on which to draw to convince people of the superiority of its news, and fewer favors of time and service to call in from its membership.

Examining the structure of network relations by itself is inadequate in a second way, because the pyramidal organization of the believers' movement itself requires explanation. HSLDA was able to coordinate the activities of thousands of volunteers because it sat at the top of the believers' organizational system—a system that had a clear top and bottom in part because the believers assumed that a hierarchical arrangement of authority was acceptable. Believers at the grassroots assumed that, as godly leaders and as lawyers, the staff at HSLDA both knew what they were talking about and could appropriately give directions to the rest of the movement. Part of the reason HSLDA was able to bank on this legitimacy was because the believers are comfortable with hierarchical social arrangements. Authoritative direction from ordained authorities is not *in itself* problematic for them. If anything, HSLDA's careful nurturing of its hierarchical net-work is but one invocation of an organizational schema that is granted general acceptability among conservative Protestant home schoolers.

The comparison case of the inclusives suggests that, absent the legiti-macy of hierarchy, HSLDA might have had less of a cause. Consider how HOUSE activists in Illinois went about alerting their constituency to H.R. 6. When Illinois HOUSE did send a mailing to its membership nearly a week after HSLDA's fax alert, its call to action left considerable room for constituent dissent. The opening lines to the mailing read: "What should you do about H.R. 6? That is something neither I or any-one, including the HSLDA can tell you. You must follow your own con-science. . . . Speaking for myself, I feel no need to identify myself as a homeschooler to anyone in the government."[34] Hardly the "urgent alert" from a named authority that ignited the believers, HOUSE's mailing ap-peared to be written by no one in particular and encouraged constituents to do nothing but follow their own consciences. The message was in keep-ing with the inclusives' broader assumptions about legitimate organiza-tion. In their movement there are few formal "leaders" at all, and in any case the informal ones are not legitimately empowered to tell others what to do. You must follow your own conscience, the HOUSE message told readers. That consciences were not in agreement was demonstrated when HOUSE never came to agreement about how to address H.R. 6.[35]

The H.R. 6 controversy richly demonstrated that the two home educa-tions have taken very different organizational forms. But the facts of the H.R. 6 story do not by themselves tell us how to explain this variation. What has made it possible for the believers to put together such a sizable and formidably organized home education? And why have the inclusives remained faithful to an organizational style that seems to bring them a lot of troubles? Finding adequate answers to these questions takes us beyond home education and into the broader cultural landscape in which home-school activists do their work.

The unchurched are sometimes surprised to learn that conservative Protestants make up at least a quarter of the U.S. population.[36] Seculars may fail to see these believers because their life rhythms and organizational affiliations set them somewhat apart from other Americans. Compared with members of mainline Protestant groups, they attend church much more regularly. They can choose places of worship among a wide array of church organizations, many of them independent operations with no for-mal ties to a denominational order. The great majority of these faithful report making contributions of time or money to world evangelism.[37]

These are people who are comfortable making commitments to novel religious causes, to leaders with vision. Many of them worship in churches founded by relatively autonomous leaders who have exploited fruitful combinations of spiritual conviction and organizational acumen. Consider, for example, that in a recent nationally representative study, sociologist Christian Smith and his colleagues found that nearly 40 percent of evangelical voters are Baptists. A denomination characterized by high levels of congregational independence, Baptists have historically maintained what might be called a free-market approach to church-planting. Unhindered by a rigid denominational bureaucracy, Baptist pastors have historically been able to start congregations as the Spirit leads and wherever they can attract followers. An additional 8 percent of the Smith team's evangelical voters are Pentecostals, another free-market tradition, and 5 percent worship in churches with no denominational affiliation—in churches, in other words, that owe their existence to considerable spiritual and organizational entrepreneurship.[38] Conservative Protestants also support a vast constellation of parachurch organizations: mission societies, colleges and universities, Bible camps and conference centers, radio and television stations. There are also publishing houses, recording labels, retirement developments, and insurance and investment plans among a large universe wide array of avowedly "Christian" businesses. In their attendance, tithes and offerings, and consumer decisions, conservative Protestants have nurtured what Smith and his colleagues aptly describe as "a pluralistic, competitive religious economy. . . . [E]vangelicalism exhibits a tremendous fluidity with which it generates entrepreneurial leaders who promote an immense array of religious products." The produce is a rich stew of organizations that enable believers to live, worship, minister, and consume in accord with their chosen faiths.[39]

Within this fertile organizational culture, such godly men and women as Michael Farris, Mary Pride, Sue Welch, Gregg Harris, and many others, have found supporters who understand and accept the mix of earthly business and heavenly service. In building their causes, Christian homeschool leaders have tended toward a particular model of organization common among conservative Protestants. Believers call them *ministries*, a term that scholars of organizations might adopt for these hybrid forms as well. Not churches and not quite (or only) businesses, ministries are pyramidal forms distinguished by a mix of charismatic and bureaucratic authority. They tend to be capped by a single person with exceptional spiritual and communicative gifts. As this leader and his nucleus accumulate followers and financial resources, they adopt more rationalized administrative structures.

Tasks are distributed by rank and office. Boards of directors (or of "elders" or "deacons") are recruited. Applications of incorporation are filed. Bureaucratization lends ministries staying power, while freeing their heads to concentrate on the work they do best: speaking and writing; winning souls, listeners, and clients; planting seeds for satellite causes. Surviving the changes, however, is the spiritual center of the organization embodied in a single person: the fiery pastor of the basement fellowship that grows into a megachurch; the articulate Christian psychologist who builds a media empire on radio; the homeschooling mom whose modest periodical grows into a glossy magazine; the ambitious attorney who invents a novel mix of religious faith and legal services. In ministries, conservative Protestantism offers a widely accepted organizational form well suited to small businesspeople, kingdom-building pastors, and political hopefuls.[40]

To homeschool entrepreneurs in particular, conservative Protestantism affords additional gifts. A second blessing is legions of potential personnel. Through four decades of liberal feminism, conservative Protestants have sustained a normative commitment to the priority of full-time motherhood. While many conservative Protestant mothers work outside the home for pay, their rate of labor force participation tends to be lower than that of the general population.[41] Even when conservative Protestant women are employed, they are continually reminded about the primacy of motherhood in women's lives. Full-time domesticity is often celebrated as an ideal from pulpits, in Bible studies, and in religious radio, print, and television programming. In this cultural context the ministry of home education has flourished. As I have already noted, home schooling enables women who are predisposed to full-time motherhood to think of themselves as more than "just moms," a considerable reward in a society that lends such ambiguous status to motherhood This affinity between home schooling and traditionalist domesticity is not lost on believer entrepreneurs like Mary Pride, who weave their rationales for home schooling into a larger ideal of a bold Christian womanhood.

These are faiths that encourage distinction from the world. The famous separatism of fundamentalists and the "engaged orthodoxy" of the evangelicals encourage both camps to be "in the world but not of the world."[42] For conservative Protestants, being a Christian often means living differently from one's neighbors. This distinctiveness is regarded as both submission to divine authority and a form of evangelism, a way of demonstrating to others the fruits of godly living. One way in which conservative Protestants manifest their lifestyle distinctiveness is in their patterns of organizational participation; compared with mainline Protestants, for example, the evangelicals are less likely to be members of volunteer organizations outside their own faith traditions but also more likely to be very active in their own church and parachurch activities.[43] In a cultural context that encourages both lifestyle distinction and active faith commitment, the prospect of home schooling seems less unreasonable than it otherwise might. Many believer parents approach home schooling as an extension of their efforts to live out a faith somewhat at odds with the surrounding culture. They receive much encouragement for doing so; the affinity between Christian distinctiveness in general and home schooling in particular is not lost on believer advocates like Gregg Harris, who often use a biblical or theological vernacular to preach the benefits of home education.

The conservative Protestant world provides a fertile cultural context for home schooling. It is a world rich with fully legitimated models for "ministry" entrepreneurship. Its celebrations of motherhood and domesticity help to create the kind of personnel that this maternal, labor-intensive movement requires. And its theology advocates a lifestyle distinctiveness that makes countercultural life choices more reasonable. But we should be careful not to see these cultural resources as having entirely determined the believers' growth and political success. Fertile soil and temperate climate can make for a rich harvest, but much still depends on the gardener. Good conditions are no substitute for hard work. The conservative Protestant world has provided opportunities for homeschool entrepreneurs, but their good fortune has come with years of labor—and rhetorical inventiveness, business sense, and, as we have seen, cooperation among the national leadership elite.

Even in the midst of great opportunity, some fortunes falter. A telling example is the late career of Raymond Moore, unquestionably the believers' first and most famous advocate. Moore's prominence dimmed as the movement matured through the 1990s. The early Moore books were initial sparks to a fledgling cause. Moore's academic credentials, avowed Adventist faith, and good communication skills made him an ideal spokesman for Christian home education. In the early years of the movement, he had speaking engagements across the country and the ongoing endorsement of James Dobson's *Focus on the Family*. The Hewitt-Moore Research Foundation augmented the ministry with curriculum products and other ancillary services.

But as the years passed and Christian home education flourished, other stars began to rise. Gregg Harris, who had begun his homeschool career as a conference planner for Moore, left his employer in a bitter business dispute and began his own fledgling ministry. Sue Welch and Cindy Short birthed and nurtured their *Teaching Home*, while Michael Farris accrued a national reputation with HSLDA, of its kind the only game in town. Christian Liberty Academy and the Calvert School had long been providing correspondence programs to homeschool pioneers, but soon parents had dozens of programs to choose from: ATI, A Beka, The Weaver, KONOS, and on and on. In this growing market Mary Pride's Big Books of Home Learning became definitive guides to homeschool curriculum.

As the field grew, it also became more explicitly "Christian." From the beginning in the 1970s, Moore had purveyed a home education whose religious undertones were amply balanced by the language of developmental science. Moore and his wife were themselves Protestant Christians, but their vision for home schooling was an ecumenical one. The next generation of believer elites had different ideas. HSLDA retained a nominal nonsectarianism, but Farris's columns for *The Teaching Home* and publications such as his *Homeschooling Father* bore witness to its founder's adamantly conservative religious faith. *The Teaching Home* and Harris's Christian Life Workshops were marketed explicitly as religious products. And while her curriculum guides spoke to a bridge market, Mary Pride showed her conservative religious stripes clearly in the books *The Way Home* and *All the Way Home*.

By the dawn of the 1990s, Raymond Moore was finding himself on the outside of an emerging inner circle of believer leaders and organizations. In 1991, Moore publicly criticized believer leaders for what he called their "'Christian' exclusivism." In a widely circulated white paper, Moore accused these leaders of subverting the unity of the homeschool movement and of promulgating a self-serving cause. Moore named names—Gregg Harris, Michael Farris, and Sue Welch among them—to paint a picture of an oligarchy doing things on their own terms. "'Christian' exclusivism . . . is a contradiction in terms, for Christ of Christianity was *not* exclusive," he declared.[44] Ultimately Moore's more ecumenical vision for home schooling lost out to a distinctively Christian home education. As an oft-read author and early champion, he retained respect among the believers, but by the mid-1990s he had lost most of his claim to homeschool leadership.

Moore's decline teaches at least two lessons. The first is that in movement building there is always a measure of uncertainty. A lot depends on who one's friends are, who else is on the playing field, and perhaps a bit on just plain luck (believers, of course, would use a different term). Even despite good odds, the road to success is always somewhat unclear.

Movement building is risky business, and while the risk undoubtedly contributes to the glamour of the work, it also means that a life's commitment can lead to outcomes one would rather not have imagined.

The second lesson, a commonplace for believers but news to many outsiders, is that conservative Protestants often and sometimes heatedly disagree. Popular media images of believers living in suspect harmony, listening blindly to their leaders, and voting with unanimity are misleading. Conservative Protestantism is a large and complicated social world with many camps and divisions. To be sure, its borders are defined by some shared theological, cultural, and organizational sensibilities, but within those borders a wide array of theologies, politics, and products vie for adherents. The believers' homeschool movement is unified, but it is a unity that has come through the organizational acumen of particular leaders, their careful use of this Christendom's remarkable cultural resources, and their successful exclusion of contrary voices.

Things have worked out quite differently for the inclusives, for a number of reasons. Unschooling's early champions were savvy and entrepreneurial, too, but they sowed the seeds of their movement in a cultural landscape less suited for rapid growth. As with Christian home education, unschooling essentially requires full-time domestic workers. But unlike among the believers, the inclusive wing of the movement does not have the luxury of recruiting from a huge population of women predisposed to full-time motherhood. Home schooling may be a troubling or even cognitively impossible choice for many secular women, who increasingly assume that their lives should include paid work. Among women who have made deep commitments to paid-work careers, home schooling may come at costs to career, identity, and economic autonomy that few are willing to pay. Consequently, the inclusives are faced with a chronic personnel problem. While conservative Protestant women sense an affinity between their notions of ideal womanhood and home education, women nearer to the cultural mainstream are more likely to see home education as incompatible with, or even threatening to, a gender identity scripted in large part by modern feminism.[45]

Perhaps this is why so many of the unschooling women I met came to home schooling from other "alternative" approaches to domestic life. Many first rethought the obligations of motherhood in La Leche League or had their own hunches confirmed in La Leche's adamantly maternalist milieu. Some, like Diana Coleman-Maxwell, came to the inclusive camp after years of seeking an even balance of domesticity and career through volunteering, art making, and part-time employment. These are women who, for one reason or another, have taken creative routes through the still-unresolved contradiction between paid work and home. Their commitment to home schooling arguably extends the palette of creative responses to this persistent dilemma.

Many of the inclusives came to the movement having already been schooled in living at some remove from mainstream culture. My field notes describe underwater births, children pure of immunizations, former communards, and family beds. I met Orthodox Jews, Buddhists, Taoists, avowed atheists, and practicing pagans. Muslim, Jehovah's Witness, and Mormon homeschool organizations were among the groups that joined the NHA's ad hoc coalition on H.R. 6. These are people with experience in questioning conventional ideas and normative lifeways. In this sense they are like the believers: they arrived at home schooling already disposed to thinking counterculturally.

Unlike the believers, however, when inclusives come together, they can assume no shared social identity, no common outlook on life beyond the homeschool project itself. Nor can the inclusives take for granted that most everyone among them has experience in similar kinds of organizations, with predictable divisions of labor and presumed pecking orders. The inclusives are diverse philosophically, but they also are diverse in their organizational experiences. This fact likely goes far in explaining why they have so often chosen radically democratic organizational forms, with weak leaders or no leaders at all, where most everything is up for discussion and anyone is free to disagree or try something else.[46]

Ultimately the form and fate of the two sides of home education are so different because the movement straddles two cultural landscapes. One is the expansive and varied terrain of conservative Protestantism, a vast kingdom of opportunity for entrepreneurial movement-builders who are attuned to the country's subtle blessings. The other is an archipelago of little islands, each composed of people who think and live distinctively. This terrain has obliged its entrepreneurs to build many bridges, navigate a wildly diverse topography, and settle for smaller returns.

As the heat of the H.R. 6 controversy faded, the inclusives seemed of two opinions regarding how their camp had managed things. Some of them thought that the ordeal had demonstrated the ability of home schoolers to work together. "I was really impressed at how quickly we were able to put the [ad hoc] coalition together," one inclusive activist told me soon after the congressional votes. "That group included people from a very wide spectrum, but we were able to pull off the coalition, really in a matter of

175

days." She also was pleased that the coalition had shown Congress that not all home schoolers were Christians. "No one can say that home schoolers are all evangelical Christians [now]. We made it very clear to legislators that there are more of us out there than that."[47]

Others found the glass half empty. Several months after H.R. 6 was done, I spoke with a frustrated Cheryl Marcus on the telephone. "I've been talking with some people in different parts of the country," she said, "and we're really tired of waiting around for consensus while HSLDA does its thing. It's like we can't get anything done until everyone agrees."

I asked Cheryl what she meant.

"Well, you know with HOUSE, and the NHA, with the consensus rules. You have to get everyone to agree before anything can get done. And I think that's one of our big problems. It slows us down. I mean, I'm not saying we shouldn't have democratic process or anything like that, but we've got to get some things done."

I indicated that I got her point.

"So we've been talking about starting our own organization. An organization that doesn't have to be run by consensus."[48]

Talk about how to make their wing of the movement function politically continued long after the H.R. 6 controversy. I did not attend the 1994 NHA national conference as I had the previous two autumns, but I learned about some of what happened there over a long breakfast with Deirdre Brown. She told me that Raymond Moore had come to the NHA conference that year.[49]

"Oh really?" I queried.

"Yeah. He flew in for the Thursday meeting and stayed through Sunday. So he was there for virtually all of the council meetings."

It seemed that Moore had come seeking an organization that might counter HSLDA politically. Over the next few days Moore apparently learned that while he shared the NHA's commitment to diversity, he differed on organizational vision. "What he really wants is a political action committee, and he thought that perhaps the NHA could do that for him," Deirdre said. "He thinks we should be more active. He wants someone to combat Farris and Harris and stand up to them, and really be more of a lobbying organization." Deirdre doubted that Moore found what he was after, since in the course of explaining to him why the NHA couldn't be a political action committee, the NHA had developed a stronger sense of the kind of organization it wanted to be.

"And in the course of explaining to him that that is not what we're about, we were forced to think about, forced to say what we *were* about," she said.

"And that is . . ."

"What we're about is diffusing power back to individuals. In a sense it's just the opposite of . . . what the other crowd is doing. Rather than pooling power and giving it to some organization to do things, we want to diffuse it back to our membership, to give it back to individuals." As she said this, Deirdre motioned to illustrate, pushing her hands out from the center of her body in the pattern of a fan. Then she reiterated the point, as if to be sure I was clear on it: "Our goal is to give power to individuals, rather than the other way around."

The tone of her voice betrayed conviction. "And it was really good to talk about that, because as we talked we got a lot clearer about what the mission of the NHA was. We really came to a better understanding, and it was like . . . a light went on . . . and some of the other decisions we had to make that weekend were easier to make. Because we had a sense of what we were trying to do." This satisfied Deirdre immensely, though she suspected that Moore might not agree with her. "I don't know what Ray thought of it all," she said. "Perhaps he gave up on us. I mean, I think he understood, but it's, you know, not what he's after."

Nurturing the Expanded Self

ON THE OUTSIDE, the Home School Legal Defense Association looked much the same in 1999 as it had six years earlier. The office was situated at the edge of a residential subdivision in Purcellville, Virginia, on the front lines of Washington sprawl. Resembling a row of townhouses, the building has the colonial embellishments typical of D.C. suburbia: brick facades and clapboard siding, window shutters added to please the eye rather than filter the elements. Passersby might have mistaken it for a condominium.

Inside, there had been some changes. In six years membership had climbed into the orbit of sixty thousand. The staff had grown apace. With the help of an employee, I had counted thirty-eight employees in 1993; in 1999 there were closer to sixty. Among the new positions was a director of media relations. A satellite office, right in the District, had been added. A new ad campaign was in place, with the caption "We do more than you may realize." "If you think that defending home schoolers in court is all we do, you're only seeing part of the picture," read a full-page advertisement in *The Teaching Home* that year.[1] And there were plans for the future, to say the least. In the summer of 1999, ground was broken in Purcellville for Patrick Henry College, described on the Web as "a ministry affiliated with the Home School Legal Defense Association." A new, colonial-style building would house the college as well as new offices for HSLDA. Patrick Henry would offer an apprenticeship program in addition to conventional classroom instruction. According to the college's publicity material, a specialty would be training men and women for government service. Also on the drawing board were plans for a Patrick Henry School of Law.[2]

I met many young people during my second visit to HSLDA. From 1995 to 1999, the organization had an internship program that drew homeschool graduates from across the country to Purcellville for twelve-month terms.[3] Many had stayed on as employees. Gavin Taylor came at age twenty; four years later, he was working full-time for NCHE. On the wall of his cubicle was a handful of photographs; there was Gavin with Dan Quayle at a homeschooling conference in Denver; Gavin with Pat Buchanan, Gary Bauer, Mike Farris. Soft-spoken and articulate, Gavin talked for an hour about the many jobs of his office: assembling the thick packages of news and political analyses sent six times yearly to regional leaders; keeping tabs on regional news through state newsletters; tracking coverage of home schooling in the national media; fielding phone calls from college admission officers with questions about home schoolers; talking to researchers like me. He said he was interested in the writing and publishing fields for his career, and that he had his eye on an internship at *World*, an evangelical news magazine.

Next door was Jason Hart, assistant director of the Congressional Action Program (CAP), parent to the H.R. 6 phone blitz. Jason first heard about CAP in 1993, when he was sixteen years old. He was a CAP volunteer through his teens before coming to Purcellville for an internship. In 1999, when I met Jason, his job entailed maintaining CAP's national network of volunteer lobbyists. CAP's goal was to have representatives in all 435 congressional districts; that spring the count was somewhere between 350 and 400, but the inevitable volunteer turnover means that the job will never really be done. "Why do people leave the program?" I asked. Jason explained that as children enter adulthood their parents can tend to become less interested in homeschool politics. And there are the "dry spells," as Jason called them, long periods during which the soldiers have little to fight, when it is harder to maintain commitment. The Internet, of course, makes everything easier, faster. Since CAP's communication system has gone on-line, Jason estimates that the network's response time is down 60 to 70 percent. Jason's work was helping HSLDA maintain its national notoriety for lobbying acumen. A year after my visit, a front-page feature on the homeschool lobby in the *Wall Street Journal* emphasized HSLDA when it called home schoolers "inside-the-Beltway pros."[4]

Despite all the new people, there were still some familiar faces. I well remembered Betsy Jensen, HSLDA's affable, razor-sharp director of communications. Under her purview are the *Court Report*, a slick bimonthly, and the endless stream of forms, schedules, ads, and brochures that are part and parcel of HSLDA's line of business. Despite her full plate, she responded immediately when I e-mailed regarding a second visit and, after my slightest inquiry, set up a roundtable discussion with several of the office's homeschooled staff.

Among those in the conference room that afternoon were Gavin Taylor, Laura Papp, Gina Farron, Derek Jones, and Peter Johanski. Talkative, smartly dressed, twenty-something all, they answered my questions with thoughtfulness and a dash of humor. I got the rough outlines of their lives in Purcellville. HSLDA maintained two residences for the interns, one each for men and women. Office life and church commitments combined, they agreed, to make for active social lives and not a little human intrigue. The jobs had their chorelike features but also their challenging dimensions; attuned as HSLDA is to the uncertainties of state legislatures and Congress, one never knew what adventure lay just around the corner at work. All of them seemed confident that their current jobs would prepare them well for the next stages of their careers. Peter, fresh from homeschool graduation in the Midwest, was already talking about a future in politics. Gina had recently begun laying plans for her own service ministry with young people in eastern Europe. Derek was applying to law school. Laura was thinking about law school, too. As far as she could tell, that was God's current plan for her life. That might change, she said, but God had taken care of things up to then, and she had every reason to think he would do so in the future. At this Gina, sitting next to her, tapped Laura on the shoulder and whispered "Amen."

After an hour of lively conversation, I offered a final inquiry. If they were to see a book published about home schooling, what would they like that book to address that wasn't covered in the national media? This one seemed to be a no-brainer. The biggest problem with the media coverage, they said, was that home schoolers were so often represented as crazy, or not well socialized, or outside the mainstream. "*Tell them we're not socially retarded,*" one voice to my left added emphatically. There were knowing laughs all around. I assured them I would do what I could.

But how, in the end, would I explain my growing conviction that home schoolers were just the opposite? That despite their traditionalist trappings they were living at a cutting edge of contemporary culture? That their movement had flourished precisely because its basic tenets are remarkably in tune with newly conventional assumptions about American childhood? I flew home, fattened notebook in hand, with several puzzles still to be solved.

In 1985, when the HSLDA interns were children and their parents were homeschool pioneers, a team of Berkeley sociologists released a provocative discussion of contemporary American character. Their book, *Habits of the Heart*, problematized a growing ethos of self-fulfillment in our culture and lamented the decline in Americans' sense of corporate obligation to a good society. *Habits* argued that the change was evident in a growing tendency to speak in a therapeutic language of personal growth, and in an evident reluctance to put the needs of a spouse, a family, a church, or community ahead of personal self-interest. The authors worried that an expansion of the individualism long central to the American character now threatened our ability to sustain a healthy collective life:

> It seems to us that it is individualism, and not equality, as Tocqueville thought, that has marched inexorably through our history. We are concerned that this individualism may have grown cancerous—that it may be destroying those social integuments that Tocqueville saw as moderating its more destructive potentialities, that it may be threatening the survival of freedom itself.

The expansion of individualism had, according to the Berkeley team, greatly attenuated "the subtle ties that bind human beings to one another, leaving them frightened and alone."[5]

Habits of the Heart found a prominent place among a number of books that assessed the recent past as a decisive period in our cultural history. Many in the national intellectual establishment celebrated particular accomplishments of the 1960s and 1970s. There was applause for the civil rights and women's movements, youth suffrage, and the ending of the Vietnam War, yet some worried that the progress of contemporary culture had a dark side. We had discarded traditional rules about commitment and national unity too quickly and had little to replace them. We were becoming dangerously narcissistic. With the emergence of identity politics, the left had lost its ability to build durable political coalitions. And across the political spectrum, an increasingly common encouragement to "do your own thing" was making for an atomized society at best and, and worst, a nation divided.[6]

Examining the full range of lifestyle experiments of the 1960s and 1970s, cultural historian Peter Clecak argued that many of the cultural developments of those decades were best understood as "the democratization of personhood":

> A quest for personal fulfillment within a small community (or several communities) of significant others: this strikes me as the dominant thrust of American civilization during the sixties and seventies. . . . The quest . . . is a multifaceted search conducted with varying degrees of intensity and different specific aims by elements of the population as diverse as born-again Christians and atheistic feminists, gay-rights activists and red-neck males, mainline Protestants and hard-line conservatives.[7]

Linking this broad plurality of groups was their mutual enjoyment of expanded protections for basic civil rights and their shared expectation that their own self-development (what Clecak called "a healthy thickening of individuality") was a worthy life goal.

During the same years, empirical evidence suggested that a psychotherapeutic conception of the individual and its needs was rapidly becoming normative. On the basis of nationally representative surveys of mental health in the United States in 1957 and 1976, Joseph Veroff and his colleagues wrote in their book, *The Inner American*, that Americans in the 1970s "had a stronger sense of the self as a differentiated being":

> Many more people take a positive view of the self and are sensitive to more psychological aspects of their strengths and unique qualities. One can think of these changes as reflecting a more integrated identity, a stronger sense of the self as an individual being with differentiated ways of responding to the world. Whereas we were a society somewhat more bound and defined by social roles in 1957, we seem to have moved toward a more personalized self-consciousness in 1976.[8]

In tandem with their new psychological sensitivity, Americans also were increasingly willing to seek expert advice for personal troubles. In 1957, 14 percent of survey respondents reported having visited a professional for help with "personal problems"; by 1976 that figure had risen to 26 percent.[9] At least as far as the surveys could measure, Americans appeared to be more concerned about who they were, and about what troubled them, as individuals.

Whether the aggrandized individualism reported in these books was something new and troubling or a minor episode in the history of modern subjectivity was a question on which academics would continue to disagree. The *Habits* authors themselves pointed out that Americans' precocious individualism was but a recent development in the complicated life of the modern self. This remarkable creature, offspring of a long Western philosophical tradition and the world-altering changes of industrialization, is so pivotal to our contemporary worldview that we tend to take its peculiarities for granted. We assume, for example, that persons have inner lives that can be hidden, or nourished, or squelched by the outside world. But we usually fail to recognize that this way of thinking about persons as having interiors is an historically situated idea.[10] We take for granted that *individuals*, not their families or other traditional authorities, rightly determine their own fates. We forget that there is significant variation over time and across cultures in the extent to which individuals are presumed to be the ultimate arbiters of their own lives.[11] Our distinctively American individualism, one rather more given to personal autonomy and more skeptical of government than its European cousins, had not been born yesterday.

But as the end of the twentieth century approached, many argued that our individualism had become more greedy, more self-absorbed.[12]

Perhaps it is little coincidence, then, that since the 1960s Americans have developed ever more elaborate means of nurturing little selves when they are children, and for accommodating their distinctiveness as they grow. One part of the cultural ferment of the 1960s generation that has seen few critics is the field of alternative education.[13] This little world saw explosive growth during the 1960s and 1970s, and while the heyday of the progressive school reform movement is over, the animating spirit of that cause—namely, a commitment to the liberation of young individuals—lives on. Over the last several decades the children of the 1960s and 1970s, now all grown up and with kids of their own, have been an eager market for educational entrepreneurs who promise new and better ways of nurturing children's inner essences and catering to their individual needs.

Sharing temporal space with home schoolers in recent educational history are several other pedagogies that preach the doctrine of childhood interiors and the importance of elaborately individualized instruction. Perhaps the most famous of these is the Montessori method. Devised in Italy by Maria Montessori in the early years of the twentieth century, this approach first met acceptance in the United States in the early 1960s. Today the International Montessori Index claims some four thousand Montessori-certified schools nationwide.[14] Central to Montessori philosophy is the notion that children have innate and powerful selves from the moment of their birth. "The greatness of the human personality begins at the hour of birth," Maria Montessori wrote in her book *The Absorbent Mind*.[15] The goal of teaching is to facilitate the development of that personality. This work can only be done through intimate knowledge of the child as an individual. As a Montessori educator explains,

> Montessori teachers do not "teach" the child in the usual way. They observe the children in order to discover their needs and interests based on their stages in self-formation and their individual personalities. They then attempt to present just the materials or activities to the children that match their developmental needs. It is in the children's subsequent independent use of these materials and activities that learning takes place.[16]

As with John Holt's unschooled child, the Montessori child leads the teacher. It is the child's own capacities and proclivities that rightly are in charge of the pedagogical relationship.

Another Italian import that is turning heads in this country is the Reggio Emilia approach, developed in the progressive Italian city of the same name. Originally conceived as one component of a comprehensive social

183

service program for all young children in Reggio Emilia, it is the pedagogical component of the approach that early childhood professionals have most eagerly carried to the United States. As with Montessori, the Reggio approach presumes the inherent potential of individual children. As an early childhood specialist explains, "The educators in Reggio Emilia view the child as protagonist. Children are strong, rich, and capable. All children have preparedness, potential, curiosity, and interest in constructing their learning, negotiating with everything their environment brings to them."[17] Reggio is arguably even more sensitive to children's individualism than its elder Italian sister, and thus more labor-intensive as well. Reggio teachers work in pairs with small numbers of children, carefully observing as the children reveal their distinctive characteristics through loosely scripted art and play activities. Teachers keep elaborate portfolios of the work of each child, both to document progress and to use as the basis for planning subsequent learning opportunities. While the approach is still novel in the United States, it is quickly gaining adherents among child development authorities and has begun to find organizational expression in a handful of schools across the country.

A third European model has found its niche in the U.S. market. Waldorf education, developed in 1919 in Germany for the children of workers at a Waldorf Astoria cigarette plant, has matured in subsequent generations as another acceptably unconventional school choice on both sides of the Atlantic. The Association of Waldorf Schools of North America claims 125 institutions in the United States. As conceived by its founding guru, Rudolph Steiner, and in the classroom practices that make it distinctive today, Waldorf education shares with home schooling the conviction that children have inner selves, as well as home schoolers' apprehension about forcing young minds to develop too quickly.

Steiner believed that before teachers ever get to them, children possess considerable knowledge of their world; it is the job of the teacher not to provide knowledge but rather to reveal what the child already knows. As with Holt's unschooling, Waldorf pedagogy embodies "the belief that everyone—assuming no obvious handicap—has the ability to do everything well, though that ability must often be discovered, or rediscovered."[18] This discovery process requires the teacher to know each child intimately, and to that end Waldorf teachers follow cohorts of children throughout their elementary school years, accumulating knowledge about individual children in an extended time window that more closely approximates parenting than conventional, age-graded teaching. Another component of Waldorf doctrine mirrors Raymond and Dorothy Moore's convictions about delayed formal instruction: Waldorf teachers are discouraged from forcing children to read and write at a particular age, under the caution that developmental damage will be caused if children are obliged to learn a skill at an inappropriate stage in their journeys to maturity.[19]

Waldorf, Reggio Emilia, Montessori, and home schooling are somewhat rarefied tastes in the marketplace of American education. Nevertheless, their growing popularity in recent decades and their shared convictions about the nature of childhood are suggestive. In all four approaches, children are assumed to have precocious inner beings whose individuality must be honored and celebrated. And all four approaches abandon conventional classrooms in favor of more flexible, less bureaucratic educational environments that give the individual learner more room. Despite the various historical eras and social contexts in which they were first conceived, all these methods have found supportive audiences in a contemporary culture increasingly enamored of its self. In keeping with the current of the broader culture, America's more innovative educators have developed novel and elaborate means for nurturing childhood selves as well. Their imports and innovations have found an eager clientele.

Growing convictions about the importance of children's individualism show up not only on the boutique margins of the educational marketplace. The tendency to conceive of students as individual cases, what political scientist David Paris calls "clientelism," is evident in a wide range of reform agendas. Curricular programs that differentiate among students on the basis of student preference or ability, such as tracking schemes, are predicated on the notion that services should be variably tailored to variable inputs. The individualized educational programs ("IEPs") that have become virtually standard procedure for children with physical or learning disabilities follow a similar logic. Notably, educational reform agendas on both left and right derive legitimacy from the logic of clientelism. On the left, the notion that schools should serve as social welfare agencies, meeting the needs of "the whole person" beyond the classroom, invites school officials to think about student needs in more case-specific ways. On the right, the argument that families ought to be able to choose schools that best fit their needs presumes that individual differences should be accommodated, not standardized away. "That such disparate kind of proposals could be simultaneously considered, as they currently are, is testimony to the rhetorical strength of arguments based on individual need," Paris writes.[20] I would add only that the rhetorical strength of clientelism is itself historically situated, in a contemporary culture increasingly given to the accommodation of distinctive individuals.

While it may be tempting to see it as a secular phenomenon, the expansion of the self is evident across the spectrum of American religion as well. A range of scholarship suggests that in the 1970s and 1980s the organization of religious life changed in ways that accommodated greater personal discretion among the faithful. In the wake of Vatican II the Catholic Church encouraged a diminishment of the hierarchy between priesthood and laity in matters of faith, as well as greater lay participation in parish administration. American Catholicism also witnessed a charismatic renewal movement that encouraged a rich spiritual life mediated less by the priesthood and more by individual connectedness with the spirit of God. Among Protestants, nondenominational movements such as Calvary Chapel, Vineyard, and Hope Chapel grew quickly. Attracting baby boomers skeptical about rule-bound religion, stiff pews, and unspoken dress codes, these movements lend primacy to believers' personal faith in Christ over adherence to worship and lifestyle convention; their grassroots organizational expressions leave individual congregations considerable freedom to govern themselves as they choose. And across the whole spectrum of faith in America, religious organizations have granted more flexibility to their congregants, who have come to expect and demand greater discretion over how to express their individual faith commitments.[21]

Not just the form but also the content of contemporary Protestant worship suggests that these believers conceive of the modern self as a more opinionated and empowered creature than have previous theological generations. Examining sermons written by Presbyterian and Southern Baptist ministers across the country, for example, sociologist Marsha Witten finds that both kinds of pastors preach a remarkably timely gospel. In contemporary Protestant theology the unsaved self, while sinful, is regarded also as having a measure of goodness. Although fallen, this self is aware of its divine needs and worthy of salvation. Conversion is described as an extension of divine grace but also a proactive, progressive effort toward greater happiness and fulfillment. Witten concludes:

> The course of the American Protestant experience has seen an increasing emphasis on the democratic and voluntarist nature of conversion, heightening the notion of the importance of individual self-knowledge and self-awareness in religious transformation. Once people become aware of themselves, this notion suggests, conversion is largely under their control. . . . [Conversion] talk serves to heighten certain characteristics that are innate in human beings and teaches listeners that they need to shed the artificial qualities that overshadow their essential selves. Once the inner self of the person

is freed from artifice, she may achieve both the desire and the competence to form the interpersonal relationship with God.[22]

Like John Holt's unschooled child, the unsaved self bears within it an essence that needs uncovering and that is capable of acting in its own best interests. Like Raymond and Dorothy Moore's homegrown kids, the contemporary Protestant self is both good and evil, needing divine direction but also worthy of love.

It is in a religious universe increasingly persuaded of the integrity and potential of the self that Christian home education has flourished. Home schooling enables believers to enact their faith's admonition about living apart from the secular world; but the practice of home schooling is itself very much in keeping with the broader culture's elaborated understandings of children's individual needs. Similarly, believer pedagogy, which simultaneously stresses children's sinfulness and goodness, has echoes both in conservative Protestant theology and in the broader culture's celebration of self-potential. These affinities by themselves, however, do not explain the extraordinary popularity of home schooling among conservative Protestants. Ultimately, it is conservative Protestants' deep commitment to full-time motherhood that has made them such a ready audience for home education.

"I was a feminist. I was going to go out there and conquer the world," Molly Ganz told me one afternoon at the very end of my fieldwork. She was talking about her college years in the mid-1970s, soon before she had children, and years before she would go on to become one of the most accomplished advocates for Christian home education in the state of Illinois. "Even at a Baptist college it was very big, the feminist movement," she explained. But "everything changed when I had my first baby. I did that nasty thing of bonding and didn't want to leave my baby." Molly's derision of the feminist doctrine that women can manage both paid work and motherhood is the evident undertone here. Elsewhere in our conversation, the distaste came to the surface.

"You see all the television shows, the magazines, pressuring women to be in a cultural war against their own families . . . so many of us have to deal with being supermom," she said. Molly had been something of a renegade even when her children were small. "I was an earth mom of sorts; when nobody was breast-feeding, I did. I did have my kids in a hospital. Had I known, I would have probably had them at home." Molly stayed home with her children during their earliest years but went back to work, at a Christian bookstore, when her husband's job situation changed and the money got tight. The children went into child care at a local church. Recounting the first day apart from her kids, years after the fact, tears came to her eyes:

> I still remember the horror. . . . I remember standing there, there was this window at the day care center . . . and I remember seeing my little eighteen-month-old just standing there with his thumb in his mouth, with his security blanket. . . . I remember thinking in my head, "They'll take care of you. I've got a boss and I've got to get going." And I remember just shutting down the emotion and leaving. I walked away.

Like millions of American mothers, Molly struggled with the contradictions inherent in trying to raise children and leave home for work. But as time passed she grew more comfortable with the emotional fault line, even grew to enjoy her job. "I was really making progress in my job. I was having my career. . . . I was moving up," she said with bitter sarcasm.

Then she got pregnant again, and was not happy about it. "I cannot afford three babies in day care," she remembers thinking. But in retrospect she describes this time in her life as one of spiritual rebellion:

> I was rebellious. . . . It's part of my spiritual journey because I was on the verge of rejecting what a woman should be. I was rejecting God's design for me. [I thought] "Oh God, you made me a woman, and I've got to deal with this pregnancy," . . . and the feminist view is so horrible, it's so horrible to make women reject the most wonderful and fulfilling thing.

The troubles that feminism attributes to the structural organization of work and family—declining male wages, inadequate workplace child care, unequal distributions of housework, and the different emotional tempos of motherhood and the workplace—Molly here ascribes to feminism itself. Like many believer women, Molly's solution to the troubles was not a critique of conventional parenting and work arrangements but rather an embrace of those arrangements along with some significant renovations. The necessary repair work entails rebuilding motherhood to make it look more like a job. Molly talks about home schooling as "a career in and of itself, even though it's not recognized. It's a career. It's a choice. . . . I don't get paid to do what I do, but it is nevertheless valuable."[23]

For Molly Ganz and tens of thousands of conservative Protestant women, home schooling provides both the means for making sense of deep maternal commitments and a way of life that celebrates those commitments. Christian home schooling has flourished at the intersection of a growing cultural sensitivity to the needs of children as individuals and a religious worldview that cautions women about the dangers of going too far astray from a traditionalist model of motherhood. The rhetorical brilliance of Christian homeschool leaders has been to subtly weave together several cultural threads that run close to these women's hearts: one about living apart from the world; one about the distinctive needs of individual children; one about the importance of motherhood and Christian families; and a fourth, feminist-inspired notion that women are entitled to meaningful work (a "career") in addition to motherhood. That the Christian homeschool movement has flourished is testament both to the appeal of this discursive tapestry and to the commitment of a veritable army of homeschooling women.

The logic of contemporary individualism presents all contemporary mothers, feminist or not, with a deep dilemma. On the one hand, conventional wisdom now encourages women to be cautious about family encroachments on the integrity of their own identities. Making too many sacrifices for husbands and children is regarded as problematic for women's own self-development and psychic health. On the other hand, contemporary assumptions about the nature of childhood oblige parents to invest ever more maternal labor in their children. At the same time that women *as women* have learned to be more defensive about their own needs, then, they also have faced increasing demands *as mothers* to honor their children's individual needs.

By making the terms of contemporary childhood into the rationale for a social movement, home schoolers have shown us what a demanding creature that childhood can be. It is cranky about standardized treatment, preferring customized service: from schools certainly, but also from churches and child care providers and the wide array of organizations that help parents nurture little selves into maturity. Our contemporary child needs to be understood in all its uniqueness, ideally by a full-time mother but in any case from some one or two grown-ups who are heroically committed to putting in the time. It is confident that, if its own needs require it, there are exceptions to every rule. In exchange for the trouble it causes, this childhood offers enormous promise. If allowed to go its way, there can be no predicting its accomplishments down the line. Nevertheless, in the meantime this precocious being requires a lot of mothering.

Moving back and forth between them over the years, I could not help but make comparisons between the inclusives' and the believers' subtly different childhoods. Both of them ask a lot from their world, but it seemed to me that the believers' demands less. The believers have a conception of children, indeed of the self more broadly, that both accommodates individual distinctiveness and obliges individuals to collective rules. Children are God's gift, made in God's image. But they also are sinful, requiring authoritative direction and correction. After all, the Heavenly Father also has given unarguable laws of conduct by which all people must live. He also has placed some persons in positions of rightful authority, from whence they can attempt to model human affairs in accord with God's design. A crucial piece of that design is that mothers and fathers have rightful authority over their children and are to train their children in the ways of righteousness. Thus the believers' conception of childhood checks some of the more untoward and unpredictable features of contemporary individualism. Because they are his children, God has imbued all people with precious and distinctive gifts, which may take a lifetime to fully discover. But humans' sinful nature means that all must also be instructed and disciplined at times.

As with unschooled kids, the believers' children are loved in all their uniqueness, and their little selves are given constant protection and cultivation. But they also are taught early on that their lives will develop in relationship with many others, that individuals will sacrifice some measure of comfort to the group as a matter of course, and that all selves, big and small, must develop within clearly prescribed moral boundaries. The believers have been able to raise this more manageable childhood in part because a shared religious worldview makes it possible for them to approach agreement, not on all the details of living, but at least on some basic house rules. To that extent their model of childhood is inapplicable in more diverse communities. Still, nonbelievers can take some important cues from these neighbors. Conservative Protestant parents are very willing to talk about imposing limits on their children, and to do so in a language of moral obligation. For a middle-class America increasingly given to accommodating not only the needs but also the desires of its children, the believers offer an instructive dissenting voice.

That said, the believers' parenting philosophy raises difficult questions about the line between parental and individual rights. Most troubling to outsiders is the issue of how far believers go in scripting their children's life choices. A Christian homeschool conference I attended as this book went to press carried the theme "Passing the Torch—That the Generation to Come Might Know." One of the guest speakers that weekend was Doug Phillips, formerly the director of HSLDA's Congressional Action Program and now the head of his own ministry, Vision Forum ("a new experiment in Christ-centered publishing and family discipleship"). In a session titled "Preparing Sons for Marriage and Life Purpose," Phillips spoke passionately about the virtues of early and lifelong wedlock. I learned that morning that adolescence was a "nineteenth-century evolutionary concept" that can prevent young people from reaching maturity on God's timetable. I was told that men and women have "a Christian obligation and duty" to get married, unless they had been granted what Phillips called the "gift of celibacy." Young women in the audience were reminded that wifely submission and full-time motherhood were the commandments and the blessings of their Heavenly Father.[24] This is a world in which many of life's big questions are answered for you. As several sensitive observers have pointed out, conservative religious communities offer contemporary men and women rich opportunities for intellectually coherent and emotionally satisfying lives.[25] But we might ask whether such lifeways are appropriately chosen, not imposed.

Perhaps because they are so intent on making sure that the torch gets passed, the believers are refreshingly explicit about the human costs of raising children. They devote considerable energy to explaining why children "need" full-time mothers, and they also are careful to celebrate the doing of that work. One need not agree with all their arguments to give the believers credit for understanding, in no uncertain terms, that the flip side of child development is maternal obligation. It is no secret that the believers get their nurturing done by categorically assigning most of it to mothers. This is a strategy that, like their childhood, is essentially unworkable for many Americans: those women who want their biographies to include more than the labors of home, and those who believe—rightly, I think—that the gendered division of child rearing perpetuates broader patterns of gender inequality.[26] Nevertheless, the believers' lively conversation about all it takes to fully accommodate the labors of parenting is one that nonbelievers can learn from. Indeed, and as others have suggested, conservative Protestantism's active engagement of the contradiction between home and work may help to explain the continued appeal of this faith tradition in contemporary American life.[27]

Somewhat paradoxically, conservative Protestantism's dualistic conception of the self may also contribute to the tradition's ongoing vitality. The simultaneity of human goodness and human sinfulness at the heart of believer theology makes it an extremely flexible cultural resource. On the one hand, the ministers and ministries of the last thirty years have been able to create Christianities that honor the broader culture's growing demand for more experiential, more psychologized, and more individualized faith experiences. At the same time, the dualistic self has made it possible for conservative Protestant leaders to legitimately call their followers to rethink some life choices, give up some freedoms, make some sacrifices for faith and family, and, sometimes, simply to obey.

But another consequence of the dualistic self is that conservative Protestants have rather distinctive assumptions about how individuals most appropriately come together. Conservative Protestants famously divide the world in two. As Carol Ingram told me that afternoon at HSLDA, "We are either saved or we're lost." The believers assume that rather different rules govern their spiritual kingdom, and because this is so they often have little expectation that nonbelievers will necessarily agree with them or make the right decisions. There is no presumption that everyone's opinion, all points of view, are equally valid. In practice, this means that when one is working in "the world" (as believers often call whatever is beyond their own), one must always be ready to walk away from the table when consensus, majority rule, or the law precludes obedience to heavenly command.

This distinction has meant that believers tend to be ambivalent about the organizational forms favored by other contemporary political activists. Home schoolers like Deirdre Brown and her colleagues in the NHA have championed organizational forms that they believe are best suited to honoring all the variation in the homeschool rainbow. But time and again, and to their sometimes uncomprehending chagrin, inclusives have found that the believers are not very interested in celebrating diversity. The believers' disinterest in inclusion is troubling to secular activists, who regard this sensibility as old-fashioned at best, and ethnocentric or even bigoted at worst. But for conservative Protestants, their division of the world has little to do with the political or human status of nonbelievers. It is instead a question of which authorities matter most: God's or men's. Our culture is increasingly given to the assumption that persons are essentially good and rightly make their own decisions; but faith in human sinfulness and in divine intention is a central feature of the believers' worldview. As the history of the homeschool movement indicates, this difference can be difficult to talk across. More broadly, it places many believers outside the coordinates of sense making by which a secular society judges social movements as modern or reactionary, humanitarian or merely self-interested, morally respectable or morally suspect.

Of course, not every believer hears God's commands in the same way. As centuries of theology and an eclectic contemporary Protestant universe demonstrate, there are multiple ways of imagining Christian life in a secular world. But when it comes to building a social movement, not all points of view can have equal sway. The imperatives of organizing oblige people to make choices about *how* to assemble their causes. This means that some visions are given concrete organizational expression, and thus more definitive power over how things will be done. In the course of opting for any particular organizational strategy, other points of view are weakened or even banished. The "Christian" homeschool movement is decidedly conservative and exclusive not because the basic tenets of Protestant theology require it but because the primary architects of the movement's organizational system have designed *their* theology into the plans. Calling their organizations expressly "Christian" discourages more ecumenical memberships in believer organizations, while fundamentalist statements of faith exclude Christians like Lissa Foster. This turn of events in homeschool history betrays a broader sociological truth: questions about how to organize are always political ones.

The inclusives have faced their own struggles about organizational questions, but the demographics of their cause have set different parameters for the politics from the beginning. In an important sense the inclusives face a more difficult challenge than the believers: inclusives have a much thinner stock of shared organizational experiences on which to draw. Consensus and other highly democratic forms have come to define the inclusives' organizational landscape, but this may be because no alternative organizational forms have elicited a constituency powerful enough to change the rules. Given the utter diversity of the inclusive cause, one might wonder where such a constituency might come from in any case. With so many different religious traditions and organizational histories represented among inclusive home schoolers, highly democratic forms may be the only ones on which any number of them can agree.[28]

As the inclusives know from experience, democracy and inclusion are not without their troubles. Sluggishness in decision making and unpredictable resource commitments are the downside of organizational forms that lend a lot of discretion to individuals. The inclusives may have to learn the hard way that pure democracy can come at the cost of organizational survival. Like many left-leaning movements of recent decades, the inclusives have perhaps been too quick to disparage bureaucratic organizational forms. In being heroically committed to the sanctity of individual discretion, they have forgotten some important lessons of social movements before them: that hierarchical divisions of labor and authority make the completion of complex tasks more efficient; that clearly scripting the terms of organizational participation makes life easier for volunteers; and that people often *want* leaders, who can help the group make sense of complicated issues, make hard decisions, and ensure that the long-term health of the cause is not occluded by people who care little about the big picture.

But if the inclusives have so far failed to capitalize on the advantages of bureaucracy, they also have developed an enviable organizational skill. They have become masters at talking across difference. Their conviction that human diversity is positive, and must be accommodated, is an appropriate organizational philosophy for an increasingly heterogeneous American society. Putting that philosophy into practice means that more time needs to be spent in conversation, and that fewer terms of organizational process can be taken for granted. But the payoffs can be significant: a cosmopolitan constituency and a greater sense of collective ownership of the cause. Finally, the inclusives deserve credit for thinking hard about what is perhaps the most formidable civic challenge of our era: the puzzle of how to sustain unity and honor difference at the same time.

The believers, on the other hand, have largely avoided the puzzle of difference. Partly because they tend to bifurcate the world into the saved and unsaved, and partly because their earthly kingdom is itself so large and diverse in its own right, the believers have not yet learned how to accommodate voices and experiences beyond their religious ken. If they are to have the impact on the broader society that their leaders increasingly demand of them, the believers simply must make theological and organizational choices that more easily bring them into commerce with their non-Christian neighbors. Otherwise they will continue to save some souls and win some political battles but will fail to change the minds of even their mildest critics. At stake is the extent to which the believers are heard as reactionary dissenters or progressive leaders in contemporary conversations about children, schooling, motherhood, and family in America. The inclusives show us that polyglot conversations on these issues are possible, but only if participants are willing to negotiate the ground rules of the discussion and to make some compromises along the way.

Throughout the homeschool movement, talk about how best to link constituencies continued through the end of the 1990s. Some inclusive advocates, frustrated by what appeared to them as the political incapacity of the NHA, maintained a years-long conversation on the Internet about how to create an inclusive national organization that could be rigorously democratic without sacrificing political muscle. On the other side of the movement, the believers became aware that their open embrace of computer technology might have important consequences for the hierarchy of authority in their cause. When the H.R. 6 controversy erupted in 1994, HSLDA had relied on a fax network with state-level organizations to disseminate the news. The explosion of the Internet in subsequent years means that HSLDA is now able to make direct contact with its rank and file. Rather than relying on state leaders to disseminate news by phone, HSLDA has the potential to reach its entire constituency in a few keystrokes. Thus it is not surprising that by the end of the decade, some state-level leaders were thoughtful about how technological changes might alter their movement's division of labor.

Even while home schoolers continued to tinker with the mechanics of their cause, some things wouldn't change, at least not by the time my work came to a close. Inclusives continued to be quietly suspicious and sometimes publicly critical of the believers' leadership elite. The believers, safe and powerful in their own organizational apparatus, continued to more or less ignore the criticism. And home schooling maintained its place on the menu of educational choices—a specialty option perhaps, but a viable one nevertheless. If anything, home schooling became more elaborated internally and more acceptable to the outside world. Inside, homeschool ministries were creating college and apprenticeship programs tailor-made for their young people. There were homeschool debate tournaments, athletic competitions, senior proms. Outside, elite colleges and universities began adding special information for homeschooled applicants to their Web sites. Major booksellers like Barnes & Noble and Amazon.com, eager to serve the growing market, designated shelves and Web pages specifically for homeschooling titles. Home schooling continued to receive media coverage, especially in the wake of tragedies like the 1999 high school shootings in Littleton, Colorado, which had reporters contacting activists like Deirdre Brown with renewed interest. And it seemed that the press attention got more favorable over the years. In 2000, a feature article in the *New York Times Magazine* likened a Christian homeschool family to the progressive cultural critics of the 1960s. Later that year, a *Wall Street Journal* editorial admonished mainstream educators to finally acknowledge home schoolers' evident academic accomplishments.[29]

As it has become normalized, the risks of actually doing home schooling have diminished. People who came in during the late 1990s joined a different movement than their compatriots had a decade before. "They don't really see all of the work that went into making home schooling what it is today," one longtime activist told me, comparing the newcomers with the old hands. "They think they can just join in relatively easily. And they can. They can do that now, but there's a different level of commitment."[30] Made more acceptable and immeasurably easier by the work of the pioneers, by the end of the 1990s home schooling had become a fully institutionalized if still unconventional educational choice. Being a home schooler now means something different and likely feels different than it did fifteen years ago. In its very success, home schooling has gained a good measure of respectability while losing some of its cutting-edge riskiness and countercultural cachet.[31]

Over the years that home schoolers have won their victories, it has gotten easier to forget that there was once a time when the theories of people like John Holt and the Moores were radical or even unthinkable, a time when our children's individualism threatened the legitimacy of conventional schooling less dramatically. It has become hard to remember a time when life was not typically imagined as an open and uncharted journey, rife with possibilities that only the individual can rightly choose for herself. Over the years we have forgotten that, not too long ago, parenting generally took place in the flow of diversified household economies. In a preindustrial era when mothers and many fathers worked at home, full-time attentiveness to one's children to the exclusion of other work was an unthinkable luxury. As our world has changed and, with it, our sense of our selves, it seems to have escaped our notice that the distinctive, autonomous, promising individualism that we now take for granted needs to be a child first. It needs to be raised.

Just why we have overlooked the reproductive costs of the expanded self is a question worth asking. We have, after all, considered at length its challenges for a healthy civic life.[32] And of course the high price of rearing individuals is right in front of us, every day. We see it in the hard choices mothers make in deciding between home and career, in the guilt some parents feel in sending their kids to group child care, and in the parenting manuals that increasingly encourage mothers and fathers to be child development experts. The total cost of developing a generation of little individuals is likely incalculable, but it is certainly high for all of us, and especially for women.

Perhaps we have failed to recognize how much nurturing little selves require, precisely because so much of that work is accomplished by women. Feminists have long understood that nurturing is gendered work and often invisible. Women disproportionately shoulder the burden of this invisibility in several ways: in lost wages, but also in diminished social status for the nurturing jobs that they do.[33] Consider, for example, that Americans rate child care workers near garbage collectors on a scale of occupational prestige.[34]

Nurturing one's own children also comes with status dilemmas. As many have pointed out, being "just a mom" brings paltry prestige in the career-oriented status system of the broader culture. But there is also evidence that the mechanics of mothering are often derided even in the more tender status economy of home. Many women report incomprehension or dismissiveness from their husbands when they talk about the mental work of mothering that no one sees. Thinking fastidiously about the daily details of parenting is work that is arguably crucial to honoring individual needs. But fathers often ignore this mental work, or else chastise their partners for "worrying" about the details to a point of obsession.[35] Whether hidden inside an ethos of sacrificial motherhood, derided as unskilled, or dismissed as maternal pathology, it may be that the labors of self-making are kept hidden precisely because they are so costly. If so, then making those costs explicit is a revolutionary activity, challenging a social system that profits from exploiting the work that women, as nurturers, do.[36]

But it may be also that the costs of raising selves have eluded us because they attend to an object called childhood, something so esteemed in modern life that at least one astute observer has called it sacred.[37] As Émile Durkheim pointed out years ago, sacred things are the primary symbols through which a society defines itself. They embody our most basic notions about who we are as a collective and who ideally we want to be. Because their meanings are so fundamental to a cultural system, sacred things are carefully protected from inquisition. Doing so is accomplished through any number of rules and rituals that preclude skeptics and the uninitiated from getting too close. Durkheim argued that one telltale mark of the sacred is an extreme reluctance to ask the hard questions about it— to voice suspicion about what's really inside that box, to wonder out loud if the gods might be appeased some other way.[38] It may be that we have not asked harder questions about our childhood because it embodies some of our most cherished beliefs about who Americans really are: free people, individuals, full of possibility, requiring little of others.

Home schoolers have asked those hard questions. And despite their very different conceptions about how best to get the work done, they share some powerful convictions about what children need. The movement they have built in the name of those convictions challenges the rest of us to some hard talk about a costly and precocious institution at the very heart of our collective life.

༻ஜ༺

Hints from my fieldwork suggest that once upon a time, home schoolers thought they were less like the rest of us, and more like each other.

Old-timers talk about the early years of their movement with nostalgia. "Those were the honeymoon days of home schooling," Michael Farris told me in an interview, talking about the early 1980s. "Everyone was trying to help each other out. Home schoolers all got along then. You took help wherever you could get it."[39] Needless to say, those days did not last forever. But testament to the character of this smart little movement, even the end of the honeymoon is instructive.

Home schoolers have always been a diverse lot. For many of the inclusives and even some of the believers, that diversity was titillating, part of the fun. It was not their ways of life or religious beliefs that divided them in the end, but rather their different sensibilities about how to organize. Home schoolers parted ways because they could not agree on who would be welcome in their associations, who would be in charge, or how decisions would be made. As with so many soured relations, the crucial points of disagreement long went unnoticed, lurking just beyond the pale of explicit discussion, even under smiling displays of unity. But the differences were evident if one took the time to look for them, cared to see. They showed up in apparently inconsequential details: the inclusives' penchant for circles, and the believers' easy use of words like *leader*. It turned out that those little things were a big deal, and a lasting lesson. The most consequential differences had to do with the arrangement of the chairs.

Notes

INTRODUCTION

1. This way of metaphorizing precocious social actors is hardly my own. See, e.g., Howard S. Becker, *Outsiders: Studies in the Sociology of Deviance* (New York: Free Press, 1963), chap. 8; Paul DiMaggio, "Interest and Agency in Institutional Theory," in *Institutional Patterns and Organizations: Culture and Environment*, ed. Lynne G. Zucker (Cambridge, Mass.: Ballinger, 1988), 4–21.

2. Scholars are just now beginning to understand how the 1960s affected biographies on the conservative right as well as the liberal left. See, e.g., Rebecca E. Klatch, *A Generation Divided: The New Left, the New Right, and the 1960s* (Berkeley: University of California Press, 1999); Maurice Isserman and Michael Kazin, *America Divided: The Civil War of the 1960s* (New York: Oxford University Press, 2000).

3. Elisabeth S. Clemens, "Organizational Form as Frame: Collective Identity and Political Strategy in the American Labor Movement, 1880–1920," in *Comparative Perspectives on Social Movements*, ed. Doug McAdam, John D. McCarthy, and Mayer N. Zald (Cambridge: Cambridge University Press, 1996), 205–26.

CHAPTER ONE
Inside Home Education

1. For a broad summary of the institutional position of education in modern life, see John W. Meyer, "The Effects of Education as an Institution," *American Journal of Sociology* 83 (July 1977): 55–77.

2. Patricia M. Lines, *Homeschoolers: Estimating Numbers and Growth* (Washington, D.C.: National Institute on Student Achievement, Curriculum, and Assessment, Office of Education Research and Improvement, U.S. Department of Education, spring 1998).

3. *Home Education across the United States* (Purcellville, Va.: Home School Legal Defense Association, 1997), 2–3.

4. Estimate of the number of charter school students is from Bruno V. Manno, Chester E. Finn Jr., and Gregg Vanourek, "Beyond the Schoolhouse Door: How Charter Schools Are Transforming U.S. Public Education," *Phi Delta Kappan* 81 (June 2000): 736–44. See also Chester E. Finn Jr., Bruno V. Manno and Gregg Vanourek, *Charter Schools in Action: Renewing Public Education* (Princeton, N.J.: Princeton University Press, 2000); Amy Stuart Wells, Alejandra Lopez, Janelle Scott, and Jennifer Jellison Holme, "Charter Schools as Postmodern Paradox: Rethinking Social Stratification in an Age of Deregulated School Choice," *Harvard Educational Review* 69 (summer 1999): 172–204; Joe Nathan, *Charter Schools:*

Creating Hope and Opportunity for American Education (San Francisco: Jossey-Bass, 1996). Thanks to Jeff Archer for suggesting the comparison with charter schools.

5. Section B-67 of the *1999–2000 NEA Resolutions* begins, "The National Education Association believes that home schooling programs cannot provide the student with a comprehensive educational experience" (http://www.nea.org/resolutions/99/99b-67.html; accessed 6/27/00). The NEA is cautiously supportive of charter schools (*1999–2000 Resolutions*, section A-26), as is the PTA (*National PTA Background Brief: Charter Schools*, http://www.pta.org; accessed 6/27/00).

6. But see Maralee Mayberry, "Characteristics and Attitudes of Families Who Home School," *Education and Urban Society* 21 (1988): 32–34; Brian D. Ray, "Home Schools: A Synthesis of Research on Characteristics and Learner Outcomes," *Education and Urban Society* 21 (1988): 16–31; Maralee Mayberry and J. Gary Knowles, "Family Unity Objectives of Parents Who Teach Their Children: Ideological and Pedagogical Orientations to Home Schooling," *Urban Review* 21 (1989): 209–25; J. Gary Knowles, "Parents' Rationales for Operating Home Schools," *Journal of Contemporary Ethnography* 20 (1991): 203–30; J. Gary Knowles, Stacey E. Marlow, and James A. Muchmore, "From Pedagogy to Ideology: Origins and Phases of Home Education in the United States, 1970–1990," *American Journal of Education* 100 (1992): 195–235. See also Jane Van Galen and Mary Anne Pitman, eds., *Home Schooling: Political, Historical, and Pedagogical Perspectives* (Norwood, N.J.: Ablex, 1991).

7. Maralee Mayberry, J. Gary Knowles, Brian Ray, and Stacey Marlow, *Home Schooling: Parents as Educators* (Thousand Oaks, Calif.: Corwin Press/Sage, 1995).

8. Ibid., 29–44. Mayberry et al.'s survey was based on a nonrandom convenience sample and is not statistically representative. I discuss this issue in the text that follows.

9. Ibid., 33.

10. Mayberry et al. did not provide complete breakdowns for respondents' denominational affiliations. They did note, however, that "approximately one third" of respondents "belong to Evangelical, Pentecostal, or other 'nondenominational' religious organizations" (35–36). Twenty-five percent of respondents were Mormon, a finding the authors interpret as an artifact of their sampling site (which included the state of Utah). In her broad survey of the national movement in the late 1980s, Patricia Lines found that most religious home educators were Protestants. See Patricia Lines, "Home Instruction: The Size and Growth of the Movement," in *Home Schooling*, ed. Van Galen and Pitman, 9–41.

11. Mayberry et al., *Home Schooling: Parents as Educators*, 36; emphasis in original.

12. Ibid., 36–37.

13. David Sikkink, "Public Schooling and Its Discontents: Religious Identities, Schooling Choices, and Civic Participation" (Ph.D. diss., University of North Car-

olina at Chapel Hill, 1998), 94–118. Sikkink cautions that his findings on home schoolers should not be regarded as definitive because only 135 families in the data set were home schoolers.

14. Reported in Brian D. Ray and John Wartes, "Academic Achievement and Affective Development," in *Home Schooling*, ed. Van Galen and Pitman, 43–62. Washington state law requires that all homeschooled children undergo a formal annual achievement assessment. Consequently, many individuals in the state have gone into the business of administering standardized tests to home educators. Wartes's findings are based on nonrandom samples of test providers, who, Wartes reports, supply him with 100 percent of the scores from tests they have administered in a given year. Reported sample sizes are as follows: 1986: N = 424; 1987: N = 873; 1988: N = 756. In no way should Wartes's findings be interpreted as statistically representative of home-educated children in Washington state, nor as official state figures.

15. Ibid.

16. Brian D. Ray, *Marching to the Beat of Their Own Drum* (Paeonian Springs, Va.: Home School Legal Defense Association), 7–9. Sampling procedures for the HSLDA SAT study were not reported in the study.

17. Lawrence M. Rudner, "Scholastic Achievement and Demographic Characteristics of Home School Students in 1998," *Educational Policy Analysis Archives* 7 (March 1999 [http://epaa.asu/epaa/v7/n8.html]). For critiques see Larry Kaseman and Susan Kaseman, "HSLDA Study: Embarrassing and Dangerous," *Home Education Magazine*, July–August 1999, 12–20; Kariane Mari Welner and Kevin G. Welner, "Contextualizing Homeschooling Data: A Response to Rudner," *Education Policy Analysis Archives* 7 (April 1999 [http://epaa.asu.edu/epaa/v7n13.html]).

18. The state of Oregon, for example, which requires standardized test scores from homeschool families, received scores for only 1,658 of its 3,102 registered homeschool children during the 1987–88 academic year. Reported in Ray and Wartes, "Academic Achievement and Affective Development," 49.

19. Mary Pride, *The New Big Book of Home Learning* (Westchester, Ill.: Crossway Books, 1988).

20. "1999 Directory of Families and Organizations," *Growing Without Schooling* 126 (January/February 1999): 49–53.

21. See, e.g., "Home-School Organizations," *The Teaching Home*, May/June 1999, 33–35. *The Teaching Home* provides organizational contact information in every issue.

22. Alma C. Henderson, "The Home Schooling Movement: Parents Take Control of Educating Their Children," *Annual Survey of American Law* 1991 (1993): 985–1009; Jon S. Lerner, "Protecting Home Schooling through the Casey Undue Burden Standard," *University of Chicago Law Review* 62 (1995): 363–92.

23. Christian Smith and David Sikkink, "Is Private Schooling Privatizing?" *First Things* 92 (April 1999): 16–20; David Sikkink, "The Public Lives of Private

Schoolers: Schooling Organizations and Parents' Civic Participation" (paper presented at the Calvin Conference on "Religion, Social Capital, and Democratic Life," October 1998); Sikkink, "Public Schooling and Its Discontents," 119–36.

24. For a succinct statement on the nature and purpose of ethnographic research, see Clifford Geertz, "From the Native's Point of View: On the Nature of Anthropological Understanding," in his *Local Knowledge: Further Essays in Interpretive Anthropology* (New York: Basic Books, 1983), 55–70.

25. Kathy Charmaz, "The Grounded Theory Method: An Explication and Interpretation," in *Contemporary Field Research*, ed. Robert M. Emerson (Prospect Heights, Ill.: Waveland Press, 1983), 109–26.

26. In most cases, interviews were tape-recorded and transcribed. On occasions when tape-recording was not feasible, I made written, detailed notes soon after the interview event.

27. This finding is in keeping with those of Ray, "Home Schools: A Synthesis"; Mayberry, "Characteristics and Attitudes"; and Mayberry et. al, *Homeschooling: Parents as Educators*.

28. NICHE, the Catholic organization in Illinois, for example, has no formal statement of faith and thus has flexible membership rules, unlike the norm for the nominally "Christian" Protestant groups. From an organizational standpoint, the Jewish group is quite informal, consisting of a handful of families, a Web site, and a contact person. From interviews with Arlene Pulaski, 8/10/99; Shoshana Reichler, 7/12/99.

29. See Nancy Tatom Ammerman, *Bible Believers: Fundamentalists in the Modern World* (New Brunswick, N.J.: Rutgers University Press, 1987).

30. Of course, the believers are diverse in lifestyle as well, but they do share a common religious identity of which they are clearly mindful and proud. For the believers, organizational affiliation parallels (and, of course, helps to constitute) a much more prominent "us" than on the other side of the cause. I assess this variation in detail in Chapter 5.

31. I visited ten organizations active at the national level: Holt Associates (Cambridge, Mass.); the Home School Legal Defense Association (Purcellville, Va.); Clonlara School (Ann Arbor, Mich.); Christian Life Workshops (Gresham, Ore.); The Teaching Home (Portland, Ore.); the Hewitt Research Foundation (Washougal, Wash.); the Moore Foundation (Camas, Wash.); the National Homeschool Association (Cincinnati, Ohio, and various locations [see Chapters Five and Six]); the Institute for Basic Life Principles (Oak Brook, Ill.); and Christian Liberty Academy (Arlington Heights, Ill.).

32. For methodological statements on this practice, see Michael J. Bloor, "Notes on Member Validation," in *Contemporary Field Research*, ed. Emerson, 156–72; Anselm L. Strauss, *Qualitative Analysis for Social Scientists* (Cambridge: Cambridge University Press, 1987), 17–20.

33. Chicago remains Chicago, but more specific locations and names of particular suburbs have been avoided or altered.

34. I made exception to this general rule only when I decided that respondent anonymity required it. These exceptions are duly noted in the text.

35. The strategy is not without precedent. See, e.g., Kristin Luker, *Abortion and the Politics of Motherhood* (Berkeley: University of California Press, 1984); Lynn Davidman, *Tradition in a Rootless World: Women Turn to Orthodox Judaism* (Berkeley: University of California Press, 1991).

36. A particularly apt example of this work is Barrie Thorne, *Gender Play: Girls and Boys in School* (New Brunswick, N.J.: Rutgers University Press, 1993); see also William A. Corsaro, *The Sociology of Childhood* (Thousand Oaks, Calif.: Pine Forge Press, 1997).

37. See, e.g., Susan Richman, *Writing from Home: A Portfolio of Homeschooled Student Writing* (Kittanning, Pa.: PA Homeschoolers, 1990); Susannah Sheffer, *Writing Because We Love To: Homeschoolers at Work* (Portsmouth, N.H.: Boynton/Cook/Heinemann, 1992); Grace Llewellyn, ed., *Real Lives: Eleven Teenagers Who Don't Go to School* (Eugene, Ore.: Lowry House, 1993).

38. Deirdre Brown, interview, 3/19/91; emphasis reflects interview.

39. For overviews of this movement, see Allen Graubard, "The Free School Movement," *Harvard Educational Review* 42 (August 1972): 351–73; Allen Graubard, "From Free Schools to 'Educational Alternatives,'" in *Co-ops, Communes, and Collectives: Experiments in Social Change in the 1960s and 70s*, ed. John Case and Rosemary C. R. Taylor (New York: Pantheon, 1979), 49–65. For a critical account of the organizational structure and interactive dynamics of these schools, see Ann Swidler, *Organization without Authority: Dilemmas of Social Control in Free Schools* (Cambridge, Mass.: Harvard University Press, 1979).

40. Radically democratic organizational forms were common, though contested, features of the 1960s and 1970s women's movement. See, e.g., Jo Freeman, "The Tyranny of Structurelessness," *Berkeley Journal of Sociology* 17 (1972–73): 151–64; Myra Marx Ferree and Beth B. Hess, *Controversy and Coalition: The New Feminist Movement* (Boston: Twayne, 1985); Gretchen Arnold, "Dilemmas of Feminist Coalitions: Collective Identity and Strategic Effectiveness in the Battered Women's Movement," and Carol Mueller, "The Organizational Basis of Conflict in Contemporary Feminism," both in *Feminist Organizations: Harvest of the New Women's Movement*, ed. Myra Marx Ferree and Patricia Yancy Martin (Philadelphia: Temple University Press, 1995), 276–90 and 263–75, respectively.

41. John Holt, *How Children Fail* (New York: Pitman, 1964).

42. La Leche League is an organization that advocates breast-feeding. I discuss La Leche further in Chapter Three.

43. Deirdre Brown, interview, 8/10/95.

44. Deirdre Brown, interview, 3/19/91.

45. Theresa Marquette, interview, 2/22/00.

46. HOUSE later changed its name to Home Oriented *Unique* Schooling Experience, to indicate that the organization did not specifically advocate unschooling or any particular educational approach. Deirdre Brown, interview, 3/19/91.

47. Deirdre Brown, interview, 7/14/99.

48. Steve and Susan Jerome, interview, 6/10/95.

49. For an overview of the movement, see Susan D. Rose, "Christian Fundamentalism and Education in the United States," in *Fundamentalisms and Society*, ed. Martin E. Marty and R. Scott Appleby (Chicago: University of Chicago Press, 1993), 452–89. For relevant case studies, see Susan D. Rose, *Keeping Them Out of the Hands of Satan: Evangelical Schooling in America* (New York: Routledge, 1988); Melinda Bollar Wagner, *God's Schools: Choice and Compromise in American Society* (New Brunswick, N.J.: Rutgers University Press, 1990).

50. *People* v. *Levisen*, 404 Ill. 574, 90 N.E. 2d 213 (1950).

51. Steve and Susan Jerome, interview, 6/10/95.

52. Deirdre Brown, interview, 8/10/95.

53. Steve and Susan Jerome, interview, 6/10/95. By the late 1980s, another explicitly Christian homeschool organization had appeared in Illinois: Christian Home Educators Coalition (CHEC), a political advocacy concern that has remained active in the state. CHEC's primary emphasis has been on serving as a homeschool watchdog in state and local politics. There have been some tensions between CHEC and ICHE over the years, but in general the two concerns have worked cordially with one another and even have shared personnel. Molly Ganz, interview, 7/15/99.

54. "Ad Hoc Committee for Illinois Home Education, Legal and Legislative Matters," flyer, n.d., author's collection, received 1989.

55. Ibid. Deirdre Brown reminded me in 1999 that Ad Hoc's basic governing rules remained operative; interview, 7/14/99.

56. Gary Wisby, "Home Schoolers Split on Protest Tactics," *Chicago Sun-Times*, February 27, 1994, 12. Claims for larger numbers were made to me by some Christian leaders during follow-up research in July 1999.

CHAPTER TWO
From Parents to Teachers

1. Tara Cook, interview, 5/16/91.

2. Eric and Marci Rayburn, interview, 8/1/89.

3. This insight is Howard Becker's. See his *Outsiders: Studies in the Sociology of Deviance* (New York: Free Press, 1963).

4. Ginny Saunders, interview, 9/13/89.

5. Penny Turner, interview, 9/1/92.

6. Pamela Eckard, interview, 9/20/89.

7. Amy Jones, interview, 4/10/91.

8. Sally Norton, interview, 8/21/89.

9. For more general theoretical elaborations of this idea, see Marvin B. Scott and Stanford Lyman, "Accounts," *American Sociological Review* 33 (1968): 46–62; also C. Wright Mills, "Situated Actions and Vocabularies of Motive," *American Sociological Review* 5 (1940): 904–13.

10. This work is what what social movement scholars often refer to as the "framing" of problems. See, e.g., David E. Snow, Burke Rochford, Steven Worden, and Robert Benford, "Frame Alignment Processes, Mobilization, and Movement Participation," *American Sociological Review* 51 (1986): 464–81; David E. Snow and Robert Benford, "Ideology, Frame Resonance, and Participant Mobilization," *International Social Movement Research* 1 (1988): 197–217; David E. Snow and Robert Benford, "Master Frames and Cycles of Protest," in *Frontiers in Social Movement Theory*, ed. Aldon Morris and Carol McClurg Mueller (New Haven, Conn.: Yale University Press, 1992), 133–55. The emotional nuance and rhetorical complexity of such work are assessed in James Jasper, *The Art of Moral Protest: Culture, Biography, and Creativity in Social Movements* (Chicago: University of Chicago Press, 1997).

11. For more detailed discussions of the general claim I am making here, see Michèle Lamont, "How to Become a Dominant French Philosopher: The Case of Jacques Derrida," *American Journal of Sociology* 93 (1987): 584–622; and Wendy Griswold, *Bearing Witness: Readers, Writers, and the Novel in Nigeria* (Princeton, N.J.: Princeton University Press, 2000). For French philosophers and Nigerian novelists as for social movement activists, the character of the intellectual product is not by itself a sufficient condition for its successful reception. But—and this is the hard part for sociologists—the character of the product certainly matters.

12. See Allen Graubard, *Free the Children* (New York: Pantheon, 1972); Great Atlantic and Pacific School Conspiracy, *Doing Your Own School: A Practical Guide to Starting and Operating a Community School* (Boston: Beacon Press, 1972); Jonathan Kozol, *Free Schools* (Boston: Houghton Mifflin, 1972). Quotation is from Graubard, *Free the Children*, viii. For surveys of the movement see Chapter 1, note 39.

13. James Herndon, *Notes from a Schoolteacher* (New York: Simon and Schuster, 1985), 110; ellipses in original. Educational historian Sol Cohen concurs, adding that the anti-Establishment sensibility of those decades also spurred the advent of parallel "revisionist" histories of education forwarded by Michael Katz, J. H. Spring, E. B. Gumpert, David Tyack, and others. Cohen notes that these critical historians "were greatly influenced by the New Left movement in politics and social thought, as well as by social and educational critics like Paul Goodman, John Holt, Jonathan Kozol, Ivan Illich, and Theodore Roszak." Sol Cohen, "Reconstructing the History of Urban Education in America," in *Education and the City: Theory, History, and Contemporary Practice*, ed. Gerald Grace (London: Routledge and Kegan Paul, 1984), 115–38.

14. Herbert Kohl, *The Open Classroom* (New York: New York Review of Books/ Random House, 1969), 12.

15. Invoking personal experience to voice dissatisfaction with given power structures, and using that experience to frame alternative politics, was fervently exploited by the civil rights, and the women's movements. See Aldon D. Morris, *The Origins of the Civil Rights Movement* (New York: Free Press, 1984); Jo Freeman, *The Politics of Women's Liberation* (New York: Longman, 1975); Verta Taylor,

"Watching for Vibes: Bringing Emotion into the Study of Feminist Organizations," in *Feminist Organizations*, ed. Ferree and Martin, 223–33.

16. Kohl, *The Open Classroom*, 12.

17. Herbert Kohl, *Growing Minds: On Becoming a Teacher* (New York: Harper and Row, 1984), 64.

18. Herbert Kohl, *Reading, How To* (New York: Dutton, 1973), 202.

19. John Holt, *Instead of Education* (New York: Dutton, 1976), 4.

20. Holt, *How Children Fail*, 167; emphasis in original.

21. John Holt, *Teach Your Own* (New York: Delacorte Press/Seymour Lawrence, 1981), 1–2.

22. Holt, *How Children Fail*, 168.

23. See Susannah Sheffer's introduction to John Holt, *A Life Worth Living: Selected Letters of John Holt*, ed. Susannah Sheffer (Columbus: Ohio State University Press, 1990), 1–11.

24. John Holt, *How Children Learn* (New York: Pitman, 1967). Sales and translation information are from the obituary for John Holt in the *New York Times*, September 9, 1985.

25. Edgar Z. Friedenberg, "How the Schools Fail," *New York Review of Books*, January 14, 1965, 12–14. Among the many glowing reviews of Holt's work were Eliot Fremont-Smith, "Scare-Eyed in the Classroom," *New York Times*, July 26, 1965, 21; and Joseph Featherstone, "A New Kind of Schooling," *New Republic*, March 2, 1968, 27–31.

26. Holt, *Instead of Education*, 4.

27. Ibid., 3; emphasis in original.

28. Holt, *Teach Your Own*, 232.

29. Holt, *Instead of Education*, 4.

30. The magazine *Growing Without Schooling* was founded in 1977. Holt's tenth, unfinished book, *Learning All the Time* (Reading, Mass.: Addison-Wesley, 1989), was published posthumously. Some of the details of Holt's life reported here are from Sheffer, *A Life Worth Living*. Sheffer's introduction provides an excellent summary of Holt's situation in the school reform movement of the 1960s and 1970s.

31. Holt, *Instead of Education*, 5.

32. I found no evidence that Holt was ever publicly critical of the Moores and their message, though it is clear from interviews with his friends and protégés (at Holt Associates in Cambridge, and in Chicago) that Holt well understood the difference between his own pedagogy and that of the Moores. Raymond Moore expresses deep respect for Holt, though he admits that they were more fellow travelers than colleagues or friends; interview, 8/16/94.

33. Raymond S. Moore and Dorothy M. Moore, *Better Late Than Early* (New York: Reader's Digest Press, 1975).

34. Ibid., 63–87.

35. Raymond S. Moore and Dennis R. Moore, "The Dangers of Early School-

ing," *Harper's*, July 1972, 58–62; Raymond S. Moore, T. Joseph Willey, Dennis R. Moore, and D. Kathleen Kordenbock, *School Can Wait* (Provo, Utah: Brigham Young University Press, 1979); Raymond Moore and Dorothy Moore, *Home Grown Kids* (Waco, Tex.: Word Books, 1981); Raymond Moore and Dorothy Moore, *Home-Spun Schools* (Waco, Tex.: Word Books, 1982).

36. Moore and Moore, *Home Grown Kids*, 14.

37. Ibid., 22.

38. Ibid., 33.

39. Ibid., 27.

40. For historical studies of Western childhood, see Philippe Ariès, *Centuries of Childhood*, trans. Robert Baldick (New York: Vintage Books, 1962); Lawrence Stone, *The Family, Sex, and Marriage in England, 1500–1800* (New York: Harper and Row, 1977); Arlene Skolnick, "The Limits of Childhood: Conceptions of Child Development in Social Context," *Law and Contemporary Problems* 39 (1975): 38–77; John Boli-Bennett and John W. Meyer, "The Ideology of Childhood and the State: Rules Distinguishing Children in National Constitutions, 1870–1970," *American Sociological Review* 43 (1978): 797–812; Viviana A. Zelizer, *Pricing the Priceless Child: The Changing Social Value of Children* (New York: Basic Books, 1985); Linda A. Pollock, *Forgotten Children: Parent-Child Relations from 1500 to 1900* (Cambridge: Cambridge University Press, 1983). Pollock is notably critical of Ariès and other scholars who take a strong constructionist approach to childhood. Read from a different perspective, however, her work suggests that preciousness has long been afforded to children. For legal-historical analyses of the parent-child relationship, see Michael Grossberg, *Governing the Hearth: Law and Family in Nineteenth-Century America* (Chapel Hill: University of North Carolina Press, 1985); Mary Ann Mason, *From Father's Property to Children's Rights: The History of Child Custody in the United States* (New York: Columbia University Press, 1994).

41. Llewellyn B. Davis, *Why So Many Christians Are Going Home to School* (Knoxville, Tenn.: Elijah Company, 1990), 60.

42. Donna Nichols-White, "Placing Our Trust in Our Children's Desire and Need to Learn," *The Drinking Gourd*, January/February 1993, 4.

43. Pat George and Lindy George, "60 Things Your Homeschoolers Might Be Doing If They Were in School Instead of 'Wasting Time' at Home," *Mentor*, December 1992, 6.

44. David Guterson, *Family Matters: Why Homeschooling Makes Sense* (New York: Harcourt Brace Jovanovich, 1992), 23.

45. Ibid., 166–67.

46. Ibid., 175–76.

47. http://www.csranet.com/vlmckie/green.htm, accessed 7/2/99 and 6/28/00.

48. Pride, *The New Big Book of Home Learning*, 11–12.

49. Fieldwork, 5/13/93.

50. Cathy Ericksen, interview, 3/28/91.

51. Sally Norton, interview, 9/21/89.

52. Gerald and Penny Turner, interview, 9/1/92.

53. Clonlara School, enrollment manual, Home Based Education Program (Ann Arbor, Mich.: Clonlara Press, 1987); emphasis in original. In phone communication with a staff member at Clonlara on June 23, 2000, I learned that the basic structure of the correspondence program had remained quite similar to what I describe here.

54. Information on the high school program from "A High School Education You Can Own," Clonlara School, n.d., received April 1994, author's collection.

55. Helen Lofton, interview, 11/13/91.

56. *The Basic Educator*, January–February 1991, 1+. Authorship of this text is credited to "Dr. Tim LaHaye," Ph.D., a leading ideologue on the Religious Right who writes often about family issues (LaHaye's wife, Beverly, is a founder of the conservative Concerned Women for America). No clear citations are given for the origin of the text. Notation is also made that the piece was "Submitted by A.S."; however, there are no further clues about the identity of the submitter. This ambiguity of authorship is not uncommon in homeschool literature.

57. Albert E. Greene Jr., "Protected Yet Exposed," *The Christian Educator*, fall 1989, 5.

58. "Home-School Questions and Answers," *The Teaching Home*, April/May 1991, 8.

59. Moore and Moore, *Home Grown Kids*, 39.

60. Davis, *Why So Many Christians Are Going Home to School*, 53.

61. Alida Gookin, "Advantages of Home Schooling," *The Christian Educator*, fall 1989, 2.

62. Kate Wilson, interview, 8/31/89.

63. Quotations from "Child Training, God's Way," produced by Mission City Television, Inc., San Antonio, Texas, 1991, videotape distributed by Christian Life Workshops, Inc. Harris's biblical allusion is to Proverbs 13:20: "He who walks with wise men becomes wise, but the companion of fools will suffer harm."

64. Kate Wilson, interview, 8/31/89.

65. The Baltimore-based Calvert School, for example, founded in 1897, has purveyed a correspondence program since 1906. It continues to enjoy a solid reputation among believers.

66. "A Beka Correspondence School," promotional material, received 1991, author's collection. A Beka curriculum texts also are available for purchase individually.

67. Preceding quotations from the *1991 A Beka Book Home School Catalog* and sample curricula (Pensacola, Fla.: A Beka Book/Pensacola Christian College).

68. Promotional literature, Christian Liberty Academy Satellite Schools, n.d. (received 8/89), author's collection. A review of CLA promotional materials received in 2000 indicated that the program was much the same, but pamphlet authors seemed less eager to imply that home *was* school. Nevertheless, the model

remains school-at-home. For example, the more recent brochure made clear that the program "is not set up in a self-study format. Instruction and schoolwork will require up to four hours per day."

69. Peter Tobin, interview, 8/21/89.

70. *1991 A Beka Book Home School Catalog.*

71. Informational literature, A Beka Video Home School, 1991–92, author's collection. As of June 2000, A Beka was continuing to offer its video program.

72. Kate Wilson, interview, 8/31/89.

73. Robert and Martha Edwards, interview, 8/24/89.

74. Eric and Marci Rayburn, interview, 8/1/89.

75. Robert and Martha Edwards, interview, 8/24/89. At the time of the interview, the program was called Advanced Training Institute of America.

76. Matthew 5:1.

77. Robert and Martha Edwards, interview, 8/24/89.

78. Ibid.

79. Harris, "Child Training, God's Way."

80. See John W. Meyer and Brian Rowan, "The Structure of Educational Organizations," in *Environments and Organizations*, ed. Marshall W. Meyer and Associates (San Francisco: Jossey-Bass, 1978), 78–109. For a more general statement of the tendency toward the "decoupling" of formal rules and practice, see John W. Meyer and Brian Rowan, "Institutionalized Organizations: Formal Structure as Myth and Ceremony," *American Journal of Sociology* 83 (September 1977): 340–63.

81. Heather Hughes, interview, 9/21/89.

82. Robert and Martha Edwards, interview, 8/24/89.

83. Tara Cook, interview, 5/16/91. Many instances of this kind of translation are as John Meyer and his colleagues might expect: home schoolers are sometimes obliged to document their work in ways required by state or local homeschool regulations. This may have been part of Tara's intention as well, but I suspect that she was doing this record keeping as much for her own purposes as for those of others; she lives in a state with a very flexible homeschooling law, and in any case she raised the issue of record keeping in a discussion of how *she* thinks about what she is doing, not regarding what others expect of her.

84. Fieldwork, 7/8/93.

85. Steve and Susan Jerome, interview, 5/10/95.

86. ICHE 1993 conference announcement, author's collection.

87. Fieldwork, 6/6/93.

88. Kenneth D. Wald, Dennis E. Owen, and Samuel S. Hill, "Habits of the Mind? The Problem of Authority in the New Christian Right," in *Religion and Political Behavior in the United States*, ed. Ted G. Jelen (New York: Praeger, 1989), 93–108.

89. See, e.g., Ammerman, *Bible Believers*; Rose, *Keeping Them Out of the Hands of Satan*; Brenda E. Brasher, *Godly Women: Fundamentalism and Female Power* (New Brunswick, N.J.: Rutgers University Press, 1998).

90. Christopher G. Ellison and Darren E. Sherkat, "Conservative Protestant-ism and Support for Capital Punishment," *American Sociological Review* 58 (Febru-ary 1993): 131–44; Christopher G. Ellison, John P. Bartkowski, and Michelle Se-gal, "Conservative Protestantism and the Parental Use of Corporal Punishment," *Social Forces* 74 (March 1996): 1003–28; Christopher G. Ellison, John P. Bartkow-ski, and Michelle L. Segal, "Do Conservative Protestant Parents Spank More Of-ten? Further Evidence from the National Survey of Families and Households," *Social Science Quarterly* 77 (September 1996): 663–73.

91. John P. Bartkowski and Christopher G. Ellison, "Divergent Models of Childrearing in Popular Manuals: Conservative Protestants vs. the Mainstream Experts," *Sociology of Religion* 56 (1995): 21–34.

92. W. Bradford Wilcox, "Conservative Protestant Childrearing: Authoritarian or Authoritative?" *American Sociological Review* 63 (December 1998): 796–809; quo-tation on 798–99. Such a dualism also shows up in studies by the Ellison team. When Ellison and Darren Sherkat asked respondents what they thought was "the most important [trait] for a child to learn to prepare him or her for life," conserva-tive Protestants were more likely than others to choose obedience, but they were no less likely to value children's intellectual autonomy. The survey evidence suggests that conservative Protestant parents simultaneously want their children to honor authority and to think for themselves. See Christopher G. Ellison and Darren E. Sherkat, "Obedience and Autonomy: Religion and Parental Values Reconsidered," *Journal for the Scientific Study of Religion* 32 (1993): 313–29.

93. Debbie Strayer, "Fanning the Sparks," *Homeschooling Today*, May/June 1993, 8–9.

94. Sally Norton, interview, 9/21/89.

95. Cheryl Marcus, interview, 4/2/91; emphasis reflects interview.

96. The 150 figure is a generous estimate, based on interviews with several prominent homeschool advocates in the state. Neither home schoolers nor the state of Illinois has kept formal count of the organizations.

97. Undated photocopy material, author's collection.

98. Robert and Martha Edwards, interview, 5/2/95.

99. As quoted in Sharon Hays, *The Cultural Contradictions of Motherhood* (New Haven, Conn.: Yale University Press, 1996), 113.

CHAPTER THREE
Natural Mothers, Godly Women

1. See Beth Anne Shelton and Daphne John, "The Division of Household La-bor," *Annual Review of Sociology* 22 (1996): 299–322; Arlie Hochschild and Anne Machung, *The Second Shift* (New York: Avon, 1997 [1989]).

2. See Susan Walzer, *Thinking about the Baby: Gender and Transitions into Parent-hood* (Philadelphia: Temple University Press, 1998); see also Carol A. Heimer and

Lisa R. Staffen, *For the Sake of the Children: The Social Organization of Responsibility in the Hospital and the Home* (Chicago: University of Chicago Press, 1998).

3. In addition to the above, see also Rosanna Hertz, *More Equal Than Others: Women and Men in Dual-Career Marriages* (Berkeley: University of California Press, 1986).

4. The literature on changing images of ideal womanhood is vast. For particularly concise accounts, see Luker, *Abortion and the Politics of Motherhood*, 158–215; Hochschild and Machung, *The Second Shift*, 1–32. For changing representations of women in the media, see Susan J. Douglas, *Where the Girls Are: Growing Up Female with the Mass Media* (New York: Random House, 1994).

5. See Hays, *The Cultural Contradictions of Motherhood*.

6. Carol Heimer argues convincingly that this distribution of parenting responsibility is the normative one. Carol A. Heimer, "Gender Inequalities in the Distribution of Responsibility," in *Social Differentiation and Social Inequality: Essays in Honor of John Pock*, ed. James Baron, David Grusky, and Donald Treiman (Boulder, Colo.: Westview Press, 1996), 241–273.

7. Jerry and Jennifer Kullom, interview, 9/13/89.

8. Jacob Maxwell and Diana Coleman-Maxwell, interview, 10/29/92.

9. Kate Wilson, interview, 8/31/89.

10. Pamela Eckard, interview, 9/20/89.

11. Robert and Martha Edwards, interview, 8/24/89.

12. "Letters to the Editor," *Practical Homeschooling*, July/August 1998, 6; emphasis in original.

13. Lissa Foster, interview, 6/23/98.

14. For a careful analysis of this choice-making process for women generally, see Kathleen Gerson, *Hard Choices: How Women Decide about Work, Career, and Motherhood* (Berkeley: University of California Press, 1985). Gerson gives little attention to some of home schoolers' primary anxieties, such as their suspicion of the bureaucratic organization of education and child care. Still, Lissa could easily be one of Gerson's subjects, faced as she is with limited day care options and the ill fit between the organization of academic careers and the obligations of parenting.

15. Diana Coleman-Maxwell, interview, 10/29/92.

16. Sally Norton, interview, 9/21/89.

17. Robert and Martha Edwards, interview, 8/1/89.

18. Diana Coleman-Maxwell, interview, 10/29/92.

19. Peg Jesson, interview, 8/23/89.

20. Fieldwork, 9/8/89.

21. Clonlara also maintains a day school program in Ann Arbor, Michigan.

22. Enrollment figure from phone inquiry to ATI, 6/8/00. The program is now called Advanced Training Institute International.

23. Lissa Foster, interview, 6/23/98.

24. Peg Jesson, interview, 8/23/89.

25. Sally Norton, interview, 9/21/89.

26. Holt, *Teach Your Own*, 1. emphasis added; Holt, *Learning All the Time*, 160.

27. Holt, *Learning All the Time*, 146; emphasis in original.

28. Grant entered Harvard in 1983, Drew in 1986, and Reed in 1988. David Colfax and Micki Colfax, *Homeschooling for Excellence* (New York: Wagner Books, 1988), xiii–xiv. This book was originally published by Mountain House Press (Philo, Calif., 1987). All following citations are from the Philo Books edition.

29. Ibid., 3; emphases added.

30. Ibid., 10.

31. Ibid., 47.

32. Ibid., xiii–xiv; emphasis in original.

33. For analysis of this process in conventional households, see Hochschild and Machung, *The Second Shift*.

34. Erving Goffman, "Where the Action Is," in his *Interaction Ritual: Essays in Face-to-Face Behavior* (Garden City, N.Y.: Doubleday, 1967), 149–270.

35. Fieldwork, 3/11/93; emphasis added.

36. Fieldwork, 9/12/92.

37. Arda Ben Shalom, interview, 3/13/91.

38. Sarah Michels, interview, 7/16/91.

39. Willa Baker, interview, 4/26/91.

40. "La Leche League Philosophy," http://www.lalecheleague.org/philosophy.html, accessed 6/28/00. For scholarly treatments of La Leche League, see Linda M. Blum, "Mothers, Babies, and Breastfeeding in Late Capitalist America: The Shifting Contexts of Feminist Theory," *Feminist Studies* 19 (1993): 291–311; Linda M. Blum and Elizabeth W. Vandewater, "'Mother to Mother': A Maternalist Organization in Late Capitalist America," *Social Problems* 40 (1993): 285–300.

41. Penny and Gerald Turner, interview, 9/1/92.

42. Blum and Vandewater make a similar analysis of the role of nature in La Leche ideology. See Blum, "Mothers, Babies, and Breastfeeding"; and Blum and Vandewater, "'Mother to Mother.'"

43. This is also why rhetoric about children is such a fruitful site for investigating the relationship between cultural innovation and social change. See, e.g., Nicola Beisel, *Imperiled Innocents: Anthony Comstock and Family Reproduction in Victorian America* (Princeton, N.J.: Princeton University Press, 1997); Theda Skocpol, *Protecting Soldiers and Mothers: The Political Origins of Social Policy in the United States* (Cambridge, Mass.: Belknap Press/Harvard University Press, 1992).

44. As with the names of parents quoted earlier, Carol Ingram is a fictional name.

45. Carol Ingram, "Schooling or Educating: Which Are You Doing?" tape recording, ICHE state conference, 6/5/93.

46. Lola Wooster, interview, 8/8/89.

47. Jerry and Jennifer Kullom, interview, 9/13/89.

48. Appeared in the *Chicago Tribune*, September 27, 1993, 12; emphasis added.

49. Titus 2:1–6.

50. Appeared in *Home School Digest*, summer 1993, 16.

51. http://www.chfweb.com/forum/Forum.asp?Section=2; accessed 7/2/99.

52. Cassette tape produced by Noble Publishing Associates (Gresham, Ore., 1993), author's collection.

53. Mary Pride, *The Way Home* (Westchester, Ill.: Crossway Books/Good News Publishers, 1985).

54. Ibid., xiii.

55. Ibid., 3–4; emphasis in original.

56. Ibid., 39–40; emphasis in original.

57. Ibid., 23.

58. Ibid., 57; emphasis in original.

59. Ibid., vii–viii, 181.

60. Michael P. Farris, *The Homeschooling Father* (Hamilton, Va.: Michael P. Farris, 1992), 1.

61. Ibid., 2.

62. Ibid., 6.

63. Ibid., 21–22.

64. Ibid., 13; emphasis in original.

65. Ibid., 19–20.

66. Ibid., 17.

67. Homeschool fatherhood is not the only site in which conservative Protestants have begun to reimagine traditionalist masculinity. See, e.g., Brian Donovan, "Political Consequences of Private Authority: Promise Keepers and the Transformation of Hegemonic Masculinity," *Theory and Society* 27 (December 1998): 817–43.

68. Phil Lancaster, "It's *Your* Home School," *Home School Digest*, summer 1993, 14–15; all emphases in original.

69. "Cover Family: Gary and Beverly Somogie," *The Teaching Home*, March/April 1994, 13.

70. *Do-It-Yourself-Fun*, book 8 (Glen Ellyn, Ill.: Walkwitz Publications, n.d.), 42, author's collection.

71. Marci Rayburn, interview, 8/1/89; emphasis reflects speaker's inflection.

72. Fieldwork, 11/8/94; emphases reflect speaker's inflection.

73. "Information and Application Booklet," Advanced Training Institute International, n.d. (received 11/8/94), author's collection.

74. Sally Norton, interview, 9/21/89.

75. See, e.g., Sally K. Gallagher and Christian Smith, "Symbolic Traditionalism and Pragmatic Egalitarianism: Contemporary Evangelicals, Families, and Gender," *Gender and Society* 13 (April 1999): 211–33; Brasher, *Godly Women*; Susan D. Rose, "Woman Warriors: Negotiating Gender in a Charismatic Community," *Sociological Analysis* 48 (1987): 245–58; Ammerman, *Bible Believers*, especially chap. 8.

76. Hays, *Cultural Contradictions of Motherhood*, 4.

77. See, e.g., John P. Bartkowski, "Changing of the Gods: The Gender and Family Discourse of American Evangelicalism in Historical Perspective," *History of the Family* 3 (1998): 95–115; Margaret Lamberts Bendroth, *Fundamentalism and Gender, 1875 to the Present* (New Haven, Conn.: Yale University Press, 1993); Judith Stacey and Susan Elizabeth Gerard, "'We Are Not Doormats': The Influence of Feminism on Contemporary Evangelicals in the United States," in *Uncertain Terms: Negotiating Gender in American Culture*, ed. Faye Ginsburg and Anna Lowenhaupt Tsing (Boston: Beacon Press, 1990), 98–117.

78. Lissa Foster, interview, 6/23/98.

Chapter Four
Authority and Diversity

1. All of the above from field notes, site visit, Clonlara School, 4/14–4/15/94.

2. Paul DiMaggio, "Culture and Cognition," *Annual Review of Sociology* 23 (1997): 263–87; quotation on 269. See also William H. Sewell Jr., "A Theory of Structure: Duality, Agency, and Transformation," *American Journal of Sociology* 98 (July 1992): 1–29. The argument that follows regarding the relationship between schemata and social structure is consonant with the basic insights of Sewell's work.

3. See Penny Edgell Becker, *Congregations in Conflict: Cultural Models of Local Religious Life* (Cambridge: Cambridge University Press, 1999), for a harmonious analysis of variation in organizational sensibility in and between local religious groups; and Paul Lichterman, *The Search for Political Community: American Activists Reinventing Commitment* (Cambridge: Cambridge University Press, 1996), for a study of similar conflicts in environmentalist groups.

4. Fieldwork, 10/21/91.

5. Fieldwork, 9/10/93.

6. Fieldwork, 11/9/93.

7. Quotations and adapted image from Mary Pride, *All the Way Home* (Wheaton, Ill.: Crossway Books/Good News Publishers, 1989), 168.

8. Quotations and adapted image from Gregg Harris, "Child Training, God's Way," produced by Mission City Television, Inc., San Antonio, Texas, 1991, video distributed by Christian Life Workshops, Inc.

9. Some of this pattern may be explained by numbers. Quite simply, gatherings of believers were consistently larger than those of unschoolers. Still, the consistency of the observation (coupled with the fact that I never heard anybody complain about such arrangements, while unschoolers sometimes went out of their way to make rows into circles) is suggestive.

10. I use the past tense in describing Christian Life Workshops. My analysis here is based on fieldwork conducted in 1994. In 2000 a phone call to the former CLW number brought the caller to an answering machine for "Noble Publishing Associates and Noble Institute." In a telephone interview with a staff member on June 15, 2000, I learned that Harris had changed the focus of his ministry some-

what. While he continued to conduct homeschooling workshops, he also purveyed other seminars on Christian family life, titled "Households of Strength." CLW no longer existed as a legal entity, having been replaced by the concerns under the Noble name. I learned also that Harris's son, Joshua, had moved to the East Coast, where his own, independent ministry was now headquartered. A bio of Gregg Harris posted on Crosswalk.com, an evangelical Web site, describes him as "Director for Noble Institute for Leadership Development, speaking in conferences and presenting seminars on home schooling, time management, household management and church reform"; http://homeschool.crosswalk.com/bio/0,2476,79,00.htm, accessed 6/15/00.

11. Promotional flyer, Christian Life Workshops, n.d., author's collection.

12. The following is reconstructed from field notes of my interview with Wendy Doyle, Christian Life Workshops, Gresham, Ore., 8/11/94.

13. "Work Flow Chart," Christian Life Workshops, n.d., author's collection.

14. With all due respect to Wendy and her colleagues, a key measure of standardization—and, hence, of organizational efficiency—is the extent of worker replicability. High replicability is an indication that organizational knowledge has been built into the job, not the worker. As Max Weber famously explained, such arrangements tend to make organizations both more efficient and more likely to survive over the long term. See Max Weber, *Economy and Society*, ed. Guenther Roth and Claus Wittich (Berkeley: University of California Press, 1978), 956–1005.

15. Promotional flyer for 1993 workshop in London, Ontario, Christian Life Workshops, n.d., author's collection.

16. Aldon D. Morris, *The Origins of the Civil Rights Movement* (New York: Free Press, 1984); Christian Smith, "Correcting a Curious Neglect, or Bringing Religion Back In," in *Disruptive Religion: The Force of Faith in Social Movement Activism*, ed. Christian Smith (New York: Routledge, 1996), 1–15.

17. Promotional letter for 1993 workshop in London, Ontario, n.d., author's collection.

18. Peggy Allen, interview by author, 8/10/94, and by telephone, 6/27/96.

19. *The Teaching Home*, March/April 1994, 3, also "10 Year Anniversary," photocopy material, dated August/September 1990 (received 8/94), author's collection.

20. *TTH* discontinued the regional newsletter features in 1998. Other than this change, the magazine looks very much the same today as it did in 1994.

21. "Illinois Update," March/April 1994, 1–2 (insert to *The Teaching Home*, March/April 1994).

22. See, e.g., "State Organizations," *The Teaching Home*, March/April 1994, 40. All references to *The Teaching Home* that follow in this section are from the March/April 1994 issue.

23. See, e.g., Rosabeth Moss Kanter, *Men and Women of the Corporation* (New York: Basic Books, 1977).

24. Staff interviews by author, HSLDA, Purcellville, Va., 12/9–12/10/93. In a survey of a random sample of HSLDA members, 93.8 percent of responding fathers and 96.4 percent of mothers described themselves as "born-again." Home School Legal Defense Association, "A Nationwide Study of Home Education," *Home School Court Report*, December 1990, 3.

25. *Marking the Milestones: 1983–1993* (Paeonian Springs, Va.: Home School Legal Defense Association, 1993), 4.

26. The following is drawn from interviews with Carol Ingram, 12/9/93 and 12/10/93.

27. Program, National Christian Home Educators Leadership Conference, November 4–7, 1993, Williamsburg, Virginia; and *Focus on Home Education* (Paeonian Springs, VA: National Center for Home Education, n.d.), a detailed summary of conference proceedings.

28. "Home Schoolers Gather for CAP Kickoff," *Capitol Chronicles*, February 1993, 1 [published by the National Center for Home Education].

29. One of many relationships linking believer home education to a legacy of far-right politics, Doug Phillips is the son of Howard Phillips, founder of the U.S. Taxpayers Alliance and a 1992 third-party presidential candidate. The elder Phillips was a keynote speaker at the Williamsburg conference.

30. Observations reported in this section are from my attendance at the NHA annual conferences, held near Cincinnati, Ohio, 10/9–10/11/92 and 10/8/93–10/10/93.

31. "N.H.A. 1992 Year-to-Date Report," *Circle of Correspondence*, winter 1992, 26.

32. Sydney Mathis, "1992 National Conference Reports," *Circle of Correspondence*, winter 1992, 11.

33. "1993 Annual Conference," *The FORUM* [formerly *Circle of Correspondence*], vol. 3, no. 4 (n.d.): 4.

34. "Bylaws of the National Homeschool Association," n.d., author's collection. Testament to the NHA's commitment to inclusiveness, the council admitted me to all its formal proceedings in 1992 and 1993.

35. Quotation from "1993 Annual Conference, NHA Conference Reports," *The FORUM*, vol. 3, no. 4 (n.d.): 9–10. My analysis here is broadly in keeping with Emirbayer and Goodwin's call for an integration of culture and network approaches to sociological puzzles. See Mustafa Emirbayer and Jeff Goodwin, "Network Analysis, Culture, and the Problem of Agency," *American Journal of Sociology* 99 (May 1994): 1411–54.

36. Informational flyer, National Homeschool Association, n.d., author's collection.

37. As reprinted in *Circle of Correspondence*, winter 1992, 7–8; emphasis in original.

38. "House Interim bylaws approved by the Council 3/9/93," photocopy material, author's collection.

39. From ICHE information packet, n.d., received 7/13/99.

40. www.geocities.com/Athens/Acropolis/7804/r01.htm, accessed 7/8/99 and 6/10/00.

41. Consider that home schooling is not a civil rights movement, nor just a family movement, nor an educational movement in any conventional sense, nor a religious movement per se. Because it is some of each of these, and all of none, movement elites have not had the luxury of borrowing an organizational model directly from one source. Instead they have had to be "bricoleurs," in Elisabeth Clemens's sense, borrowing organizational ideas from multiple traditions simultaneously. See Clemens, "Organizational Form as Frame."

42. My argument here is essentially a transposition from the work of Clemens, who developed the insight from a study of movements in a different historical era. Elisabeth S. Clemens, *The People's Lobby: Organizational Innovation and Interest Group Politics in the United States, 1890–1925* (Chicago: University of Chicago Press, 1997).

43. I learned as this book went to press that the NHA was dissolved on September 15, 2000 (http://www.n-h-a.org/, accessed 12/19/00).

44. Fieldwork, 9/10/93. Council members' hometowns have been changed in this section.

CHAPTER FIVE
Politics

1. "Unclassifieds," *Home Education Magazine*, May–June 1993, 60–61.

2. Larry Kaseman and Susan Kaseman, "A Manageable Approach to Political Action for Homeschoolers," *Home Education Magazine*, January–February 1993, 19–23.

3. "Support Groups and Organizations," *Home Education Magazine*, January–February 1993, 60–61.

4. "Homeschooling Freedoms at Risk" (special section), *Home Education Magazine*, May–June 1991, 25–42. All quotations in the following section are from this *HEM* feature.

5. Transcript of Internet conversation, 11/1/92, author's collection.

6. Interview, Robert and Martha Edwards, 5/2/95; emphasis reflects speaker's inflection. For survey data on the religious orientations of home educators, see my discussion in chapter 1.

7. See my discussion of this organization in chapter 1. Through my fieldwork with the National Homeschool Association (NHA), I learned of a similar instance of collaboration between inclusives and believers. In Massachusetts, a wide range of groups worked together to create a common fact sheet, "Massachusetts Home Education Law and Practice" (flyer, 7/19/93, author's collection), used by constituents in both camps. According to the activist who told me about the project, the two-page fact sheet "took 2 years to write!" (personal correspondence, 3/28/94).

8. Fieldwork, 10/8/93.

9. Fieldwork, 6/5/93.

10. Fieldwork, 11/11/93; emphasis reflects speaker's inflection.

11. Fieldwork, 1/13/94; emphasis reflects speaker's inflection.

12. Robert and Martha Edwards, interview, 5/2/95.

13. In addition to firsthand field study during the course of events surrounding the H.R. 6 controversy and post hoc interviews with several involved activists, the account provided here is based on the following sources: Phil Kuntz, "Home-Schooling Movement Gives House a Lesson," *Congressional Quarterly Weekly Report*, February 26, 1994, 479–80 (I rely heavily here Kuntz's succinct narrative and illuminating quotations); "Blitzing Congress," *CQ Researcher*, September 9, 1994, 783–84; "Lawmakers Renew and Revamp 1965 Education Act," *Congressional Quarterly Almanac*, 103rd Cong., 2d sess., Vol. L (Washington, D.C.: Congressional Quarterly, 1994), 383–96; *Congressional Record*, February 24, 1994; "The Anatomy of a Victory," *Home School Court Report*, March/April 1994, 4–7+; and numerous other printed materials distributed during the course of events by HSLDA/NCHE, the National Homeschool Association, Illinois HOUSE, the Christian Home Educators Coalition (CHEC), Clonlara School, Holt Associates/Growing Without Schooling, and the Wisconsin Parents Association (WPA).

14. For a scholarly appraisal of Farris's place in Virginia politics, see Mark J. Rozell and Clyde Wilcox, *Second Coming: The New Christian Right in Virginia Politics* (Baltimore: Johns Hopkins University Press, 1996).

15. "Urgent Alert," fax sent from the headquarters offices of HSLDA/NCHE, 2/15/94, photocopy, author's collection.

16. Fieldwork, 2/18–2/20/94.

17. Letter dated 2/20/94, photocopy, author's collection; emphasis in original.

18. Letter dated 2/23/94, photocopy, author's collection.

19. "How Federal Bill HR 6 would affect private schools, including home schools," Wisconsin Parents Association, 2/18/94, author's collection.

20. As reported in Kuntz, "Home-Schooling Movement Gives House a Lesson," 479–80.

21. As quoted in "Home Schooling Wins Emphatic Assurance from the House," *New York Times*, February 25, 1994, A14.

22. As quoted in Kuntz, "Home-Schooling Movement Gives House a Lesson," 479.

23. PRAIRIE, April 1994, 2. PRAIRIE is a newsletter produced by the Kasemans.

24. Letter dated 2/22/94, photocopy, author's collection; emphases added.

25. As quoted in Kuntz, "Home-Schooling Movement Gives House a Lesson," 480.

26. As quoted in ibid.

27. As quoted in ibid.

28. A search of the NEXIS database revealed that the Associated Press released

five different stories about the H.R. 6 controversy. Released from February 19 to 25, none of the stories mentioned the strategic split among home schoolers, nor did any of them discuss the independent lobbying efforts of the NHA coalition.

29. "Home Schooling Wins Emphatic Assurance from the House." One Chicago newspaper did carry coverage of the inclusive-believer split; as it read, the article was based on information supplied by activists on both sides of the movement in Illinois. See Wisby, "Home Schoolers Split on Protest Tactics." The following September, the *CQ Researcher* included a dissenting perspective from Larry Kaseman in its retrospective coverage of the H.R. 6 scenario. See "Blitzing Congress," 784.

30. For a good, and enduring, summary of the lines of debate about the cultural dimensions of social movements, see Ann Swidler, "Cultural Power and Social Movements," in *Social Movements and Culture*, ed. Hank Johnston and Bert Klandermans (Minneapolis: University of Minnesota Press, 1995), 25–40.

31. From my research I have no reason to believe that HSLDA's dues-payment rate is as low as 80 percent. Nor did I meet any families who said they had free memberships to HSLDA. But the revenues are impressive even if we grant a 20 percent margin of researcher error on this point.

32. Fieldwork, NHA annual conference, 10/8/93–10/10/93.

33. HSLDA's national membership roster, its palette of member services, and its fax and phone web constitute precisely the kind of organizational apparatus that recent scholars of the Christian Right suggest is crucial for turning moral sentiment into political action. See, e.g., Mark D. Regenerus, David Sikkink, and Christian Smith, "Voting with the Christian Right: Contextual and Individual Patterns of Electoral Influence," *Social Forces* 77 (June 1999): 1375–1401. The organizational sophistication of HSLDA suggests that its leaders have long understood the importance of maintaining a well-oiled organizational instrument through which the Lord might do his work.

34. HOUSE mailing, n.d. (postmarked February 21, 1994), author's collection.

35. Ironically, the mailing included the verbatim text of HSLDA's first fax alert—testament to the degree to which HSLDA had achieved definitional control of the issue, even among inclusives. HOUSE's lack of agreement over H.R. 6 was reported in the March 1994 newsletter, a Chicago HOUSE chapter (author's collection).

36. Robert D. Woodberry and Christian S. Smith, "Fundamentalism et al.: Conservative Protestants in America," *Annual Review of Sociology* 24 (1998): 25–56. The authors summarize a wide range of studies that employ different measures of religiosity (denominational affiliation, beliefs, and personal identification with a religious movement) to derive this estimate.

37. Christian S. Smith, Michael Emerson, Sally Gallagher, Paul Kennedy, and David Sikkink, *American Evangelicalism: Embattled and Thriving* (Chicago: University of Chicago Press, 1998).

38. Denominational data are from Smith et al., *American Evangelicalism*, 231.

For a brief depiction of the organizational features of the Baptist denominational tradition, see Roger Finke and Rodney Stark, *The Churching of America, 1776–1990* (New Brunswick, N.J.: Rutgers University Press, 1992), 169–98. A more detailed organizational history of the Baptist Church in the United States can be found in Nancy Tatom Ammerman, *Baptist Battles: Social Change and Religious Conflict in the Southern Baptist Convention* (New Brunswick, N.J.: Rutgers University Press, 1990), chaps. 2 and 3. Ammerman's account aptly depicts the variation within the denomination regarding issues of how to organize.

39. Smith et al., *American Evangelicalism*, 86. Not surprisingly, race divides conservative Protestants as much as it does the rest of the society; some of this division is organizational. Largely as a consequence of systematic white exclusion, African-American believers have long maintained their own organizational universe. See, e.g., C. Eric Lincoln and Lawrence H. Mamiya, *The Black Church in the African-American Experience* (Durham, N.C.: Duke University Press, 1990). My analysis here is essentially of a white conservative Protestantism; many interesting questions about the organizational configuration of African-American Protestantism, and the relationship between black and white religious organizational universes, await their scholars.

40. Of course, the mix must be executed properly. Too much vision and not enough business sense likely make for a shaky organization, while dollar signs can occasionally occlude the light of divine intention. Skeptical outsiders tend to too easily assume the latter: that entrepreneurial ministries are primarily in it for the money. This greatly underestimates the sophistication of followers, who in general are quite adept at detecting spurious value in the religious marketplace. We tend to forget that some ministries fail, on the one hand, and on the other that many are fruitful for years, untainted by the financial scandals so beloved by the mainstream media. It is notable additionally that this entrepreneurial tradition in conservative Protestantism bears affinities with the populist, small-business entrepreneur ideology touted by the U.S. Republican Party. This may help to explain the courtship between conservative Protestants and the party over the last two decades.

41. For a useful summary of the literature on conservative religious women and work participation, see the introduction by Nancy Tatom Ammerman and Wade Clark Roof to their edited volume, *Work, Family, and Religion in Contemporary Society* (New York: Routledge, 1995), 1–25. See also Bradley H. Hertel, "Work, Family, and Faith," 81–121, in the same volume.

42. *Engaged orthodoxy* is the term Smith and his colleagues have created to describe evangelicals' commitment to remain distinctive from the broader culture while simultaneously participating in it. Theologically the intent is to inform, and potentially transform, the wider culture through Christian witness. Conservative Protestants use such Bible verses as Romans 12:2 to frame their separatist and quasi-separatist theologies: "Do not be conformed to this world but be transformed by the renewal of your mind, that you may prove what is the will of God. . . ."

43. Robert Wuthnow, "Mobilizing Civic Engagement: The Changing Impact of Religious Involvement," in *Civic Engagement and American Democracy*, ed. Theda Skocpol and Morris P. Fiorina (Washington, D.C., and New York: Brookings Institution Press and the Russell Sage Foundation, 1999), 331–63.

44. Raymond Moore, "White Paper—History on Homeschooling," unpublished manuscript, February 1991, photocopy, author's collection.

45. I did not conduct research that might test this claim, but informal conversations with many professional academic women suggest its validity. Female colleagues often found home education a quaint or exotic cause. Their comments to me indicated that they thought of home schooling as something that only *other* women, unlike themselves, might consider.

46. The point of this paragraph owes much to Paul Lichterman's work in *The Search for Political Community*. Examining the collective sensibilities of the U.S. Green Party, Lichterman argues that for these activists an organizational culture of "personalism" "worked as a logic of unity amidst diverse social identities and cultural allegiances" (70).

47. Telephone conversation, winter 1994, and in conversation, 10/24/94.

48. Cheryl Marcus, telephone conversation, summer 1994.

49. Fieldwork, 10/21/94; emphasis reflects speaker's inflection.

CHAPTER SIX
Nurturing the Expanded Self

1. *The Teaching Home*, January/February 1999, 32.

2. In fall 2000, Patrick Henry College welcomed its first entering class. Information about the college was drawn from http://phc.hslda.org/overview.asp, accessed 8/9/99 and 6/29/00; promotional material received 6/2/00; and Amy Argetsinger, "College Faces Test of Its Own," *Washington Post*, October 2, 2000, 131+.

3. I was told during my visit that the internship program would cease with the opening of Patrick Henry College; the college's apprentice program would continue to provide volunteer workers to HSLDA. Site visit, 4/6/99.

4. "Social Studies: Home Schoolers Learn How to Gain Clout inside the Beltway," *Wall Street Journal*, April 24, 2000, 1+.

5. Robert N. Bellah, Richard Madsen, William M. Sullivan, Ann Swidler, and Steven M. Tipton, *Habits of the Heart: Individualism and Commitment in American Life* (Berkeley: University of California Press, 1996 [1985]); quotations from xlii and 284, respectively.

6. See, e.g., Daniel Bell, *The Cultural Contradictions of Capitalism* (New York: Basic Books, 1976); Christopher Lasch, *The Culture of Narcissism* (New York: Norton, 1979); Phillip Rieff, *The Triumph of the Therapeutic: The Uses of Faith after Freud* (London: Chatto and Windus, 1966); Daniel Yankelovich, *New Rules: Searching for Self-Fulfillment in a World Turned Upside Down* (New York: Random House, 1981).

7. Peter Clecak, *America's Quest for the Ideal Self* (New York: Oxford University Press, 1983), 9; subsequent quotation is from page 8.

8. Joseph Veroff, Elizabeth Douvan, and Richard A. Kulka, *The Inner American: A Self-Portrait from 1957 to 1976* (New York: Basic Books, 1981), 138.

9. Joseph Veroff, Richard A. Kulka, and Elizabeth Douvan, *Mental Health in America: Patterns of Help-Seeking from 1957–1976* (New York: Basic Books, 1981), 78–80.

10. See Charles Taylor, *Sources of the Self: The Making of the Modern Identity* (Cambridge, Mass.: Harvard University Press, 1989), esp. part 2, "Inwardness"; also John W. Meyer, "Self and the Life Course: Institutionalization and Its Effects," in *Institutional Structure: Constituting State, Society, and the Individual*, ed. George M. Thomas, John W. Meyer, Francisco O. Ramirez, and John Boli (Newbury Park, Calif.: Sage, 1987), 242–60.

11. See, e.g., Boli-Bennett and Meyer, "The Ideology of Childhood and the State," 797–812. For a lucid picture of cultural variation in the importance of individualism, see Joseph J. Tobin, David Y. H. Wu, and Dana H. Davidson, *Preschool in Three Cultures: Japan, China, and the United States* (New Haven, Conn.: Yale University Press, 1989).

12. For a contrary view to that of the *Habits* team, see, e.g., John W. Meyer, "Myths of Socialization and Personality," *Reconstructing Individualism: Autonomy, Individuality, and the Self in Western Thought*, ed. Thomas C. Heller et al. (Stanford, Calif.: Stanford University Press, 1986), 208–21. For a recent historical study that locates the cultural innovations of the 1960s in the broad sweep of American history, see Dominick Cavallo, *A Fiction of the Past: The Sixties in American History* (New York: St. Martin's Press, 1999).

13. But see Swidler, *Organization without Authority*.

14. For accounts of Montessori in the United States, see Margaret Howard Loeffler, ed., *Montessori in Contemporary American Culture* (Portsmouth, N.H.: Heinemann Educational Books, 1992). Schools estimate is from http://www.montessori.edu/FAQ.html#QUESTIONS, accessed 6/20/00.

15. Maria Montessori, *The Absorbent Mind*, trans. Claude A. Claremont (New York: Holt, Rinehart, and Winston, 1967), 4.

16. Paula Polk Lillard, *Montessori Today* (New York: Schocken Books, 1996), 22. See also Loeffler, *Montessori in Contemporary American Culture*.

17. Louise Boyd Cadwell, *Bringing Reggio Emilia Home* (New York: Teachers College Press, 1997), 5. See also Lella Gandini, "Fundamentals of the Reggio Approach to Early Childhood Education," *Young Children* 49 (1993): 4–8; Deborah L. Cohen, "Preschools in Italian Town Inspiration to U.S. Educators," *Education Week*, November 25, 1992, 1+.

18. David Ruenzel, "A School with Balance," *Education Week*, October 18, 1995, 24–29.

19. Information on Waldorf education was derived from the Association of Waldorf Schools of North America (AWSNA), http://www.awsna.org, accessed

7/19/99; Freda Easton, "Educating the Whole Child, 'Head, Heart, and Hands': Learning from the Waldorf Experience," *Theory into Practice* 36 (spring 1997): 87–84; Ruenzel, "A School with Balance"; David Ruenzel, "The Waldorf Way," *Teacher Magazine*, October 1995, 22–27.

20. David C. Paris, *Ideology and Educational Reform: Themes and Theories in Public Education* (Boulder, Colo.: Westview Press, 1995), 149.

21. On changes in American Catholicism since Vatican II, see Roger Finke and Rodney Stark, *The Churching of America: Winners and Losers in Our Religious Economy, 1776–1990* (New Brunswick, N.J.: Rutgers University Press, 1992), 255–61. On the charismatic renewal in Catholicism, see Mary Jo Neitz, *Charisma and Community: A Study of Religious Commitment within the Charismatic Renewal* (New Brunswick, N.J.: Transaction Books, 1987). On the Protestant movements, see Donald E. Miller, *Reinventing American Protestantism: Christianity in the New Millennium* (Berkeley: University of California Press, 1997). For analysis of these changes across the broad sweep American religious life, see Wade Clark Roof, *A Generation of Seekers: The Spiritual Journeys of the Baby Boom Generation* (San Francisco: HarperSanFrancisco, 1994).

22. Marsha G. Witten, *All Is Forgiven: The Secular Message in American Protestantism* (Princeton, N.J.: Princeton University Press, 1993), 127–28.

23. Molly Ganz, interview, 7/15/99.

24. Conference quotations are from field notes, Sixteenth Annual Convention, New York State Loving Education at Home (NYS LEAH), Syracuse, June 2, 2000; also from *Covenant & Cross: The Vision Forum Catalogue 2000*, received 6/2/00 (quotation on page 3).

25. See, e.g., Ammerman, *Bible Believers*; Davidman, *Tradition in a Rootless World*.

26. See, e.g., Nancy Chodorow, *The Reproduction of Mothering* (Berkeley: University of California Press, 1980); also Hochschild and Machung, *The Second Shift*, especially chaps. 16 and 17.

27. Judith Stacey, *Brave New Families: Stories of Domestic Upheaval in Late Twentieth Century America* (New York: Basic Books, 1990); also Gallagher and Smith, "Symbolic Traditionalism."

28. Again, there is a strong echo here of Lichterman's work in *The Search for Political Community*. But rather than seeing radical democracy as a solution to the puzzle of difference, as Lichterman does, I am suggesting that in some cases it might be a default form. We may find radical democracy simply because a movement's standing elites favor it, or because it is the only thing everyone can agree to, or because there is no constituency powerful enough or interested enough to change the rules.

29. Margaret Talbot, "A Mighty Fortress," *New York Times Magazine*, February 27, 2000, 34–41+; "Home Works," *Wall Street Journal*, June 6, 2000, A26.

30. Fieldwork, 6/95.

31. This process is a generic one for social movements whose causes win

some degree of institutionalization. See Debra Friedman and Doug McAdam, "Collective Identity and Activism: Networks, Choices, and the Life of a Social Movement," in *Frontiers in Social Movement Theory*, ed. Morris and Mueller, 156–73.

32. For an excellent summary of this ongoing conversation, see Paul Lichterman, "Beyond the Seesaw Model: Public Commitment in a Culture of Self-Fulfillment," *Sociological Theory* 13 (1995): 275–300.

33. Those who nurture make wage sacrifices even when they receive financial compensation for their work. Sociologists Paula England and Nancy Folbre found in a recent study that, other things being equal, jobs that can be described as having nurturance as a central component are compensated less than other occupations. See England and Folbre, "The Cost of Caring," *Annals of the American Academy of Political and Social Science* 561 (January 1999): 39–51.

34. James Allan Davis and Tom W. Smith, *General Social Surveys, 1972–1993: Cumulative Codebook* (Chicago: National Opinion Research Center, 1993), 927–45.

35. See Walzer, *Thinking about the Baby*.

36. The argument here is very similar to the one offered by Marxist feminists regarding the contemporary organization of housework and child rearing; I extend this thinking just a bit to encompass the work of self-making. See, e.g., Heidi I. Hartmann, "The Family as the Locus of Gender, Class, and Political Struggle: The Example of Housework," *Signs* 6 (1981): 366–94; Meg Luxton, *More Than a Labor of Love* (Toronto: Women's Press, 1980).

37. Zelizer, *Pricing the Priceless Child*.

38. Émile Durkheim, *The Elementary Forms of Religious Life*, trans. Karen E. Fields. (New York: Free Press, 1995).

39. Michael Farris, interview, 8/9/99.

Index